Richard Bangs'

Adventures
with Purpose

Library of Congress Cataloging-in-Publication Data
Bangs, Richard, 1950–
Adventures with purpose: dispatches from the front
lines of the Earth / by Richard Bangs.–1st ed., 1st printing.
p. cm.

ISBN 10: 0-89732-735-7 (cloth edition)
ISBN 13: 978-0-89732-735-0 (cloth edition)
ISBN 10: 0-89732-736-5 (paperback edition)
ISBN 13: 978-0-89732-736-7 (paperback edition)

1. Bangs, Richard, 1950– 2. Voyages and travels.
3. Adventure travel. I. Title.
G465.B367 2007
910.9'033–dc22
2007018040

Menasha Ridge Press
P.O. Box 43673
Birmingham, AL 35243
www.menasharidge.com

Richard Bangs'

Adventures with Purpose

dispatches from the front lines of earth

Menasha Ridge Press

*To the pillars of my vale, Laura and Walker, whose strength
I drink with unstinted abundance. An alliance they possess
with the air in the promotion of mettle and well-being.
Many people think they bestow the gifts of magic well,
a belief I accept at once without further scrutiny.*

Contents

ACKNOWLEDGMENTS

Over the span of this piece I tried quite vainly to color in the map, but were it not for the hereto mentioned, I should have counted the cats in Zanzibar (or the elephants of Mandevu) from the cush and comfort of my book-lined office. Notwithstanding the digital notion that if you liked my baby wait till you see her picture, I do believe there is no substitute for raw reality, for the squish of other soil, the cologne of tropic isles, the sweat of effort and anxiety, the pounding of the senses that can only happen when actually present. I can never adequately thank those who kindly helped me make these journeys, but I can cite their heroic reserves of patience in answering one simple, endlessly repeated query: "How do I get *there?*"

First of all I want to express unending gratitude to Scott Moore and Paul Maritz, the friends and visionaries who supported these concepts, and who made enormous efforts, and took significant risks, to make what appears between these covers possible.

I also want to make special notice of folks who traveled with me and made the media possible, including longtime collaborator Christian Kallen; undaunted explorers Pasquale Scaturro and Jim Slade; gifted director and video-maker Didrik Johnck; media Sherpa John Canning; BBC reporter and producer Laura Hubber; videographers extraordinaire Scott Finley, Jon Brick, Andrew Locke, and Max Block; and super-publisher Cyrus Krohn.

Of course while no act of kindness goes unpunished, no act of adventure goes without Mountain Travel Sobek, the adventure

company that made many of these expeditions possible, and I
especially want to thank Special Ops Director Nadia LeBon and
President Kevin Callahan, who forever have endorsed my fanati-
cal schemes and helped to make them real.

And no travel is complete without celebrations of my longtime favorite suppliers: Ex Officio (whose unstoppable shirts I
have worn to every continent); Eagle Creek, whose durable lug-
gage seems to have a half-life; and Teva Footwear, who have
stepped with me around the globe.

For **Expedition Rwanda** I want to thank Daryl Hannah who
lent her celebrity, time, and sincerity to the project, lifting it to a
much-needed higher consciousness. Also Greg Cummings and
his wife Jillian Miller who have been working tirelessly to save
the mountain gorillas for over two and half decades, and the Dian
Fossey Gorilla Fund which hosted us. And a special thanks to
Rosette Chantal Rugamba, the director general of the national
office of tourism and parks. I also want to thank Swiss International Airlines for getting us to Africa, the president of Rwanda,
Paul Kagame, for his support, as well as the Rwanda Tourism
Board. And my friend Peter Guber for making *Gorillas in the Mist*.
And lastly Yahoo!, which funded the building of the cistern.

For **Expedition Bosnia** I want to thank one of the greatest
environmental champions I know, Tim Clancy, and his organization Green Visions. Then there is Samir Krivic, owner of Rafting
Europe, who paddled us through paradise. I also want to thank
USAID for supporting this and taking a stand for the good of
nature, especially David King, Chief of Party at the Emerging
Markets Group, and his colleague Snjezana Derviskadic.

For **Expedition Thailand** I want to thank John "Caveman"
Gray who is a true hero, and the Tourism Authority of Thailand
who helped us get to some unusual places. I also want to call
out Casio which supplied the digital cameras used throughout
this expedition, and also for the Eiger and Panama expeditions.
Travelocity was also a major supporter, as they were for several
of these expeditions. And China Airlines helped us find our way
across the Pacific.

For **Expedition Libya** I want to thank Mr. Solieman Abboud, owner of Tripoli-based Sari Travel, who made the impossible possible. Also Paolo Balduzzi for helping to put this outlandish notion together, and to Bruton for the solar panels that worked so well in the Sahara, Sandisk and Ken Castle for digital storage, and fellow intrepid travelers Alix Hartley, Robert Wright, Bastien Stieltjes, Ludovic Bousquet, Cheryl Sulima, Ann Duncan, Hugh Westwater, and Frank Headen.

For **Expedition Eiger** I want to thank John Harlin III for allowing us into his family and to his very personal but epic story; and to his wife Adele Hammond and their daughter Siena, who put up with me and my crew. And to Greg MacGillivray and MacGillivray Freeman Films who had the vision to let us join in their media project. Lori Rick did an amazing job coordinating, and Stephen Judson was the brilliant director/editor. Thanks to super-climbers Robert and Daniela Jasper, who allowed me into their home and lives; Brad Ohlund and Michael Brown, the great shooters; and the film's executive producer, Alexander Biner of Four Eyes 4iS; Sammy Salm and Marina Tonn from Grindelwald Tourism and the Jungfrau Region; Swiss International Airlines who winged us there; and Maja Gartmann of the Swiss Tourist Board who made magic.

For **Expedition Panama** I want to thank the pirate king, Barry Clifford, and Richard Cahill, a superb naturalist and cofounder of Ancon Expeditions, our host. I also want to acknowledge the Wild Thornberry's in the flesh, Scott and Jo Seagren and their kids, Parker and Josie Dee, who shared every adventure throughout the isthmus, and Rachel Cohen, our able escort.

For **Expedition Jordan River** I want to thank Gidon Bromberg, the Israeli Director of Friends of the Earth Middle East, and Mira Edelstein, the Resource Development Manager; and Tova Wald and Lina Deshilton of the Israeli Tourist Board, who assisted us mightily. And then my kindred spirit, Lahav Blouh of Neharot Expeditions, who took us rafting, and Professor Haim Goren, who taught us well. And Native Eyewear for supplying the sunglasses.

For **Expedition Australia** I want to thank my friend and astonishing photographer, Jonathan Chester, who showed the way throughout. I want to thank QANTAS Airways for helping us get down under, and Tourism Australia for its ever ready assistance, and especially Lisa Gregory and Kristen Malaby who orchestrated it all. Also assisting were Tourism Victoria and Tourism New South Wales. I want to tip my hat to the Daintree Eco Lodge and Spa, Voyages Wrotham Park Lodge, Holiday Inn Cairns, Hotel Lindrum, Hartley's Crocodile Adventures, Raft 'n Rainforest, Australian Wild Escapes, Queensland Parks and Wildlife, the Melbourne Aquarium, Philips Island Nature Park, Global Ballooning, Taxi Restaurant, and Cairns Limousine.

For **Expedition New Guinea** I want to thank Bob Bates, owner of Trans Niugini Tours, and the man who first showed me the highlands over three decades ago. I also want to thanks HP who supplied the digital cameras and printers, and QANTAS who got us there. And can't forget fellow explorer-photographers Norm Singer and Patrick Giamanco. And finally my late mom, Louise, who was a passionate photographer, and who inspired this expedition.

For **Expedition Nahanni** I want to thank one of my inspirations, John Blachford, as well as my fellow canoe mate Dave Shore, and other boaters Dan Lockwood, Sean Greene, Leslianne Carbary, and the rest of the gang. I also want to thank Monica Campbell-Hoppé, Director, U.S. Media Relations for the Canadian Tourism Commission, who helped with arrangements, and to Blackfeather, the outfitter of the adventure.

For **Expedition Missouri River** I want to thank Ford for supplying the Escape Hybrid, Peggy Dulany for letting us stay on her amazing ranch, and Charlie Tillinghast and Kyoo Kim of MSNBC for making this survey of Western America possible.

For **Expedition Zambia** I want to thank Yaffa Maritz for letting us go, and Justin Seymour-Smith, who took time away battling for his rights in Zimbabwe to join and teach us; and Chriss Wienand, the MacGyver of Africa. Also want to thank South

African Airways who helped Pasquale and me wing across the Atlantic. And June Thomas and Jacob Weisberg of Slate.

For **Expedition Macedonia** I want to thank Exploring Macedonia.com and Sasha Gavrilovic; Vasko Kronevski and Nora Buklevska of NextSense; Hal Yaeger, Teresa Albor, and Zarko Pop-Iliev of USAID, and all the Greeks who accept Macedonia for what it is and was.

For **Expedition Annapurna** I want to thank Ed Viesturs, just shy of a sun god, and our outfitter in Nepal Stan Armington, and our logistics coordinator in the United States, Narendra Gurung. I also want to thank fellow trekkers Erik Blachford, Russ Daggatt, David Whitlock, Dean Alper, Lindsay Yaw, Kristy Severance, and the gang. I also want to credit Sony, whose digital gear we used, and Cisco Systems for supplying some high-tech communications support.

For **Expedition Egypt** I first want to express huge gratitude to John Givens who believed in this concept in its earliest conception and devoted time and considerable resources to make it happen. To Sue McNally and her husband Richard, a creative and logistics-team nonpareil, and Karel Bauer, the exceptional cameraman who shot the companion special to this chapter. And a grand and gracious gesture of gratitude to Mr. Nour and Madame Omayma El Husseini of the Egyptian Tourism Authority, as well its chairman, Ahmed El Khadem, and also Sakkara Tours of Cairo, and Egyptologist and guide Maher Haggag. In Egypt I must thank Dr. Zahi Hawass, Secretary General of the Supreme Council of Antiquities, Dr. Willeke Wendrich of UCLA, Dr. Sherif Baha El Din, and Eva Dadrian of the BBC. And not least I want to thank Crocs for supplying the super comfortable but gripping footwear.

And for **Expedition Dream** I can only thank the elephants for their respect to a trespassing foreigner.

Others who helped and made a difference include Michael Kinsley, Patty Stonesifer, NPR and their Culver City Studios, Lloyd Braun, Julia Romano, Lynne Hentemann, Jess Baron, Steve

Enders, Ezra Palmer, Elaine Fortier, Bonnie Carlton, Valerie Brossard, Farah Ravon, Amy Iorio, Nathan Myhrvold, John Russell, Keli Stuckart, Steve Cvengros, Jeff Dossett, Steve Marks, Janine Robertson, British Airways, my sisters, Patricia and Cindy, and all my colleagues at Microsoft, MSNBC, Slate, MSN, MSNBC, and Yahoo!.

Lastly I want to turn up the music for Russell Helms of Menasha Ridge Press, who was bitten by the bug while exploring in Ethiopia some years ago, and his infection with adventure brought him to help this book come to be.

INTRODUCTION

I once sailed by rubber boat down the Grand Canyon of Asia Minor, the Kemer Khan of Turkey's Adiyaman Plateau, a spectacularly striated gorge of sedimentary and volcanic rock through which the upper Euphrates cut and purled for tens of thousands of years. It was such a stunning passage, it hurt my eyes and stole my breath away. Yet, when a few years later I planned to return with friends, I was shocked to discover this vault of history, the Grand Canyon of the Euphrates, had been dammed in a styptic blink, when nobody was looking, and the river flowed no more.

In 1770, the Scottish explorer James Bruce, in his search for the source of the Nile, came across the 150-foot-high Tissisat Falls in Ethiopia. He described it thusly:

The river . . . fell in one sheet of water, without any interval, above half an English mile in breadth, with a force and a noise that was truly terrible, and which stunned and made me, for a time, perfectly dizzy. A thick fume, or haze, covered the fall all around, and hung over the course of the stream both above and below, marking its track, though the water was not seen. . . . It was a most magnificent sight, that ages, added to the greatest length of human life, would not deface or eradicate from my memory.

Yet when I scrambled to this magnificence last year, a thin ribbon of water scraped down the cheek of a dark cliff. The immense cascade was gone, 90 percent diverted into a power scheme built by Chinese and Serbian contractors, erected without knowledge of or critique from the rest of the world. The river was redeposited a few hundred yards downstream after pouring through penstocks and turbines, but it had left the great falls bald and sallow.

This has been a cheerless theme to my travels and explorations over the past thirty years. So often I would stumble to spectacle so bravura, it would speed the blood and validate existence, but then upon return discover it was less so, or gone, because of non-sustainable commercial concerns set to exploit the earth. There is no waterway on the planet uncoveted for diversion or damming; there is no forest that's not lusted over for felling and development. It is a paradoxical notion that the places we wish to remain protected and wild cannot become so unless visited and appreciated.

Over the decades, I have witnessed many special places preserved and lost, and the critical vector in their survival or demise was more often than not the number of visitors who trekked the landscape or floated the river and were touched deeply by their unique beauty and spirit. When such a space became threatened, there was a constituency for whom the place was personal, a collective force ready to lend energy, monies, and time to preservation. The Colorado still dances through the Grand Canyon largely because those who rafted this cathedral rallied against a proposed dam. The Tatshenshini in British Columbia, a river I pioneered in the mid-1970s, which has the highest concentration of glaciers, grizzlies, and bald eagles in North America, was almost victim to an open-pit copper mine, but those adventurers who had made its passage fought fiercely and won protection. Culturally intact Dayak villages in Borneo and their counterparts throughout the tropics sustain themselves because visitors who witnessed their magic made public battle against timber and oil companies otherwise poised with bulldozers.

Yet in my sleep there is lament that falls drop by drop upon my heart. I am haunted by the losses and question if I could have done more to entice people to come and see. In the 1980s, I explored the Alas Basin in Sumatra, running through the largest orangutan reserve in the world. Timber poaching has reduced the once luxurious habitat to a scrawny shadow, and the "men of the forest" are on the brink of extinction. In the late 1970s, I led the first descent of Chile's Rio Bio-Bio, a tumbling gem that offered some of the finest white water in the world. I tried to persuade as many folks as possible to come glide this course, but not enough, as a local power company rolled over resistance and broke the wild water with a series of dams.

In 1981, I joined President Kenneth Kaunda at a function in Lusaka to help save the last of the black rhinos of Zambia. I pledged to motivate more to come and see, but I never really made good on the promise. When I returned last year, all the rhinos were gone.

A recent census estimates the lion population in Africa has decreased 95 percent since the 1950s. In the 1960s, the Luangwa Valley was home to 100,000 elephants, largest concentration in the world. Today, because of poaching, an estimated 15,000 remain. In Madagascar, 90 percent of the forests are gone. And as we gaze about the world it is not just trees, rivers, and animals vanishing. The Dead Sea is drying up; variegated coral reefs are bleaching; glaciers are retreating.

One bona fide way to save the extraordinary, but sometimes distant, natural assets of our world is to hearten enough people to see and tap and be tapped. Then the concept becomes real and personal, not academic. The value of wonder and the inter-connectedness of all things become patent. It is those who have discovered these places who have been key to saving them, and a part of themselves.

I've spent a career designing and conducting adventures with purpose, travel that is expectantly meaningful and designed to make a difference. But the graveyard of my own sacred places gone speaks to regrets and quests not fulfilled.

So this book is an invitation, a summons to come and hear the raw, deep voices of nature and behold architecture supported by the brilliant beams of rainbows. In making that step beyond the equipoise of provisional comfort there is the chance to be swept away by glorious displays of flocks and herds, to be baptized into the marvels of the natural life. And then I hope when the time comes for volunteers to save what those travelers have seen, their hands and voices will be raised to the sky.

Richard Bangs'

Adventures with Purpose

1

The Quest for the Lord of the Nile
Egypt

It is the wisdom of crocodiles, that shed tears when they would devour.
—Francis Bacon, "Of Wisdom for a Man's Self"

The whole business began with an entirely improbable cosmological conjunction, a Nilotic lord in the house of a men's magazine.

In the early 1970s, I was a river guide on the Colorado River through the Grand Canyon, and somehow between trips happened across a copy of *Argosy* magazine, one of those pulp rags that depicted brawny men bare-handedly fighting off large predators, often a grizzly or mountain lion, while scantily clad nymphs swooned in the background. This issue reported on a 1968 rafting expedition down the Blue Nile by a British Army team, a military-style enterprise distinguished for its lack of river-running experience and fatal blunders. One success, though, was with the crocodiles that cruised the eddies. As the unchallenged lords of the river, they would instinctively charge the passing rafts, but as the British hurled baseball-sized rocks back, the crocs would submerge and retreat, perhaps in puzzlement at such counterattack behavior. But the explorers fared less well with the river itself. They flipped boats, sacrificed gear to the boiling currents, and lost one member to drowning. While reading the piece, I realized I knew more than anyone on the British expedition about white-water rafting, and that perhaps I could make a successful descent of the Blue Nile where they had failed.

So I spent the next several months preparing to head to Ethiopia to run the Blue Nile, poring over books describing the many ways I could die attempting such. I learned there were a raft of nasty obstacles that might do damage. The rapids were certainly a given. They were big and dangerous. But then there were hippos, second largest land mammals after elephants, and infamous for turning over boats and snapping occupants in two. The wild buffalo in the region had a reputation for charging unprovoked. I read about puff adders, black mambas, and spitting cobras and about legendary twenty-foot pythons that capsized canoes. And there were a score of documented exotic tropical diseases, from onchocerciasis (river blindness) to elephantiasis; from trypanosomiasis (sleeping sickness) to trichuris (whipworm); from yaws to several fatal forms of malaria. There were the local peoples, some with fierce reputations. The Blue Nile corridor had taken a toll of explorers who had fallen prey to the ruthless *Shifta,* the roaming bands of bandits who ruled the outback. In 1962, a Swiss-French canoeing expedition was attacked in the middle of the night. Four of the party escaped in a single canoe under a hail of gunfire, while the rest lay dead in the campsite.

But the one danger cited over and over was the risk of death by crocodile. The most deadly existing reptile, the man-eating *Crocodylus niloticus* has always been on man's "worst enemies" list. More people are killed and eaten by crocodiles each year in Africa than by all other animals combined. Crocodile hunters, upon cutting open stomachs of their prey, often discovered bracelets and bits of jewelry and human remains. Huge, ravening predators, armed with massive, teeth-studded jaws, strong, unrestrainable, indestructible, and destructive, crocodiles, if given the chance, eat people. It's their nature. The river is their turf, and we would be trespassers. I found myself in cold-sweat nightmares imagining the yellow, chisel-sharp teeth of a giant croc ripping my skin apart. This would be the most awful way to die. But I thought about the alternative—law or graduate school leading to a real job—and facing crocodiles seemed the delightful evil of two lessers.

I read as much as I could find about crocodiles, though I quickly discovered not many people had ever navigated white water in Africa, and of the few who had, and survived, less than a handful had left reliable accounts of their experiences with crocs. I discovered there were two major schools of thought about how to cope while floating a crocodile-infested river: 1) Be as noisy as possible when passing through a crocodile pool to scare them off. 2) Be as silent as possible when passing through a croc-infested area so as not to attract attention. The rationale for the latter method was that since crocodiles have fixed-focused eyesight—they can see things clearly only at one specific distance—a noiseless boat floating past at the proper distance could probably go unnoticed. One expert at the National Zoo even warned not to laugh in a certain manner, as it resembled the sound of an infant croc in trouble, and the noise would alert all larger crocs within hearing distance to rush to the rescue. He demonstrated the laugh, and it sounded eerily like my partner's high-pitched nervous laugh, so I silently vowed to keep topics serious if sharing a raft with John Yost.

Another account was graphically presented in the bestiary *Eyelids of Morning: The Mingled Destinies of Crocodiles and Men*, written by Alistair Graham and photographed by Peter Beard, two researchers who might be considered the anti-Jane Goodall and Dian Fossey in that they studied their charges by hunting them (they shot 500 in the course of a year). In their summary, they recount the saga of a Peace Corps volunteer, Bill Olsen, a recent graduate of Cornell, who decided to take a swim in Ethiopia's Baro River, an eventual tributary to the White Nile, against the advice of locals. He swam to a sandbar on the far side of the muddy river and sat there with his feet on a submerged rock. He was leaning into the current to keep his balance, a rippled vee of water trailing behind him, his arms folded across his chest as he was staring ahead lost in thought. A few minutes later, his friends saw that Bill had vanished without trace or sound. A few more minutes later, a big croc surfaced with a large, white, partially submerged object in its jaws, whose identity was in no doubt. The next morning, a hunter on safari, a Colonel Dow, snuck up on the croc, shot it, and then dragged the carcass to the beach. He cut it open and inside found Bill Olsen's legs, intact from the knees down, still joined at the pelvis. His head, crushed into small chunks, was a barely recognizable mass of hair and flesh. A black and white photo of Bill's twisted, bloody legs dumped in a torn cardboard box drilled into my paraconsciousness, and for days I would shut my eyes and shiver at the image.

In the end, I was not comforted by what I learned in my research—if anything, I was a good deal more afraid.

It was while I was casting about for a name for my expedition that a thin book on the gods of ancient Egypt wrought inspiration. There was Ra, the sun god, but that had been taken by Thor Heyerdahl's recent expedition. There was Hesamut, the hippo goddess depicted in the act of demolishing a crocodile. But *Hesamut Expedition* didn't resonate. One chapter spoke of the crocodile god Sobek, worshipped along the Egyptian Nile. A temple was built to the deity on the island of Kom Ombo between Aswan and Luxor, where mothers of children eaten by crocodiles felt privileged to have provided something for Sobek's delectation. And there were sacrificial pools at a city in the Fayoum Valley called Crocodopolis. The story went that once upon a time, Menes, first king of all the Egyptians, was set upon by his own dogs while out hunting. In his flight he came to the Nile, where lay a large croc baking in the sun. The croc, rapidly sizing up the situation, offered to ferry the desperate king across the river.

With all saurian ceremony, Menes was sculled over to found a city in about 3000 BC that would worship crocodiles, a city that was christened Crocodopolis. Henceforth, it was believed that if Sobek were appeased, he would allow the fragile papyrus boats used to ply the Nile to remain unharmed. About 321 BC, when the army of Perdiccas was crossing the Nile at Memphis, it forgot to pay Sobek homage, and 1,000 soldiers were killed and eaten. Naming my expedition after a deity that would protect boats from sharp-toothed serpents seemed like a good idea to me, so Sobek we became.

The eponym served us well. For the next ten years I made a number of first descents of upper stretches of African rivers, including a section of the Blue Nile that had defeated the British, and though all the rivers were populated by man-eating crocodiles, for the most part they left us alone. Okay, we had a few rafts bitten by crocodiles, but more by hippos, and we suffered no mortification of the flesh. It seemed Sobek was indeed looking kindly upon us, and so in 1983, for our ten-year anniversary, I organized a trip to visit Kom Ombo, the Sobek temple, to pay proper tribute.

It was a quick three-day excursion on a cruise boat, and once at the nearly vacant house of Sobek, where only a few foreign researchers milled about, I drank in the seemingly mystical exhibition of the crocodile god in a gallery of ancient Nilotic scenes. I left an offering of a Sobek catalog, an inscribed Sierra Club cup, and a T-shirt at the base of an engraved depiction of the god. But one thing left me wondering. Throughout the journey we saw not a single live crocodile on the Nile, and when I queried the captain, he said there were none left—they had gone like the pharaohs. In Egypt, he explained, they had all long since vanished, hunted or died out from environmental shifts.

For the next two decades, my colleagues and I continued to run expeditions around the world under the Sobek imprimatur, and for the most part they were successful. But as Sobek saw us through, I wondered about the source of the mythology and about what had happened to the river dragons, so indestructible, so revered, closest living relatives to the dinosaurs, existing little changed since long before man walked along the Nile, yet now gone.

Then in 2003 I helped organize an expedition that hoped to make the first full descent of the Nile from its Blue Nile source in Ethiopia to the mouth near Alexandria, Egypt. My friend Pasquale Scaturro led the five-month-long voyage, and as I waved good-bye to him on the banks of Lake Tana in the highlands of Ethiopia, he promised to check in every few days on his satellite phone. "Watch out for the crocs. They're always looking for a handout," were my departing words.

Indeed the expedition was charged by several large crocodiles as it made its way down off the Abyssinian plateau and into Sudan. A kayak paddle was chomped at one point. But the real surprise was when Pasquale passed into Lake Nasser in Upper Egypt. He called and reported, "You wouldn't believe the size of the crocodiles here. They're monsters!" I was surprised and in some strange way delighted with that news. I had thought crocodiles were gone from Egypt, but they were, according to Pasquale, coming back, in a big way.

So it was I crafted a confection, to travel to Egypt and follow the Nile upstream from Alexandria to Upper Egypt and Lake Nasser to inquire a little into the crocodiles in myth and history, and know why they disappeared and how they might be returning, a quest for the Lord of the Nile. I owed a lot to Sobek and wanted to see if I might mine some understanding and perhaps find a way to give back.

The Eastern Harbor of Alexandria curves like a scimitar at the edge of the Nile Delta. It was here that crocodiles in great numbers lingered at the stitch of fresh water and salt water, a seam rich with nutrients and fish. During the annual flood, some were swept seaward and found their ways to shores as distant as the Aegean and the Levantine Coast.

In the time of the Ptolemys, this port was the center of learning of the civilized world, and texts and manuscripts were brought to its library from everywhere writing existed. But during the time of Julius Caesar, the library was burned, and the city fell into decline.

The ancient library has been replaced by a new one, the Bibliotheca Alexandrina, spearheaded by UNESCO and completed in 2002.

Crossing the wide boulevard of the Corniche, I head into the tilted, circular building that with a squint looks like a rising sun. I find my way across the cantilevered study halls to one of the hundreds of computer terminals and there begin to scroll through the titles, assuming that if there is a repository of information on the reptiles of the Nile, and Sobek, it would be here.

After I pore over tomes, a possible explanation for one of the riddles of the Nile begins to emerge. It was the crocodile, in a fashion, that was responsible for the pyramids and the great tombs of Egypt.

The ancient Egyptians watched helpless each summer as the life-giving Nile receded and left their fields barren. Then come September, under clear blue skies, the river would run in spate, bringing swarms of crocodiles and the rich soil and nutrients that would replenish the black and dead soil. It was a mystery from where the crocodiles and the new soil came, and why, but the Egyptians looked on as lifeless land was reborn and crocodile eggs were laid with the season.

Just as the sun died and was reborn each day, so the soil was resurrected along the Nile each year as the crocodiles came. Crocodile eggs hatched and created life out of nothing. These annuities, it might be conjectured, gave the Egyptians the idea that the crocodile was the agent for this rebirth, giving them reason to believe they too could restart life after death.

So Sobek became a god of fertility and rebirth, and Egyptians inferred that if Sobek could give the land a new life, then he could do the same for humans. Accordingly, the pharaohs endorsed the concept of an afterlife and believed they could bring possessions with them. So they built enormous tombs, filled them with their effects, and had themselves mummified in preparation for the journey. Perhaps as guides to the afterlife, crocodiles were also embalmed in sarcophagi in these tombs, placed alongside canopic jars filled with vital organs necessary for the hereafter.

If this theory is true, I am not the only one who owes a debt to Sobek. So does everyone who has ever admired the pyramids, or the tombs of the Valley of the Kings as well, monumental aesthetic gifts that have endured for millennia.

Of no surprise, this library carries the Egyptian Book of the Dead, the cheat sheet to the afterlife for dynastic Egyptians, rich with references to Sobek. In one passage the crocodile god speaks:

"I am the owner of seed who takes women from their husbands whenever he wishes, according to his desire. I am Sobek, who carries off by violence."

A key description in chapter 125 of the Book of the Dead is that of the weighing of the heart, a precursor to the Christian concept of the Last Judgment. The heart of the newly dead was placed on one side of a scale. On the other side was a feather from the goddess Maat, who represented order and justice. Looming nearby was the hell mouth of a crocodile-headed monster.

If the scale balanced, the god of the underworld, Osiris, would lead the deceased to reanimation in the next world. If unbalanced, the heart was tossed to the crocodile-headed monster and devoured.

Sobek as a spirited demiurge was associated with death, but also sex. In the Pyramid Text (spell 510), Sobek's lusty stealth and sexual potency are described, wherein the king changes into a crocodile before robbing husbands of their wives. Another passage speaks to Sobek's contravening powers: women would use the dung of crocodiles as contraceptives.

Still other texts suggest it is a stroke of good fortune to be gobbled by a crocodile. And so it is that the relationship with the Nile crocodile is a conflicted one; the croc was feared and worshipped, seen as an instrument of death, fertility, regeneration, and channel to the next world.

The brilliance of the ancient imaginings of Sobek is that their current of moral energy ran both ways, just as the Nile for navigation. Creator, destroyer; good, evil; a god, the devil. Like its amphibious nature, between land and water, the god evoked ambiguity, a place between and of, a duality in motion, ultimately a spiritual device that covered all bases.

After scouring the library, I can find no reference to crocodiles returning to the Nile, so I set out upstream to see if I can find the lost beast and make some sort of approbation.

From Alexandria I wind up the estuarine Nile to Cairo, where the river turns like some grave thought threading a dream. Here the Nile grinds and clanks with an incessant bass note at the frame of the delta, polluted, noisy, demanding. If a crocodile wanted to live in the noxious waters here today, it couldn't. Past sand-colored mosques and beneath the mullioned windows, I comb the streets looking for any evidence of a crocodile, but come up with nothing, save a popular extract of crocodile, a philter ointment whose label says, "For you and your happiness." Finally, I step down an alley into the heart of the Khan al-Khalili bazaar, a frantic mélange of old smells and snaking Arabic sounds.

I encounter a man in a beaded robe who tells me I can find a crocodile at El-Fishawi Café and offers to guide me there. I imagine a crocodile, traded like a slave from the south, in some tub in the back, and if so, I know I will want to negotiate to set it free. But as I step into the hazy, hookah-filled cafe and ask where I might find this wayward animal, a waiter nods to a candy-striped arched doorway. As I lift eyes above the archway, I spy a five-foot crocodile stuffed and nailed as though in a Victorian trophy room. He is the closest thing to an intact crocodile I will find in Cairo.

Deeper in the bazaar, among the pricelessly bad tourist baubles, I ask the merchants if they have any crocodiles to sell. Ever since Herodotus, Egyptians have welcomed foreigners with an admixture of banter, hearty browbeating, effusiveness, and the sort of insincere familiarity associated with people trying to become intimate enough to pick a pocket. So when one man offers to take me up the narrow stairs to his shop, I proceed with caution. There he sits me down and offers me tea. In the furbelows and folderol of the chat between the first cup and the second he shows me several interpretations of crocodiles in soapstone and wood, but nothing real. Then into the second cup he asks me to wait and disappears down the stairs. A few minutes later, he emerges with the gnarled, rolled skin of a seven-foot crocodile. His price is $2,000, and I pass, declining to bargain. He won't tell me where he got it, or any details. It was likely poached, and just negotiating could encourage the illegal trade. So I instead bid on a beautiful, handmade Egyptian-cotton abaya. I manage to get him down to half his initial price and feel pretty good with the deal until the next day when I eye the same robe in the hotel window for another half off the price.

Before I arrived in Egypt, there was a flurry of e-mail exchanges with Eva Dadrian, a Cairo-based reporter for the BBC. I had asked if she could track down any experts on crocodiles, and she found but one: Dr. Sherif Baha El Din, an environmental consultant and herpetologist who has been surveying the scaly wildlife of Lake Nasser.

In his cluttered Cairo apartment, ornamented equally with toddler toys and renditions of reptiles, I ask Dr. El Din what happened to the crocodiles of the Nile.

"A combination of things. Certainly human population pressure over the centuries . . . increasing numbers of people competing with wildlife for the river, and winning." Dr. El Din continues to elaborate, citing the first Aswan Dam, finished in 1902, as a primary culprit. It effectively blocked the annual floods, which washed down new populations of crocodiles each year. Now crocodiles are locked upstream.

But it is the lust for crocodile leather that really wiped out the crocodiles in the twentieth century, a madness for handbags, shoes, belts, and other pelt accessories. By the 1950s, professional hunters from all over the world were coming to Egypt to bag crocodiles, not only for their valuable skins, but also for their meat, a delicacy to some gourmands, and their fat, used as a curative for rheumatic diseases. By the early 1980s, the crocodiles of the Egyptian Nile were all gone. That coincided with my 1983 Sobek anniversary trip.

"When did they start to return?"

"In the mid-1980s, Egypt passed a ban on hunting crocodiles, in the wake of CITES [the Convention on International Trade of Endangered Species of Wild Fauna and Flora] putting Nile crocodiles on the list of endangered species. Since then, crocodiles have started to reappear on Lake Nasser, but not yet in the main Nile. The fishermen hate the crocodiles, who compete for their fish, get caught in and cut their nets, and sometimes attack and eat them, so they continue to kill the crocodiles when the government isn't looking. And there is still a lot of poaching and smuggling going on, even professional hunting safaris for well-heeled foreigners."

"If they are such deadly menaces, why not just hunt them to extinction?"

Dr. El Din argues that crocodiles are an integral part of our natural heritage and ecosystem, a link in the chain of global diversity, and have as much right to share space on the planet as any other creature. They were in fact here millions of years before people and could claim first rights. They were in a fashion the first Egyptians. Through the rise and fall of empires, from the ancient pharaohs to the Ptolemys, through the epochs of the Greeks, Romans, Persians, Arabs, Ottomans, French, and English, only the crocodiles stayed the same, until recently.

But I wonder how the fishermen can ever be convinced? The returning crocodiles affect their livelihood, their well-being.

"Ecotourism" is Dr. El Din's answer. He thinks a viable economic alternative to fishing would be making the wild crocodiles a tourist attraction, just as the gazetted paradises of sub-Saharan Africa have done with lions, Australia's Great Barrier Reef has done with sharks, and the Canadian outpost of

Churchill has done with polar bears. "Crocodiles are a very valuable resource and can be a significant tourist attraction. People want to see wild crocodiles in the sun."

Dr. El Din then describes how he has confiscated crocodiles from traders in the Aswan area and liberated them back to the Nile. He concludes by advising, "If in your travels you find a captured crocodile, set it free, if you can. Set an example. It could be a small gesture that saves a life, sends a message, and makes a difference. And the crocodile will then pray for you."

On the outskirts of Cairo is Giza, where I hire a camel and clop to see the great pyramids in the soft coral flush of dawn. Built some 4,500 years ago as way stations to the afterlife, they are the lineaments of gratified desire. No matter how many images one's seen of the pyramids, when in their presence the mind is slendered by awe. If there is architecture of happiness, it is the pyramids, ancient elevators to a higher life.

I continue then south to Saqqara, through a land that looks like the scrapped hide of a camel, bits of hair still tufted to its tawny back. Saqqara is a vast, ancient burial ground featuring the world's oldest standing step pyramid.

While Memphis was the capital of ancient Egypt, Saqqara served as its graveyard. It remained an important complex for burials and cult ceremonies for more than 3,000 years, well into Ptolemaic and Roman times. It is here I hook up with Dr. Zahi Hawass, head of the Supreme Council of Antiquities, and a man temperamentally disinclined to keep any achievement quiet. Hawass wears brushed jeans, a pressed denim shirt, and his signature Indiana Jones hat, one he tells me is about to be licensed under his brand by a Chicago haberdashery. His famous enthusiasm bubbles when I ask him about Sobek.

"Sobek . . . that is so interesting. Nobody studies Sobek, but he was an important god. In fact, I just made two discoveries. Let me show you."

I follow Dr. Hawass's hat down into a dig in progress, where workers are sifting through a mud-brick tomb that dates back

4,200 years, to the start of the Fifth Dynasty in the Old Kingdom. Grave robbers unearthed this tomb a few months previous, making it the newest major archaeological discovery in Egypt.

Dr. Hawass uncorks his theory that three royal dentists are interred in these tombs, and points out hieroglyphs of an eye over a tooth, the symbol of the men who tended teeth.

Then he says the tomb is marked with a curse and points to a depiction of a crocodile with a beautifully curved tail, one of the oldest illustrations ever discovered of a crocodile: "The dentist put an inscription to say: 'Anyone who enters my tomb will be eaten by the teeth of Sobek.'"

"What about you?" I ask Dr. Hawass.

"Well, the thieves went to jail. As for me . . ." And he stretches a smile like a hammock, hanging out his belief in his own immunity.

Dr. Hawass then signals a couple of his workers, who carry down into the excavation site what looks like a large loaf of bread wrapped in a linen bandage. It is a crocodile mummy found in the house of an antiquities dealer near Giza recently. "The crocodile was the god of rebirth, and in the ancient Egyptian quest for immortality, bringing Sobek with you secured a safe passage to the afterworld."

Dr. Hawass's dig is off in an isolated, anhydrous patch, but just off the road is the famous tomb of Mereruka, a popular tourist walk-through. I join the throngs and file through the labyrinthine chambers and catacombs, past storyboards of a hippopotamus hunt, fowling in the marshes, dwarfs making jewelry, scenes of fishing, gardening, and farming, an ancient catalog of harmonic balance that reverses the telescope from today's hardships and irredentism.

There are enough plot elements in these halls to fill a periodic table. As I sweep my flashlight about, I keep looking for the long-nosed image, and there at last it is, in a fight scene in which a hippo is breaking the back of a crocodile, a not uncommon eschatological picture. Without death, of course, there can be no resurrection. In the Egyptian Book of the Dead, the deceased pass through a series of gates guarded by crocodiles. The correct answer to a riddle opens the gate and leads the way to the everworld.

From Saqqara, I trundle down into the Fayoum Valley, a depression some fifty miles southwest of Cairo and well below sea level, a place burly with old heat. It was here the greatest worship of Nile crocodiles took place, in a city founded by Menes of the First Dynasty and named Crocodopolis. The rulers under the Ptolemys took Sobek to a new level, claiming he was the father of Zeus in the Greek pantheon.

At a withering resort on the edge of Lake Qarun, we sip mint tea and look out at brightly painted fishing boats. Although you would not know from the graciousness and hospitality, this is an oasis where Muslim fundamentalism runs deep into the subsoil, and recent terrorist acts were supposedly plotted along these shores. This valley has long been a fertile bed for severe ideas.

Just up a tor above Lake Qarun, under a glare so fierce it roasts the eyes, I meet Dutch-born archaeologist Dr. Willeke Wendrich, associate professor at UCLA, who is overseeing a dig at Karanis in the heart of Crocodopolis. Karanis was the first Greco-Roman site excavated in Egypt, starting in 1895, and more than 100,000 archaeological objects have been recovered to date.

As she sweeps her hand along the dusty ruins, she says, "This area was once infested with crocodiles." She explains that not only did the annual deluge wash in hordes of crocodiles, but also when the waters retreated the crocodiles remained, lurking in puddles, pools, and fields, creating a constant threat. In an attempt to control this powerful and highly evocative beast, the people deified the crocodile, building at least two large pedestal temples to Sobek here to pay homage, often through sacrifices on altars.

We are standing in one, the limestone-based Southern Temple, in the central temenos of which rests a large stone altar, where one can only imagine what took place. Alongside is a concealed opening where, some speculate, priests hid and gave oracles, pretending they were Sobek, a sort of Wizard of Oz behind-the-curtain spectacle. Anatomizing a temple, though, like interpreting a hieroglyph, risks missing the unanalyzable spirit of the thing, its beautiful and hazardous play in a time we can never know.

On each side of the altar are ovenlike compartments, niches where sacred crocodiles, mummified with natron, were placed on biers. Out in the courtyard is what looks like a pool, and we know from Herodotus and other travel writers of the day that crocodiles were kept in pools and bedecked with golden necklaces and bracelets, glass earrings and pendants and other jewels, and hand-fed grain, meat, and wine mixed with milk and honey. It was an early form of ecotourism, a Roman holiday, so to speak, in that pilgrims from the other side of the Mediterranean came here for a chance to see a croc up close, and they paid for the privilege.

The temple seems to have been abandoned around the middle of the third century AD, about the time faith in Sobek as a god and savior waned, coinciding with one of the intervallic droughts. The droughts seemed to prove not only the pharaoh's vulnerability, but also the fact that no matter what homage was paid to Sobek, he didn't, or couldn't, bring the all-important flood sometimes.

From Fayoum, I drive back to the Nile proper and sail up the waters early texts cite as the sweat of Sobek, toward old Thebes, Luxor, and the Valley of the Kings. The middle section of the Nile is unhurt by wonder, defined by the sweat of the working class, full of factories, pylons, roofless brick dwellings, and mud huts adorned with satellite dishes.

Passing to Upper Egypt, the river again spills its romance, sighing around a bend shaped like a crocodile tail. At the water's edge is a colony of reeds, glistening and dancing as the current strolls the margins, stroking stems with fluid fingers. And there is a feast of birds—weavers, kingfishers, darters, cranes, herons, and of course, Egyptian geese flying in wedges around our craft.

Stepping into the Valley of the Kings at dawn, it is quiet and cool, as though the whole of the Nile Valley is holding its breath. The alabaster shops are closed; no urchins tug at the cuffs. Within the shafts of sunlight, platelets of dust move as if in obedience to the rhythms of ancient, silent slaves carrying their burdens.

But then the first of the tourist buses arrives, and then the next, and next, and on and on.

No summer theme-park crunch can describe the experience at the Valley of the Kings: waves and waves of tourists, like warriors from Middle-earth, pour into the tombs, and just when it seems there may be an ending to the crowds, another wave rolls in, tourists from every faucet of the world. Amid this valley of babble I manage to squeeze into a couple of tombs, and there, among many tales from the crypt, I find some vivid renditions of Sobek, seemingly guarding the entrance, open jaws facing outward. Sobek was seen as a powerful protector of tombs from not only raiders but also the deceased in the next life, just as the crocodile seemed to protect the fields. The crocodiles swept throughout the fields during the flood, keeping grass eaters such as hippos and livestock at bay.

In one tomb there is a crypt holding the mummy of a long-tailed crocodile. In another there are neat rows of drawings of the clawed beast in dramatic, frangible moments, scenes of life that reach across the centuries and move today's viewer because the backdrops seem in many ways so contemporary. We may worship different gods, but we still eat, drink, dance, hold hands, and hope there is an afterlife.

The pharaohs gave Sobek his due, but the veneration continues today, in different forms. From the cruise-ship dock I hire a high-masted felucca, one with a sail promoting a local beer, to take me a couple of miles to Crocodile Island, where the worship is alive and well at the Mövenpick Luxor Resort. Everything is croc-themed, from the tiered garden walls decorated with an infinity of crocodiles to "Sobek Hall," the conference center, to the swampy pool on the grounds that houses a lone live crocodile to the famous Crocodile Bar, where under a tapestry of a hungry croc with mouth agape I pay my homage and order a weapons-grade fruffy fruit drink and toast the mighty god.

Refreshed, I chuff upriver to the greatest temple to Sobek ever built. Six hundred miles south of Alexandria, the Ptolemaic ruin of Kom Ombo stands on a bend of the river, looking almost painterly upon approach, like the watercolors of nineteenth-century Nile explorations. While now a jut of mainland, the site was once an island for much of the year with the Nile's high water. Because it could be defended, it was also a main trading center for gold, spices, even elephants moving from Nubia in the south to the ports of the Mediterranean in the north. But while Egyptians here had protection from human invaders, their boats were often seized by crocodiles, and so they built a temple to Sobek in hopes he might look kindly upon their passages. In one surviving text, a man instructs his son to study so as to avoid menial jobs such as that of the washerman who "launders at the riverbank in the vicinity of the crocodile" or the fisherman "who is at his work in a river infested with crocodiles."

In a small shrine within the temple, mummified crocodiles from a nearby sacred animal cemetery are on display, their great scutes and withered limbs the color of antique wood. A hundred years ago, a workman excavating tombs flung aside a mummified crocodile, and it burst open. Papyrus with fragments of lost works from Sophocles, Homer, and Euripides spilled from the belly of the beast.

Now the cruise ships debouch tourists, thousands upon thousands who hungrily snap images of Sobek with their digital cameras and cell phones as they are processed in crocodile files through the sandstone arches, some not knowing where they are. I overhear one tourist ask a local guide, "Is this the Parthenon?" Wandering about myself, I feel as though I've returned to an old play but am no longer playing the same part, recast now as the audience. Sobek seemed almost a sacred secret to me more than two decades ago. Now he is an amusement park ride in a culture of massclusivity.

From Kom Ombo, I unravel the Nile once more, sailing south, the wind at my back, companioned by time and the river flowing. I purl past blistering cliffs and folding pages of orange sand, past feluccas puffing by islands, up a river that dreams along like a giant sleeping. The parted water rejoins unchanged at my stern's trailing edge, but the still shore whispers of a wilder time. Once these banks were crawling with crocodiles.

I arrive at last at the First Cataract, the site of the two Aswan dams. The second, the 364-foot-tall High Dam, was completed in 1970. Without the Nile, the desert would swallow Egypt like a pill. But the dams have tamed the desert. The crocodile was for millennia the most formidable creature in Egypt. But the dams have conquered the beast.

The Nile backs up for almost 300 miles now in one of the largest man-made lakes in the world, some 162 billion cubic yards of water in storage. The rising lake drowned towns and temples, buried significant archaeological sites, and dislocated some 90,000 Nubians, one of the largest human rights abuses in the history of dam building.

The still water behind the dam has become a brew-pot for schistosomiasis, a deadly disease transmitted by infected snails. The mineral-rich silt deposits from the yearly floods, which made the Nile floodplain fertile, are now held behind the dam, and the downstream water is becoming increasingly saline. Where there were once twenty-four kinds of fish, only twelve remain. The mongoose and otter have gone the way of the crocodile. Fishing throughout the whole of the Mediterranean has declined without the nutrients that used to flow freely into the delta.

Then there are the global repercussions. There is an accelerating erosion of coastlines (due to lack of sand, once delivered by the Nile) all along the eastern Mediterranean. And the whole Mediterranean Sea has seen an increase in salinity, with altered current quality traced hundreds of miles into the Atlantic. Some scientists predict the dam's effect on this outflow may contribute to the next ice age, a cog in an engine chugging toward global weather change.

I cross the engineering feat of the High Dam, commemorated by a jagged concrete lotus poking harsh petals to the sky, proclaiming friendship to the Soviet builders of the dam. The zenith of that god, the Communist one, has also passed.

Security here is extreme, as the dam is perhaps the most prominent terrorist target in Africa, yet after much negotiation, and some baksheesh, I am able to make it to the shores of Lake Nasser behind the dam, where I meet a group of fishermen. They have fished these waters all their lives, as did their fathers and their fathers' fathers. I ask about crocodiles in the lake, and they say they are indeed coming back, and in such numbers and size they are more than a nuisance. They find no spiritual utility, no sentiment or fancy with the crocodiles. The crocs' presence makes their traditional fishing waters a stew of anxiety. A colleague was pulled into the water during the last Ramadan and chomped to death. One fisherman shows me his hand, which is missing a thumb, torn off by a crocodile snagged in his night net. Although it's illegal, they sometimes kill the larger crocodiles, and smaller ones they sell to Nubians as tourist attractions. I ask them about tourism as an alternative to their own livelihoods, and they just give me a blank stare. Remote from the temples of preservation, they can't imagine doing anything other than what they do and what their families have always done.

That night I head to the pulsing potamic souq, more unruly and wanton than the counterpart in Cairo, where the shop-keepers hustle visitors like dice, shaking and prodding until the right answer rolls. Through a foyer done in Egyptian porphyry there is a shop called Che Guevara, kept by a smartly dressed young Nubian named Moustafa Abd El Kader. He waves me in and attempts to vend cobra, cheetah, and crocodile goods: belts, handbags, wallets, even the recombinant art form of a dagger with a baby crocodile claw handle. Flush with unearned famil-iarity, he describes the quality and puts a flame to a belt to prove it's not plastic. He lets me fondle a purse, sturdy and sensual, and volunteers that he personally hunts for the goods in his shop, and offers he could broker a live crocodile by tomorrow.

I ask him about ecotourism as a substitute for killing the

crocs, and he dismisses the concept with a wave. He holds up a belt and says there is just too much money in the crocodile trade, and business is booming; tourism will never compete.

The next day I find myself at a Nubian village as Disney might have imagined it. It consists of a series of families moved just downstream of the dam as Lake Nasser filled. They have recast their lives as tourist attractions, and their homes are filled with baubles and kitsch to hawk to the crucible of tourists who pass through each day.

Nailed above the doorstep to one home is a five-foot crocodile stuffed with straw, his teeth in a death grip around the neck of cormorant. Not long ago, crocodiles were hung thusly as talismans to protect inhabitants from the evil eye, but now they are simply tourist draws.

In a neighbor's home I meet Ahmed, a watery-eyed man in a white turban who shows me a glass cage with a bamboo lattice top stuffed with adolescent crocodiles, folded and bent to fit into the cramped space. If crocodiles are relics and symbols of the savagery we mean to rise above, these little reptiles defy that notion, their eyes fogged with discomfort and helplessness, their eyelids of mourning. Ahmed pokes one with a stick, and back it sends a disconsolate hiss. These crocodiles, smuggled from the lake, are tourist magnets, until they become too big, when they are killed for their leather and offered to brokers and the shops in the bazaar. This is not the ecotourism that Dr. El Din imagined.

So I ask what it would take to liberate one of the crocodiles. Ahmed says it is expensive and difficult to poach these "protected" creatures and offers to allow the release for $1,000. I counter with $500, and with little hesitation he agrees. So he chooses one of the crocodiles, a relatively docile one about three and a half feet in length, and hands him to me as he fetches a cardboard Aquafina box. I clutch the little monster with one hand tight around his bulging neck, the other gripped at his pitted tail, his power coursing up my arms. Then he thrashes his body about, driving his nose into my chest like a mallet to a tent peg, and I wrestle in terror, not knowing if he is attempting to attack or flee. He snaps his 64 sharp teeth and lashes his tail for a few awful seconds, but then calms, as though in trust, or waiting. I quickly drop him into the box, which I recognize in a flash as the same size and shape as the one in which Bill Olsen's legs were dumped along the Baro River. Ahmed quickly shuts the lid. Then to a remote edge of the lake we drive, to a spot safe from the blessings of civilization.

The shoreline has a pale, sun-sucked color, shadowless and uniform. We set the box on the coarse sand, pull back the cardboard, and lift out the lucky crocodile, his cold scales like the heads of small nails. Gently we place him on the ground, careful to avoid a snap, and on the count of three release him. He seems uncertain. He skitters forth a bit, but then stalls a few feet from the water. The lake is making small lapping sounds, like a giant taking sips from a mug.

I give the little croc a boost with my boot, and he sculls along the hot sand, makes a little leap into the water, and begins to propel away to freedom. Watching his little ripple deliquesce, it's hard to appreciate the antipathy for crocodiles, the human urge to rid the world of such life, though I well know this fellow would easily bite the hand that frees him, and in a few years' time would hesitate not a lick to swallow me whole. Yet in some way we must know there is a complexity, indeterminacy, and interconnectedness to all living things, and that it is a mistaken belief that humans are apart from nature. We have for millennia sought dominion over all wildlife, but by eliminating a natural torment, altering a balance that has endured since the morning of humankind, as did the dams with the Nile, there are results unforeseen, consequences that could raze that which was meant to be safeguarded in the first place. Once you mess with equilibrium, as when opening an Egyptian tomb, the essence is liable to crumble, and the world may well turn out to be a more dangerous place for all our efforts to tame it.

Ahmed offers a gap-toothed smile, the wrinkles of his face cracking like a windscreen hit by a stone. He lifts his hand and waves to the departing crocodile, who melts away into the green water. The sublime question is his postdeliverance fate. He may be recaptured and end up in another cage. He may be hunted. He may hunt a fisherman or more. He may become the magic glass into which our fears pour and out of which mythic beasts step. Or he may simply live a long and prosperous life, becoming once again a reason for tourists to come to Egypt, to be awed once more by the Lord of the Nile.

2

CAN WATER SAVE GORILLAS?

Rwanda

I t all boils down to water.

By some estimates, more than two billion people, a third of the world's population, are threatened by a scarcity of clean, potable water. And in a tiny swath of highland rain forest smack in the center of Africa, the last of the mountain gorillas, some 350 in all, are threatened as well.

It may seem enigmatic that gorillas living on the slopes of fertile volcanoes that receive rainfall almost every day could be in jeopardy over water issues. Mountain gorillas don't even drink— they slake their thirst from a salad bowl of wild celery, thistles, nettles, and bamboo. But it is the richness of the environment that has preserved this rare primate, and that same richness may be the vital cause of its demise.

Greg Cummings, the fifteen-year director of The Gorilla Organization, believes there may once have been 1,000 gorillas that roamed the Virunga Mountains. Gentle vegetarians, they had no predators, knew no borders, and lived in tropical afflu-ence, all their needs supplied from the swaddling forest.

That all changed in 1902. A German officer, Robert von Beringe, was the first to sight and shoot a mountain gorilla, set-ting off an era of trophy hunting. (In a rude bit of eponymous taxonomy, the primate is named *Gorilla gorilla beringei* for the man who may go down in history as the catalyst for its extinction.) By 1925, at least fifty gorillas had been taken, and in a moment of progressive sanity the Belgian government established Africa's first national park in the Virungas as a sanctuary for the gorillas.

Today, that sanctuary is divided into three parks in three countries, Uganda, the Congo, and Rwanda, and it is a fraction of its original size. And while today sport hunting no longer exists, other, more insidious forces are pushing the gorillas to the edge of extinction.

Habitat reduction is the modern curse. The area that butts against the park boundaries in Rwanda is the most densely populated in Africa, some 400 people per square kilometer, and those people are desperately poor, living on less than a dollar a day. When I fly over Rwanda, it is like flying over a circuit board, with little delineation between farm plots and cattle ranches, and only the cloud-eating Virungas the exception. When the mists clear, the volcanoes look as though they have been draped with ragged green tablecloths, the only uncultivated land in the country. Rwandans have an average of six children per family, and there is no place left to go. In 1958, the park was 340 square kilometers; by 1995, it was reduced to 125 square kilometers, the rest lost to the match, machete, and plow. And, as with the people, there is no other place for the gorillas to go. None has ever reproduced outside this unique afromontane lair; none live in captivity.

Even after the madness of 1994, in which a million people were murdered in a hundred days and another 2 million fled the country, Rwanda remains Africa's most overpopulated country, with some 8.5 million people in a landlocked tract the size of Vermont. Some accuse the wildlife conservationists of neocolonial myopia. Why make all these efforts to save 350 gorillas when millions of people are pounding at the door of survival? Greg Cummings argues that gorillas in fact may be a savior to the disenfranchised. Gorillas have become a major tourist attraction—Rwanda hosted 25,000 visitors in 2005, generating twenty-six million dollars, and a portion of the revenues went to community-based projects to improve crop yields, education, and health care. Greg's own organization raises significant money from a raft of American billionaires and funnels the cash to local endeavors that improve lives. "When I first came to Rwanda in 1992, I picked up a postcard that showcased the country's wildlife, and gorillas were conspicuous in their absence," Greg remembers. Few Rwandans had ever seen a gorilla or even an image of one. One of Greg's goals, he says with tongue only slightly in cheek, is to help usher in an "all-singing, all-dancing, gorilla-loving nation." Gorillas may be the country's greatest natural resource, and Greg contends that "if people champion and defend the gorillas, their own future is secured. Gorillas are Rwanda's gold."

But there is a blight that may be the dreaded knell for the survival of the gorillas, and in a seemingly oblique way it has everything to do with water. As we drive through the tropical savagery of an afternoon rainstorm, Greg explains why.

As in much of the developing world, where the human population has burst beyond its seams, people have slashed and burned the forests to plant. With the arboreal root system gone, the rich topsoil quickly washes away, and a natural catchment is gone. Runoff from the rain is immediate, and despite two rainy seasons here, villagers have found themselves with not enough water to endure. "Today, the greatest illegal human incursions into the gorilla park are not poachers, not firewood seekers, not planters, but water gatherers," Greg explicates. "Every day, villagers walk for hours deep into the park to volcanic sills and streams to fetch water."

But how does that harm the mountain gorillas? Because just as avian flu, Ebola, even AIDS may be the scourge of the human race, novel diseases are the biggest threat to the survival of the little kingdom of gorillas. The gorillas have few immunities, and exposure to villagers on a water quest can have dire consequences. Not long ago, eight gorillas were lost to measles. Others have died of flu, scabies, and other human-borne diseases, far short of their forty-five-year life expectancy. Some seven million years ago, we evolved from a common ancestor of these great apes, whose DNA is 97 percent shared with our own. A miniplague could wipe out the remaining gorillas in a flash, a portent perhaps of our own fate writ small.

The solution? Greg thinks it is providing a reliable source of freshwater to the communities surrounding the park, forestalling water quests into gorilla zones, lessening unsupervised contact. (When tourists make the treks, they are screened for coughs and ill-health symptoms, obliged to keep a distance of several yards from the apes, and not permitted to defecate near water in the sanctuary.)

The UN has designated March 22 as World Water Day, with a different theme each year ("Coping with Water Scarcity" in 2007). In that spirit, my colleagues and I have invested in Greg Cummings's vision for helping the mountain gorillas of Rwanda by building a cistern that will collect rainwater and supply a dependable source of clean water for one of the human communities just outside the park. It is but one coin in a vast and complicated coffer of coexistence and species survival, but like a reservoir that shines like silver, it will be an asset that makes a difference. Actress-turned-environmental-activist Daryl Hannah is making the long trek to this equatorial outpost, a village that straddles the watersheds of the Congo and the Nile, and she, along with Greg Cummings, hopes to see the water flow not away to giant rivers, not away from the realm of the mountain gorillas, but into the cooking pots and mouths of Rwandans in the mists.

Silverback Mountain

As we make the long, bumpy ride to the headquarters of Parc National des Volcans, our driver, Alex, wrestles the wheel like a captain in a typhoon, trying to miss not only the ruts but also the river of people pouring down this track. A great many of them are carrying yellow plastic jerry cans, water jugs, looking for the precious element. Some are on rusted bicycles with as many as ten jerry cans strapped to every available bar. Many are headed into the park on an illegal hunt to find the water that will help feed their families.

At one point, near the Mountain Gorillas Nest lodge and golf course, we stall at the edge of a craterlike fissure caused by erosion, its twisted mouth looking as though waiting for a catch. As Alex shifts gears forward and reverse, a hundred children surround the vehicle and press their faces against the glass; most are smiling as they reach out, palms up for some sort of acknowledgment. But others look angry, as though we are insulting them by driving past, as foreigners do each day, on $1,000-a-day safaris to see the gorillas. I am swept away with disorientation, as though we have veered off into an illusion, and don't know what to do. I roll down the window, and a dozen hands push through as though trying to claw their way out of poverty. I offer a plastic bottle of water, and it is snatched away by one of the boys, as though it were a thousand francs, a fortune in this terribly oversubscribed piece of the world.

There is a constant tug of conscience and imperative here. We've come to meet the mountain gorillas and understand their plight, but it is impossible to not be affected by the human stories, and there are so many it simply crushes the psyche. It's almost some sort of reverse caste system at work: it is the tiny population of gorillas that gets all the world's attention, and millions in donations, while the seething sea of people is, in relative terms, marginalized and ignored.

Once at park headquarters, we meet our guide, François Bigirimana, who has been tracking gorillas for twenty-six years and knew the famously misanthropic Dian Fossey. While studying gorillas from the late 1960s to the mid-1980s, Dr. Fossey made it a personal crusade to stop the poachers, a campaign that brought world attention and may have led to her own grisly murder when she was macheted six times to the head in her bed just after Christmas 1985.

Just before this trip, I breakfasted with Peter Guber, the producer of the Fossey biopic *Gorillas in the Mist,* which he cites as the film of which he is proudest in a long catalog of features. He remembered that when he pitched the movie, the executives at Warner Bros. were skeptical of his conceit. He wanted to film the lead, Sigourney Weaver, in situ with the authentic gorillas for six weeks and then write the script around what actually transpired. "That's backwards," Guber was told. "We write the script, then hire actors in gorilla suits and film on a soundstage in London. Nobody will know the difference." Guber prevailed, and viewers were awed by the verisimilitude. The film went on to inspire millions, fund several gorilla conservation organizations, and influence the hosting governments to make efforts to eliminate poaching.

To a degree it has worked. During Fossey's era, the gorilla population shrank to about two hundred fifty, teetering on the brink of extinction. Now there are about three hundred fifty, but there is still loss to poachers, who kill gorillas to sell their heads for wall mounts, their hands for ashtrays, and their babies as pets. François says he caught a poacher three weeks ago who had crossed over from the Congo. The poacher had snagged a baby, and François returned it to the forest and put the poacher in jail. The more menacing poacher, though, is the father looking for bush meat to feed his family. He lays snares inside the park to capture duiker and bushbuck, and the gorillas sometimes step into one and end up losing a limb or dying from infection. And then there are the bamboo poachers who cut down one of the major food sources for the gorillas. François says if caught, bamboo poachers get five years in jail, antelope poachers get ten, and a gorilla poacher goes to jail for life.

After an orientation in a tin hut in the midst of a rainstorm, we begin our trek up the volcano in search of the Sabyinyo group of eleven gorillas. It is a slosh wading through thick primary forest, screaming at the stinging nettles as they stick through pants, shirts, even gloves. We tuck our pants into socks to keep out the safari ants and stop every few minutes to catch our breath in the thin air. We're at 9,000 feet, winching ourselves upward through a matrix of mud and montane jungle.

After ninety minutes, we lurch over a ridge and practically into the arms of the largest silverback in Rwanda, Guhonda, thirty-five years old and 400 pounds, the alpha male of the Sabyinyo group, who is sucking water from a wild celery stalk. François makes a rolling grunt-hum, "*Mmmmm,*" and I repeat, as he says this is gorilla language for "I'm a friendly visitor."

Guhonda lopes to a glen where seven members of his group are resting after brunch, and François guides us down to a gallery just a few feet away. For the next hour we watch and photograph with our array of digital cameras as the gorillas do their thing. Two babies, looking like plush toys, tumble and bite and roll about just as my own son, Walker, used to do as a toddler. The mothers patiently discipline and groom their charges, while Guhonda lounges in the middle of it all, the king on his thistle couch. Individually, they stare at us with their large, knowing eyes, and it seems as though we've stumbled upon a neighborhood of mirrors, or of lenses to a different time in our lives. While below the park the eyes of the young seem to telegraph a winter landscape in a tropic paradise, the soft, brown eyes of the gorillas speak of an unfallen place and time.

As we trip down the slippery volcano, Greg Cummings, who has made some fifty treks to the mountain gorillas, sums it up: "You come here with all this high-tech gear and think the gorillas will be impressed; instead you are overwhelmed by how much we've lost."

GORILLA TACTICS

When Greg recently met Bill Gates Sr., father of the Microsoft cofounder, at the Bill & Melinda Gates Foundation, and Bill learned that the fee for an hour's visitation with the gorillas is $375, he balked: "That's more than I get as a lawyer."

Donations and fees to save the gorillas are in the millions of dollars each year. One billionaire benefactor, when told how many gorillas were the recipients of his largess, remarked, "I just gave enough to put up all the gorillas in Claridge's [hotel] for a year."

The money for gorilla salvation goes to many good works, such as training trackers, clothing and arming antipoaching squads, removing snares, researching behavior, even giving inoculations. But The Gorilla Organization, which Greg heads, is devoted to what he calls "a holistic solution," one that invests in community development surrounding the park. His theory is that if the lives of the two and a half million people who live in the shadow of the Virungas are improved because of the presence of great apes, they will come to say to the more shortsighted, "Hell, no. You're not coming into the gorilla habitat. The gorillas are our bread and butter here." And the gorillas' presence is the reason for a local supply of clean water, as we are to witness.

"I think that sometimes environmentalists can be out of touch with the reality of poverty, of the challenges that face people who have just emerged from civil war. Wildlife conservation can't happen in isolation," Greg postulates as we trundle toward the village of Gitaraga, just below the 13,540-foot-high Muhabura volcano, home to several gorilla groups.

Greg's organization employs what he calls *gorilla tactics*, investing in a number of community projects, such as farmer training for better crop yields, artisan schools so villagers can make handicrafts to sell to tourists, microcredit loans to entrepreneurs, environmental education, poacher reform, school building, and, especially significant today, the building of cisterns. "We've built twenty-six cisterns, all attached to the long roofs of schools, all within two kilometers of the park." It's the children who make the long, illegal journeys into the park to fetch water, the children who put the gorillas most at risk with exposure.

And as we grind up the last muddy hill to Gitaraga, it is the children who meet us, some fifteen hundred in all who attend this tiny, tin-roofed school. They come swarming to our vehicles, a sea of smiles, backdropped by the storybook volcano that looks lifted from a Japanese silk. None recognizes Daryl Hannah, who has lent her name and energy to this day and this project. But they make the connection between our presence and the construction that has been going on for the past fifteen days next to their school, a twenty-five-cubic-meter cistern that is in its final moments of fashioning, here in a village with no springs, no source of clean water within five kilometers.

Out of the ruck of cheering children emerges Peter Celestin Muvunyi, the lead engineer for the building of the cistern. He leads us down a path littered with yellow jerry cans to the new cistern. Peter is proud of this work, built in record time, and it is only the second in the series built with stones rather than brick. "It's more expensive to build with stones, but it is better for our environment," Peter boasts. "The bricks need to be cooked, and that requires cutting down trees to fuel the kiln, and fewer trees mean less catchment."

The circular cistern is a beautiful sight, almost elegant in its simple design, bordering on art. A plastic pipe runs from the school roof eaves, feeding rainwater to the contained reservoir, which then releases its bounty through a spigot three meters from the base. It is here the children who used to walk so far each morning, missing school, will now find the water for their families, and that is more beautiful than art.

Like the black space between stars, the effectiveness of one more cistern on saving gorillas is difficult to measure. But at least one star is willing to believe theory over imprecise data. Daryl Hannah has flown halfway around the world to participate in the opening of this cistern because she is a supporter of World Water Day, and because the concept of being involved in a project that could contribute to the future well-being of mountain gorillas is irresistible. Daryl has most of her life been involved in saving animals. She grew up on the forty-second floor of a high-rise in Chicago, but even there when she found broken-winged birds and other small creatures in need, she would take them home and nurse them to health. When she was seven, her family was on a road trip and stopped at a restaurant off the freeway. She wasn't hungry so she stayed in the car, but when she saw a trailer of cattle she wandered over and began to commune with a big-eyed calf. She spent a half hour petting and speaking with the young cow, and when the driver emerged she turned to him and asked the name of the animal. "At seven o'clock tomorrow, 'Veal,'" the driver replied. Daryl never ate meat again and became a lifelong friend and savior to animals.

As an adult, Daryl has hugged a manatee, swum with dolphins, petted a moose, and been kissed by a wild wolf. Now she takes in strays and rescues animals of all stripes—dogs, cats, horses, turtles, tropical birds, even a South American tree frog she found in a Los Angeles swimming pool. So when, just a few weeks ago, I told her of our project to help finance a cistern at the edge of the gorilla habitat, working with Greg Cummings and The Gorilla Organization, she volunteered to help. "I've always wanted to see the gorillas!"

Now it is time. It is a preternaturally sunny day in a part of the world usually swirling in mist. There is a ribbon across the entrance to the cistern, and Daryl is presented with a china plate covered with embroidered linen. Inside is a pair of scissors, which she gently removes, and with which she attempts to cut the ribbon, which is stubbornly resistant. But after a few attempts, it falls away, and Daryl and the mayor and the governor and the director general of tourism and national parks, and all sorts of other keen parties, walk to the basin below the cistern, where a shiny silver tap awaits. Daryl is handed a plastic petrol container, which she positions to drink. As she turns the spigot, there is a sound like compression brakes. All of Gitaraga holds its breath; we all sense an intangible atmosphere of imminence, as though a huge charge of lightning is building up within a thundercloud. Then, a whoosh, and cool, clean, clear water issues forth. The sun strikes, the water bursts into a million gems . . . it is pure, pure magic. I reach my hand into the cascade and feel the vitality and power as it courses up my arm, into my chest, and up into my brain. The lives of several hundred families, and perhaps as many gorillas, are at this moment changed, even if by but a bucket's worth in a wide and stormy sea.

MONKEY WRENCHING

> *And the gorillas themselves are too shrewd to talk . . .*
> *They have a very healthy wariness about people in gen-*
> *eral and government people in particular. As one of*
> *them told me once, "If it got out that we can talk, the*
> *conservatives would exterminate most of us and make*
> *the rest pay rent to live on our own land; and the liber-*
> *als would try to train us to be engine-lathe operators."*
> —Robert Shea and Robert Anton Wilson,
> *The Golden Apple*

As a storm of people gathers to celebrate the cistern, I imagine the gorillas on the volcano above looking down in amusement, wondering among themselves what all the fuss is about.

More than two thousand Rwandans have come to the grounds of Gitaraga Primary School near the Ugandan border to rejoice in the new cistern, some from as far away as the capital, Kigali. There are film crews, photographers, dignitaries, a movie star—this is the biggest thing to ever hit town.

There is a crude PA system with a swarm of feedback. There is an entire Goodwill store of fashion. There are speeches (they could use the Academy Award rules for duration) and thank-yous and acknowledgments. Failure is an orphan; success has many fathers, and we seem to have a whole haunt of silverbacks here today.

The governor, like the mayor before him, cites gorillas as the great natural asset that generates money for community projects such as this, and he stresses the gorilla habitat must be kept sacred. When the governor asks if anyone still hunts in the forest, an old man raises his hand and says he has been culling his subsistence from the park his whole life. The governor asks him to come forward and offers to buy him a hoe if he promises to stay out of the park. The old man is suspicious, but agrees only if the governor gives him the money right there, right now, and to

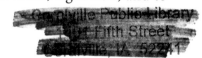

the amusement of the crowd the governor reaches deep into his pocket and produces a few thousand francs.

This is an auditory country. There are no movie theaters in the shadow of the Virungas, no video stores, and the few televisions are in hotels for foreigners. Magazines and newspapers are rare; most people don't even read. So the primary source for information is the radio. It was the radio that served as the critical tool to incite the genocide of 1994, provoking the ruling Hutu to kill neighbors, families, and friends, anyone with rival Tutsi heritage, up to a million in little more than three months. Now the radio is used to spread a different kind of propaganda, that of conservation and celebration of the gorillas, and it has infused itself into school curricula and the consciousnesses of young minds as the golden rule has for western schoolchildren.

When the speeches are done, the music and dancing begins. There are *ingoma* drums, choruses, and a one-stringed instrument called an *indingidi,* a sisal-snared fiddle whose sawer could beat Charlie Daniels to Georgia. All the songs are themed with water as the source of life. There is a kind of Rwandan rap, wherein a young girl from the wildlife club challenges her peers:

"You children, what is your plan now?"

"We want to live in a healthy Rwanda with clean water and a protected environment. Conservation is the only way we can protect the sources of life, of water and trees."

"Who told you all this?"

"We are students, and we have our own club. Dian Fossey is also helping us to learn more about the wildlife of Rwanda."

Then there is a peculiar rendition of "Jingle Bells," with the words altered a bit for local relevancy but the spirit in some ways the same: "Because the cistern has come there will be no more sleeping without food. Because the cistern has come there will be no water you can't cook. There will be lots of cleanliness now, and everything is going to be fine with the people of the area and of the kids of this school."

Next there is a kind of ballet, simple yet expressive, dignified

but provocative, a delicate poem of subtle arm movements, genteel turns, and graceful swoops, arms rippling, supple bodies
undulating, a dance full of politeness, all set to customized lyrics:
"Come and see. We are happy because we have water." It seems
a refined and elevated art, coming from one of the most remote
villages on the planet. It seems so hard to draw the circle from
preserving the gorillas by honoring their habitat through providing alternative sources of water for adjacent communities from
money generated by gorillas, but somehow the music and dance
do so elegantly.

The grand finale is the *Ikinimba* dance, a venerated bop that
tells the stories of Rwandan kings and heroes, with rotating arm
movements like rice blowing in the wind and impossible foot
moves. I know, because the Rwandan dancers invite the American visitors to the floor, and most of us look like the "wild and
crazy" Czech brothers attempting an interpretive dance to "Flight
of the Bumblebee." The exception is Daryl Hannah, who has the
long limbs of a gazelle and chooses not to attempt imitation, but
rather does her own funky pronk that somehow makes sense in a
place that seems a physical manifestation of jazz.

We end our day with a visit to His Excellency Paul Kagame,
the president of Rwanda. Greg Cummings wears a tie with more
gorillas on it than survive in the Virungas, Daryl wears sneakers
without shoelaces, and I don my only clean shirt, an ExOfficio
Buzz Off. Paul Kagame lived in the Virungas for several years
when he led the rebel Tutsi forces and made forays back and
forth from Uganda. But during that time he never saw a mountain gorilla. It wasn't until he came to power in 2000 that he made
a gorilla trek, a four-hour slog in the rain. When he saw the
gentle giants in their own private demilitarized zone, he found
religion. He went on record later that year saying that the nation's
two highest priorities were conservation and HIV prevention.
So when we asked how he has managed to oversee a national
change of conservation consciousness in the midst of so many
pressing human problems, a transformation that has resulted

in a lessening of poaching and encroachment and a significant increase in the gorilla population, he ties it back to the 1994 genocide. He has made a harsh-light policy of remembrance of that time, making sure people look into the face of evil and understand it so it cannot happen again.

"When something so horrible happens, it allows people to start over, to reevaluate priorities. Gorilla tourism is the third largest source of foreign exchange, and we value gorillas now in a way we didn't before the war. We have a unique asset in the gorillas, and by helping them they can help us."

Somewhere up high up in the Virungas, I'm convinced, the gorillas are celebrating, sucking water from thistles and celery, rolling about the bamboo, exchanging commentary about the humans below. Tomorrow, with Daryl, we'll climb to these innocent landscapes and learn what we can from our cousins and their lofty, leafy kingdom of grace.

GORILLAS IN THE CLEAR?

> *You may drive out nature with a pitchfork, yet she'll be constantly running back.*
> —Horace, *Epistles*, Book 1, Epistle 10

Visiting the mountain gorillas is an exercise in devolution. We fly halfway around the world, drive for several hours to the base of a set of tropic volcanoes, hike for a number of hours, and then crawl the final steps up into the lair of our ancestral kin.

On the trek toward the park, we pass several wattle-and-daub huts roofed with what looks like witches' hats. They seem hastily constructed and give the impression they would get up and leave if they only had the energy and something did not block their way.

We pass long-horned Achole cattle, who until recently regularly mowed down gorilla vegetation (Dian Fossey famously shot thirty head at close range in her private effort to preserve the gorilla habitat). But the cattle no longer roam upward.

We wade through a field of what looks like daisies, but they are in fact pyrethrums, a cash crop that yields a natural insecticide. Not long ago, 22,000 acres, roughly half of the protected gorilla habitat, were given over to a European scheme to cultivate an alternative to DDT. But the fields encroach no further.

All have been stopped by a fetial wall. From fees generated by ecotourists and donated money from nongovernmental organizations, a five-foot-high, volcanic stone wall has been fashioned that surrounds most of the park and is on the path to completion. Ostensibly designed to keep buffalo and forest elephants from raiding crops, it serves another, perhaps greater, purpose of delineating the park boundary so farmers, hunters, rangers, and antipoaching squads know the armistice line. Rwanda has a zero-tolerance policy for unauthorized visits to the park, though the mandate is still violated with some regularity. A few days ago, our team followed six young girls on a dangerous water quest into the park, not just because they were at risk of being arrested, but also because the slippery landscape is so severe a fall could be fatal. Unsupervised exposure to gorillas on these quests has the potential to transmit disease in both directions. One villager on a recent water quest was bitten by a venomous snake and lost his leg. But with alternatives, such as the village cisterns now being constructed, water quests may become a thing of the past.

At the zigzag passage through the wall, we step over a scattering of porcupine quills—some wildlife still travels both directions—and begin the steep climb up the volcano. We swat away branches, cling to creepers, slide through muck, and whack the biting safari ants as we reel up into the richest ecosystem in Africa. Daryl, who lives in an off-the-grid home at 10,000 feet in Telluride, Colorado, has fewer problems with the elevation than the rest of us, and she is quickly at the front of the pack, eager for first contact.

Somewhere in the middle flanks of the volcano we hear a

rustling, and within a few steps a black ball of fur flies from the top of a bamboo stalk. It is Daryl's first mountain gorilla sighting, and her eyes grow with the moment. The gorilla knuckle-walks by us within a couple feet, and we proceed to follow. Suddenly we are surrounded by gorillas, from babies to blackbacks and silver-backs, thrashing about in their own guiltless ways. We listen to a baby whimpering as its mother refuses it back passage, an attempt at weaning. We watch as two young males wrestle, fur flying and leaves scattering as they tumble about the forest. "Monkeying around," Daryl says with a laugh, and for a moment one of the gorillas looks at us and seems to display a toothy smile. Another baby strolls to one of our video camera microphones, covered in synthetic fur as a wind screen, and reaches out to touch what seems a fellow creature. A mother with disproportionately huge eyes stares at Daryl as though she's seen her in some movie but can't quite place her, and puffs of condensation steam from her mouth. Two other apes rise up and thump their chests with a sound like mallets on wood, and Daryl thumps her own chest back. The sway-bellied silverback watches all the activity dispas-sionately, with eyes that nature seems to break through, then falls back to chill on a springy bed of vegetation. When Daryl sits near the lounging ape and begins to explain her delight, the sil-verback seems to punctuate each sentence with a disapproving grunt. Then, when another criminally cute baby wanders by, I ask Daryl, "Don't you just want to take it home?"

"No. I'd rather stay here."

Violence just seems missing here. At this moment there is not a breath of brutality in these long-haired beings. The vast for-est seems motionless as in a picture, caught in a continuous now, living in the churns of mists with neither past nor future. Then our hour is up.

As we gather our packs, we hear another sound that doesn't quite fit the milieu. We stop moving and listen, and a tinkling fills the air, as though something is pouring into a bowl. It is beautiful music, like a small spring singing to itself, and we realize it is the sound of children singing down the slopes, down at the village of Gitaraga, where the new cistern is installed. At this moment there seems a balance, one that may have existed two centuries back before French naturalist Paul du Chaillu, after encountering a family of lowland gorillas, described them as "hellish dream creatures," an impression that remains today and is reinforced through cliché and popular film. But here in Rwanda, a culture shift is underway, precipitated by tourists, politicians, nonprofit organizations, and local communities. For the moment, the gorilla population is stable and growing; the habitat is mostly protected. Life for the surrounding communities is improving. Hope wafts the air.

Back in 1996, I shared a dinner with Bill Gates Jr., and he had recently returned from trekking to see the mountain gorillas. He proclaimed the sight one of the wonders of the world, but he was pessimistic about the prospects. He was aware of the political problems in the region and the enormous population pressures, and he thought the trend not good. At the end of a long conversation that spiraled through dessert, Bill bet me one hundred dollars that within ten years the mountain gorillas would be extinct. Well, Bill, I am happy to report you were wrong (a rare event, admittedly), and I would request that the hundred dollars be sent to The Gorilla Organization, one of the good-works groups that has done so much to make a future for the gorillas possible through investment in community projects, such as the Gitaraga cistern. Because of the empowerment of villagers alongside the volcanoes, the people have come to appreciate the asset in their backyard and now make efforts to preserve this breathing, thumping, black and silver currency.

As we reach the buffalo wall on the return trip, Daryl stops short. "I'm just gonna stay here now. Say hi to my family. I'm gonna go live with the gorillas." And she turns toward the volcano and walks back into the forest, to perhaps a more splendid state of imagination and nature's own infinite but gracious imperfections, the habitat of the mountain gorillas of Rwanda.

3

PEACE IS HELL ON NATURE

Bosnia

The Bosnia we know from images of the war—the bombed and bullet-ridden buildings, the scars from the 1,200-day siege of Sarajevo—has kept from view a Bosnia we don't know, a place where nature has been bighearted with its gifts. The country described sometimes as the heart between the mouths of two lions hosts one of the two greatest tracks of primeval forests in Europe, unmatched biodiversity, daunting mountain faces yet to be climbed, wild rivers with water so pure you can cup your hand to drink, some of the highest concentrations of wildlife, and perhaps the last highland tribes of seminomadic peoples on the continent.

But the political thunderstorms that have crashed over this country for millennia have not been kind to these vast natural assets, especially of late. Only 0.6 percent of the country is protected, but even that is a dubious designation. The war ended more than a dozen years ago, but it left a country devastated economically, and, some would say, morally. In the rush to find a new economy, natural resources are being exploited at record rates, usually for nonsustainable, short-term benefits, often illicitly. Every hour of the day, belching diesel trucks bearing timber trundle down passes on their way to Italy or to other buyers of hardwoods, some of which is from irreplaceable primary forest. Even the international community is complicit, purchasing cheap local lumber to rebuild houses in Kosovo and other devastated neighborhoods.

Few in the world even know of these issues, or of the exceptional natural wonders of Bosnia now threatened, and those who do more often than not turn blind eyes. One man, however, is leveling his stare, waging his own war against crooked activities and doltish policies, dedicating his life to saving what he considers inimitable international treasures: a slight, ponytailed American, a vegetarian in a land of meat-eaters, a man who suffers from hay fever, a bad back, and a virtuous and vital obsession—Tim Clancy.

After graduating from Florida State in 1992 with a degree in English literature and creative writing, Tim took the obligatory year off to backpack abroad. While crashing with friends in London he heard about efforts to help the Muslims of Bosnia, who were being attacked from two sides, Serbia and Croatia, in the crumbling country of Yugoslavia. He'd never heard of these places, but his heart told him to help, so he found himself volunteering for relief work in refugee camps, driving ambulances, conducting medical evacuations, and shuttling baby packages through the Sarajevo tunnel, often under fire. Some of his colleagues and friends were killed, and he had many close calls. When the war ended with the Dayton Peace Accords in 1995, Tim went to work for Save the Children. When after a couple years he quit, disillusioned with agendas and priorities within the organization (and shaken by a death threat from an Albanian), he decided to take a year off and explore the wilderness of Bosnia, which he had only glimpsed from afar during the war.

Despite the land mines, Tim hiked and climbed throughout the country and was dazzled by the wildness and intoxicated with the exquisite beauty. He found his own peace of mind and purpose. With some like-minded friends, he founded Green Visions, the first ecotourism company in the country, and wrote several books extolling the sights of backcountry Bosnia. And he became an outspoken advocate of quelling corruption when it came to stewardship of natural resources, a tireless blaze for conservation in a ring of counterfire, a voice in the wilderness for such.

I meet Tim in Sarajevo, where he has just purchased a plot of land. This is his home now, and he shows me about the city, pointing out the marks of the war, the countless bullet holes and blasted remains of buildings, including the once-great library and the once-grand Hotel Europa, splashed in phosphorus-scorched black, almost like a piece of art. We dial back further into the city's fierce past and cross the bridge where Archduke Franz Ferdinand was assassinated in 1914, sparking the First World War. We go by the Forestry Service Building, where outside the Bosnian flag hangs upside down, and we pass the invisible Ministry of Tourism, which has yet to establish a physical office. And we make our way up over the natural bowl of hills surrounding this city, up where snipers once crouched, beyond the rows of pointed tombstones where many of the ten thousand dead from the longest city siege in modern history lay buried.

Tim has invited me on a bear quest in his favorite hiking haunt, Sutjeska National Park, about two twisting hours by car, accompanied by James Taylor and Bob Dylan in the player, his father's poets, and also his, he says. Tim is thirty-five.

The park is 17,500 hectares, larger than some small countries, with no trail maps or guides. When we step into this cathedral of old-growth beech and black pine, Tim offers that we are probably the only ones here. We make our way to an overview at the base of Bosnia's highest peak, the 7,828-foot-high Maglic Mountain on the Montenegrin border, the last great sigh of the Alps extending south from Switzerland. "This is my church, my mosque, my synagogue." He spreads his arms to the landscape. Then we make our way to a mountain hut on a serene lake, next to an old lodge that had been burned to its stone base during the war.

At daybreak, we set out to hike to an alpine aerie to look for bears, wolves, and wild goats, chamois. Before the war, Bosnia had the second highest concentration of brown bears in the world, after Canada, and perhaps the greatest number of wolves in Europe, and chamois were so ubiquitous they would sometimes leap over hikers' heads. Now, nobody knows how many remain, but Tim guesses perhaps as many as one thousand bears, which would still rank highest in the region. However, hunting is allowed in the park, as are off-road Jeep rallies, and Tim believes there is illegal timbering as well, under the auspices of "sanitary cuts," which is felling a swath of forest around an infected tree. "There is no culture of conservation here," Tim rants. "There is no environmental education. Bosnia has an identity problem . . . What history should be taught; in what language? Ecological awareness is low on any priority list."

But we find no bears on our quest. Nor wild goats, nor wolves. Just waving fields of wildflowers, the alpine wind, and the sounds of timber trucks rumbling through the trees. "Twelve years ago we were killing people. Now we're killing the environment," Tim laments.

Tim then wants to take me to one of the first eco-lodges in the country, Motel Sunce, up a long dirt road atop the windswept Podvelezje Plateau in the southwest. Its proprietor, Ismet Stranjak, a Bosnian Muslim, met Tim during the war when they both volunteered at a mobile hospital, and they became fast friends. The lodge is modest and fashioned from concrete—not the western vision of an eco-lodge, but the food is organically grown, and certainly the staff is local. No money being sucked away to multinationals here. And it is quiet and peaceful, a place to clear the mind and feed the soul. The little lodge sits beneath the stunning mountain ridge called Velez and in front of a stark memorial to the villagers who died in local battles—some one hundred fifty names are inscribed—and on the path for local sheepherders, who pass by each night around sunset.

After we sup on organically grown peppers stuffed with beef and rice, traditional salad and soup with hypercrisp fresh vegetables, and farmers' cheese, and share a glass of homemade Herzegovinian rakija, Ismet tells a story that makes his mission to find solace and a salve in the wilderness more achingly evocative than any other.

Two years ago, Ismet's ten-year-old son, Imtias, was playing on this plateau with a friend. They found an explosive left from the war and began to fool around with it. It blew up, killing both boys.

Ismet received nothing from any government, from any aid organization, from any nongovernmental organization, for his personal loss. He had no place to go for escape or succor, save here. So he runs his little lodge, hoping it respects the land that killed his son, hoping it attracts people who will travel a bit off the beaten path to find peace of mind on a wilderness plateau in back of Bosnia.

THE LEAP OF FAITH IN BOSNIA

(*Dive,* he said.)

Although many had died violently in the volleys and fire-fights across the river, when the mortar hit the slender, pale lime-stone arch and the old bridge collapsed into the cold, teal-blue river, most everyone cried.

The Neretva River, Tim Clancy says, is the Nile of Bosnia. For centuries it was the passageway from the sea to the riches of the interior, the river road up which sailed explorers, settlers, traders, and conquerors, from the Illyrians to the Romans to the Ottomans to the Austro-Hungarians to the Serbs and Croats, in attempts to plunder or possess this land.

And just as the Nile has the pyramids, the Thames its London Bridge, the Seine its Eiffel Tower, San Francisco its Golden Gate Bridge, all emblems that transcend the tyranny of geography and politics, Bosnia for five hundred years had Stari Most, the gracious single-span link across the Neretva. Commissioned by Suleiman the Magnificent in 1557, completed nine years later, the elegant bow withstood earthquakes, floods, battles, and two world wars. But on November 9, 1993, Croat forces pummeled the little foot-bridge with tank shells, and after long resistance, it fell like a proud

warrior into the crying, hissing currents. For a moment, denominations on all sides were united in grief over a cherished monument
destroyed. The hearts of thousands sank with the stone.

Tim Clancy was nearby when the bridge went down. He was
volunteering at a refugee camp for mothers and children. One of
his colleagues, Colleen Webster, a young American from Michigan, had shown up to help as well, packing a five-year supply of
toiletries. But the month before Mostar was shelled, she was hit in
the stomach with a rocket-propelled grenade. She died instantly.
Tim knew many killed in the madness. Everyone here does.

But on July 22, 2004, nine years after the war ended, the bridge
reopened, and the sky was lit not with the lights of conflict, but
with fireworks, the pyrotechnics of peace. The symbolism happily cried with cliché, the bridge over the ethnic gap, connecting
East and West, church to mosque, the past to the future. And it
brought back a proud tradition that dated back to the Ottomans:
the Mostari bridge divers.

The Mostaris were the original bridge keepers, who main-
tained the one-hundred-foot span and took tolls from those who
passed. In the seventeenth century, however, a Turkish travel
writer described how young men would jump from the eighty-
foot-high bridge as a rite of passage. Today, the Mostaris jump for
tourists and their touro-euros.

On the bridge's western abutment at the entrance to the
Mostari Divers Club, we meet Ermin Saric, one of the eight official bridge divers, meaning he dives professionally; it's his job.
He's been diving since age fourteen. He is twenty now and says
he will dive as long as he can. He thinks the body can handle the
punishment until around fifty, at which point the shock of the
cold water might trigger a heart attack. Ermin says about one or
two people die each year diving, and there are many injuries, but
all these casualties are from nonprofessionals—swaggering tourists, locals on a dare, Saturday night drunks. As long as Ermin
can remember, there have been no fatalities among club members, as they know how to dive it right.

Ermin offers to demonstrate. He skips the part where he passes a floppy hat to tourists lining the parapets—ever since the bridge was listed as a World Heritage Site the number of visitors has steadily increased, as have the fortunes of the divers. As he stands at the apex, he drenches his head and limbs in cold, cold water from a big bottle to acclimate his body for the freezing Neretva. He climbs over the matrix of metal bars that protects innocents from the precipice, and then he "enters into the world of diving." There are butterflies in his stomach; they have yet to go away after all these years and countless jumps. Then he spreads his arms as though flying in the wind and leaps into the void, feet first.

About two-thirds of the way down, he draws his arms tight against his sides and firms his legs straight and fast against one another. He tucks his chin against his chest and points his toes to the fast-approaching water. Then he hits the river "like a bullet," and with a sound like glass shattering he disappears. There is an awful silence as all who watch hold a collective breath . . . and then, *whoosh,* Ermin's head pops to the surface, and he swims to shore. If the demand is there, Ermin will jump six or seven times today.

There's no health care or insurance with this job, certainly no job security. But in a country with 40 percent unemployment, Ermin is thankful to be a Mostari, and he admits there are perks: no local women are divers, but they admire the men who are, and Ermin is never without girlfriends, he says with a grin.

Although Mostar is far and away the most famed feature of the Neretva, Tim wants to show me more. He takes me to the delta of the river, where it begins its fan into the Adriatic, right on the Croatian-Bosnian border. Not only have waves of armies flowed up this waterway, but also thousands of birds, which biannually migrate, first from Africa, across the Mediterranean, and up this corridor into Europe for the summer, then back again.

Tim points upstream and says he wants to take me up this limestone-encased, emerald-hued river to show off its rare beauty. He says there is nothing quite like it in Europe, or even in the whole of the world. It is a ribbon of adventure, where one can raft down pieces of white magic, climb soaring sedimentary walls, and hike through "the most unexplored gorge in Europe." And near its highland headwaters, up a narrow tributary canyon, lies the isolated village of Lukomir, where people have lived a seminomadic life for centuries and are little changed in customs, dress, and cosmology for the passage of time.

All these, Tim says, are threatened by politics, by misplaced priorities, by corruption, by desperation, as Bosnians strive to reconstruct a nation and construct a viable economy in the aftermath of war.

Our first stop traveling up the river is Pocitelj, an art colony among the fig trees, shaded by the labyrinthine walls of Sahat-kula, the Ottoman fort strategically situated above the Neretva so that watchmen could see approaching invaders for miles. The mosque in the fort has been superbly rebuilt after being razed during the war, but the grand watchtower is crumbling and scarred with trash and graffiti—someone suitably named Darko had an urge to let visitors know every stone window through which he gazed. There is everywhere the edgy smell of must and uric acid. Tim says the government would like to preserve this ancient architectural monument, but it lacks the funds, so the fort falls victim to vandalism and is slowly dissolving into the Neretva.

A little farther up the valley, we again stop at Mostar for a cup of syrupy Turkish coffee just upstream of the bridge, which appears as a pastel rainbow. The rushing water below looks clear as local brandy, but Tim says it is actually quite polluted. The war knocked out the sewage systems, and now all the waste from the town disembogues into the river. This, Tim laments, is an example of how the residuum of war affects the environment. A Japanese aid group offered to pay for a sewage system serving both sides of the bridge, but while the Bosnian Muslims agreed, the Bosnian Croats on the western bank did not, so the project has not gone forward. The bridge may be repaired, but a chasm persists, and the Catholics did not want to share their feculence with nationals of the other side.

Up the Buna River, a Neretva tributary near Mostar, there is a karst cave that seems to deliver cherished secrets as clearly as if uttered with a voice. At its side shines the seventeenth-century Velagic House, a dervish monastery. The water, filtered by the porous rock, spills like the translucent eyes of an eagle. Swallows sing and flit. This is a back eddy of Bosnia, spared the wounds of war. Glades of trees stand tall, the stream runs pure, and the monastery lusters as it has for four hundred years. "This the way Bosnia used to be," Tim sweeps his hand across the mystic tableau. "And this is what Bosnia should aspire to be again in the future."

RIDGE OVER TROUBLED WATERS

> *Grey is all theory; ever green is the tree of life.*
> —Goethe, *Faust*

There is a theory that war sharpens the senses to such a drug-gedlike state that everything afterward is like sleeping. In Bill Broyles's post-Vietnam book, *Brothers in Arms,* he argues that being in battle is such an overpowering thrill intoxicant that survivors spend lives in the wake either reliving or trying to recapture those adrenaline-packed moments. The same has been said of extreme adventurers, who create their own life-and-death battles with Everest, with the Amazon, with unexplored rivers, and with untamed wildlife.

"I came here for the boom-boom," Tim Clancy half-jokes as he drives about the ruins of Mostar, pointing out where he ran down streets amid sniper fire, where he dodged mortars. Tim came here to help people—no debate—but most Samaritans help the diseased in Africa, the deprived in Asia, the disenfranchised in Brooklyn, without the prospects of flying artillery.

It's easy to draw false analogies here, but as Tim defiantly struts into the sand quarry, I can't help but think it is an act of righteous thrill-seeking that harks back a dozen years. And I'm guilty as well. I pace just a few steps behind.

We are in the mountain valley of Diva Grabovica, just off
the Neretva River, in the stony heart of the Dinaric Alps. Behind
us is Velki Kuk, the largest rock face in the Balkan Peninsula,
over 3,400 feet sheer, taller than Yosemite's El Capitan. Framing it
are ragged beech and pine-covered peaks, which Tim has tagged
the Herzegovinian Himalaya. This is a wilderness track that in
1985 was proposed as the mnemonically inhospitable Prenj-
Cvrsnica-Cabulja National Park, after the three mountain chains
that connect here, along with the interface of the Mediterranean
and alpine ecosystems. But the war interrupted the process of
park designation, and though Tim, who has hiked extensively
here and describes it as his personal cathedral, has picked up the
mantle, the official appointment has stalled. And like a gaping
battle wound in the face of this wilderness, here festers the Prominvest sand quarry.

Prominvest, a large prefab construction company, started
digging here in 1996, a year after the war ended, and has been
profitably supplying the core of concrete for rebuilding the country ever since. The problem, Tim says, is that Prominvest has no
permit to operate on government lands on the path to protection,
and it disrupts the sands of silence with its activities. This was
once the hunting grounds for Tito and his Communist elites—
packed with European mouflon, chamois, boar, and bear—but
rackets of exploitation have scared the animals away. The fresh
stream that runs down this valley into the Neretva is now polluted from the mining. The roads Prominvest has blazed are used
by bootleg timber operations to fell the ancient forests. Tim has
made saving this stunning corridor his personal crusade. He has
railed in articles and books, debated Prominvest's director, Enver
Becirovic, on national television, been party to lawsuits, and peti-
tioned international conservation groups for help, all to no avail.
Although the Bosnian Supreme Court and other legal entities
have sided with Tim and sent cease-and-desist orders to Prominvest, the company has ignored them and continues to operate
with seeming impunity, to Tim's great aggravation.

So it is that Tim crosses the line in the sand into Prominvest's wildcat operation. Almost immediately a truck driver returning from delivering a load sees Tim and halts for a confrontation. They begin to argue, decibels rising with each verbal bastinado, and it seems on a bad trajectory when I step to the back of the truck. Tim introduces me as someone from the American media. The driver is quickly all smiles and heartily shakes my hand. He then hops back in his cab and bumps down the road into the gouge. Tim fumes and remarks he might just chain himself to a rock in protest. Then he quotes Gil Scott-Heron from "Work for Peace": "Nobody can do everything, but everybody can do something."

As we're hiking back to the car, Tim speaks to himself in a murmur, though the caterwauling of the quarry is such he could be howling. "I'm going to go back to school and get a master's in environmental studies. That way, I will no longer be just a guy who likes nature babbling in the wilderness. People will listen if I have the credibility of an advanced degree."

We continue our trek up the Neretva River, past four dams in the first forty miles of the spinning course. The Neretva, filtered to a glassy sheen by its limestone frame, almost seems lit from beneath as we glance down from the precipitous road. At the little way station of Konjic we stop at a riverside restaurant and meet Samir Krivic, owner of Rafting Europe. Even though afternoon thunderclouds are gathering, Samir offers to take us on a fourteen-mile bolt down the Neretva, the river he calls the best rafting run in the world. He's prejudiced, he admits. He's been running the Neretva for thirty years, since he was eight. Now he is a physical education teacher at the nearby elementary school in the winters and runs his rafting operation in the summers, mixing the two as often as he can, teaching students environmental education during school, then taking them down the river on cleanup expeditions during vacation.

At the put-in, Samir brags that the run is ranked Class III–IV, with one Class V "jump," which would place the course in same league as the Rogue, Selway, Tuolumne, and many of the other great white-water rivers of the American West. But the wimpy Slovenian life jackets, and the thousand-cubic-feet-per-second river volume, seem to belie the boast.

Minutes later, we're riding through a glacially carved canyon where once a river spilled, then froze, cracking the gorge like an egg. The sail is dreamlike, down a delirium of blue-gray limestone, with trout-filled, vitreous pools and sudden springs spewing from the walls. At one spout Samir pulls us over and tugs a bouquet of wild mint from the ground, grinds it in his palms, and then mixes it with the cold, clear water, creating instant iced tea, or a mojito without the rum. There remains virtually no rafting river in the United States where drinking its water doesn't risk ingesting *Giardia lamblia* or some other nasty flagellated protozoan parasite, but here the luminous water is eminently potable, and we all drink with wild abandon.

At last we ride the vectors into the rapids, and thankfully they are not the uncorked tempests Samir seemed to describe. Instead they are delightful drops of interference waves, little sacraments of crests and troughs. But what the Neretva lacks in muscle it more than makes up in the spectacle it has scrawled from the rock: towering walls, temples, buttes and monuments, feathery waterfalls, and gardens of wildflowers and stately trees inhaling the warm coastal breezes.

In the slanted light of evening, a mist begins to gyre, and as we drift closer we see it doodling lazy curlicues up the abutments of a bridge. Tim allows this is a dam site, one of three proposed on this section of the Neretva by Elektroprivreda, the state-run electric company, which intends a series of concrete insults that would level all the life from these currents, but supply cheap energy to Italy and others. If, as some have postulated, water is the next oil, the precious global resource in limited supply, then Bosnia might be a one-country OPEC with its luxury of freshwater fonts. Nonetheless, the whispers of this river could be soon be replaced by the hum of turbines, generating energy that has not nearly the worth of a clear-flowing stream, so says Tim, and having sipped the spirit of this river, I find it hard to disagree.

As we make the last paddle strokes, we glide over the rusted magazine to an AK-47 among the colored pebbles, and I ask Samir if he fought in the war. Everyone we've met in Bosnia over thirty harbors memories of the horror and typically wants to tell the stories, to relive the searing moments. But Samir says he doesn't want to talk about the war. "We're all in the same raft now. We all breathe the same air, drink the same water. Let's just enjoy our river. It is the best river in the world."

CONFESSIONS OF AN ECO-WARRIOR

At the height of the siege of Sarajevo, Tim Clancy was sequestered in an office building in downtown Sarajevo. One day he had the urge to escape the claustrophobic quarters and decided to go out for a fresh-air walk, knowing that snipers surrounded the city and that citizens were being picked off each day. He took a shower and headed for the door when several Bosnians stopped him and begged him not to proceed. "Your hair is wet, you'll catch your death of cold!"

Tim believes when it comes to the environment, Bosnia is a culture of misplaced priorities, and that belief is never more manifest than this morning, when Tim receives a phone call with bad news. The government has just announced it is tendering bids for the construction of two new dams on the Neretva, the river he believes is the clearest and cleanest in Europe, the last of its kind on the continent. Tim fumes. His mood seems to fall into a crevasse, which his staff blames on lack of coffee. Then, in a moment of seethe, he says he is going to quit Green Visions, the eco-adventure company he cofounded to show travelers the wilderness marvels of Bosnia, and work full-time to save the Neretva. He rants that those who waste this sacred waterway are scrofulous and self-pitying, and that he needs to carry the sword against them. And he wants to show us why.

Our first stop is the little village of Sunji, hanging prettily above the Tresanica River, another tributary of the Neretva. The village elders called Tim three weeks ago to solicit help, as they felt duped by the power company, which was bulldozing a steep zigzag road at the village frontage. The company had come to the villagers with a proposal to build a microdam on a nearby water-fall and had extolled the benefits of an environmentally sound power scheme. The village signed on, but then was shocked when the contractors showed and started plowing down a landslide area to the river, where the diversion project was now to be placed. We follow one of the elders down the freshly turned dirt to a growl-ing orange Atlas backhoe, whereupon a workman confronts us and claims we must leave, as this is private property. Tim calmly says no, that this is public land, and continues to step down to the river as the workman gets on his cell and calls for backup.

Within minutes, several men from nearby Konjic, includ-ing Feda Sahinpasic, the project manager, show up at the river to defend the work in progress. They say that they have proper permits for the undertaking, that the scheme is environmentally sound, that any damage the road-clearing makes will be repaired, and that the villagers are complaining simply because they want to squeeze the company for more money. Tim argues the transi-tional concept that Bosnians should be preserving the Neretva, not compromising it. "You don't understand. We have what the rest of Europe has lost!" Tim then offers to cut off his right arm if they can name one river in Europe as clean. The contractors don't seem to have an answer, or really care. For them the enterprise provides a job, a good one, and likely putting food on the table is more important than the integrity of a river. Tim bluntly knows this—he calls theirs the existential fight—but curses at what he calls the endemic ecological illiteracy, and suggests we move on.

As we're driving along the tree-lined lineaments above the river, I wonder what could we expect to find next except fresh dis-appointments. As if to accommodate the coil of thought, we find ourselves on a steep incline stuck behind a Prominvest cement truck. As Tim tries to pass the truck, there is a beating sound that is either a set of bumps on the road or a drum of revolving anxieties. Safely in front of the cement truck, Tim confesses he battles with himself all the time. He says that a part of him enjoys the moral fights, that he is inexplicably drawn to these sharp struggles, but that another part of him just wants to abstain from the selfish sticks of society, to retreat to nature, where he can underwrite his own joy, where he can hike and read and live his own quiet life in peace. And he wonders aloud if he should have a child, or if it is too late.

Up another tributary of the Neretva, beneath a high eddy of crows, Tim pulls over and suggests we grab neckerchiefs. As we step from the car, an overpowering stench assaults, whacking my nose like a sledgehammer. Around the corner is an animal carcass dump, piled high with the bloated, decaying remains of cows, sheep, and other creature features. Tim says this is the dump for a local butcher and restaurateur, and though the land is state owned, site of the proposed Igman Bjelasnica National Park, and the dump is a health hazard that could spawn an epidemic, his efforts to have it removed have fallen on deaf ears.

Then Tim grinds his truck up a dirt road high above the Neretva River canyon and stops at various overlooks, where we gaze down at screaming rafters on the limpid ribbon, and then upward to great disfiguring swaths of clear-cut forest, scars across a green countenance of one-hundred-year-old pines and beeches. "This is an obscenity," Tim cries. "By law, timber companies must plant four trees for every one cut. Look at these hills. There's no replanting here. Just wanton cutting to sell grade A hardwoods to the European market on the cheap. Politicians, bureaucrats, the Mafia, even war criminals are financing themselves through illegal foresting here."

What, I ask, are the alternatives? I've spent the week traversing these confusing colors, soaking in the ravishing beauty of Bosnia, but also witnessing firsthand the desperate efforts to find social and economic answers for a people picking up from the wreckage of war.

"I'll show you." Tim grins for the first time today.

We wind higher and higher, rising fluently into an immense horizon, until at last we spill across a rocky plateau above the tree line, into the village of Umoljani. The tiny Muslim community near where several events were staged in the 1984 Winter Olympics was ethnically cleansed during the war, virtually all its homes burned to the ground. But it has rebuilt itself and, with Tim's help, discovered new economies for a traditional way of life. Spread across the tableland are gardens of organically grown potatoes, carrots, onions, lettuce, cabbage, and wheat, fertilized with manure, grown without pesticides or herbicides or chemicals of any kind. It is the method of growing they've practiced for centuries, yet Tim has introduced the notion of exporting these crops to groceries and restaurants in Sarajevo and beyond for a market increasingly willing to pay premiums for organically grown food. Looking about the village, Tim points out several buildings in various stages of construction. He has been bringing his adventure clients on treks to this scenic outpost the last few years, and now village entrepreneurs are building eco-lodges in childlike bright colors to accommodate the visitors. Already seven homes have added rooms for the onslaught.

"The people of Umoljani see ecotourism and organic farming as their future," Tim swanks while leaning against a haystack of freshly scythed grass. "These could be the alternative sustainable economies to felling forests, damming rivers, to abusing this singular land for short-term profits. This, I believe, could be the hope and opportunity for Bosnia."

THE LAST VILLAGE

> The greatest tragedy is not the doings of evil men but rather the silence of good men.
> —Martin Luther King Jr.

One of the harsh little sleights of logic in the wake of the Bosnian war is that land mines may have saved the country's greatest asset, its large swaths of old-growth forest. As we wend our way up the edge of the Rakitnica Canyon, a tributary gorge to the Neretva that Tim Clancy calls the most unexplored in southern Europe, we pass a seductively alluring, leafy copse marked with a red sign sporting skull and crossbones: *Pazi* ("Beware"). Here, loggers fear to tread.

We're in the boundaries of the proposed Igman Bjelasnica National Park, and in another seeming illogicality, Tim Clancy, Bosnia's greatest eco-champion, advocates reducing the size of this impending parkland. He says it would be suicide to sanction a national park that has land mines within. All it would take would be one hiker blown away, and the park would be void of visitors, and with no visitors it would soon be auctioned off to the highest bidder. "The politicians here all have signs on their heads that say, 'For sale,'" Tim critiques. Instead, he proposes the park be shrunk to boundaries that are known to be mine-free and the rest be made a buffer zone until the mines are gone.

Tim relishes contrarianism in almost every quarter. "I seem to have a chemical imbalance when it comes to authority and convention," he says while wrestling the wheel of the truck over a barren pass. At one point he switches the music on the CD player from American 1960s folk to early twentieth-century Bosnian shepherd music. Then, in the middle of what seems the end of the world, Tim pulls to a wide spot, jumps out, and starts walking down a rough and rutted but perfectly drivable clay road. "I like to walk into Lukomir," he exclaims. "It's like walking onto the set of some medieval movie."

And, indeed, as we turn a corner and step over a rise, there before us spreads something from a fairy tale: the highest and most remote community in Bosnia, perhaps in the Balkans, the little feudal village of Lukomir.

As we step toward steep-roofed stone buildings, a few of the old villagers pass by carrying hand-carved tools, and each grins toothlessly, laughs heartily, and gives Tim a big hug. He is family here. Tim says he has been here one hundred times since he first stumbled into it while exploring the Rakitnica Canyon in 1999, and now it is his favorite place in the world, and his destiny. "I dreamed I lived here before I ever found it," Tim says with a sigh.

The village itself seems hung with rusty nails to the rim of the Rakitnica, with collapsed roofs, pieces of tin patched over broken tiles, rotting timbers, abandoned wood carts, even an ancient red Yugo that looks as if it took a wrong turn in the quondam Yugo-slavia and ran out of gas. But there are no bullet holes, no torch ashes or black stains of mortar blasts. This was the only village in the region spared during the war, demonstrating the power of geographical isolation over malice.

But the village is suffering in other ways that can be traced to the war. Young men were recruited for battle; mothers and chil-dren were evacuated for a time. Now, those young people who left are not returning, having sampled the comfort and tempta-tions of life beyond the hard village. All that remains year-round are a handful of grandparents and their sheep and cows. In the summer, children and grandchildren come up for visits.

Tim shows us around Lukomir, which looks more relic than real, pointing out the roofs crafted of cherry wood shingles, a technique dating back hundreds of years; the men cutting grass as the women gather it into mounds, preparing for the harsh, six-month winter when the snowbound village is cut off from the outside; the *stecci,* medieval tombstones, that have washed down from the hill and are now adjacent to a newer cemetery where I can't help but notice that most of the occupants lived to ripe old ages. "There is very little stress here, and the food is as healthy as you can get. No added hormones, the air is pure, the water clean. Everything is authentic and simple. A village such as this is a door to our past, and the key to our future."

As if to prove this evangelism, we're invited into the Euro-pean home 1,000 years ago. It has just three low-ceilinged rooms and an attic. First is an all-purpose mudroom for footwear and clothes, and for preparation of raw food. The second room has a wood-burning stove, a worn Persian rug, and a low round table where the family dines cross-legged. On the wall hangs a sheep-skin prayer rug, as this room is also for worship. The third is the bedroom, where our host, Rahima Comor, raised her six children. We peek into the dark, smoky attic and see hanging cheese and shanks of meat. There are no chimneys in the Lukomir homes; the wood smoke circulates in the attic to act as a sealant and to cure food. There is a clock ticking through the quiet somewhere in the house, but it has no need—time has stopped here.

Rahima turns a coffee grinder as a potato pie cooks in the stove. She wears clothes suitable for a Renaissance fair, though this is her daily ensemble: a head scarf, wool pantaloons, a cotton nightgown shirt, a wool vest, and socks, all handmade.

As we sup on pita and yogurt and sip fresh raspberry juice, I ask Rahima how she feels about the shrinking size of the village. She says she thinks Lukomir will be a ghost town in a few years unless something changes. There is no school, no health clinic, and no reason to stay. Her knees hurt now, and the children are gone. She volunteers that if she had the money she would leave, but all she has to her name is one hundred sheep.

Tim has a different vision. As he fights to preserve an environment older and purer than anyplace else he has seen, he includes in the ecosystem this ancient culture, whose people he calls the last seminomadic white tribe on the continent. Just as he believes a certain kind of tourism can be a savior to forests and wild rivers, the same could be the knight for saving Lukomir. Already he treks here with clients as often as he can schedule, and the villagers have found a modest market in selling hand-knitted socks, sharing their homes for overnights, and serving traditional shepherds' meals. "If they can make a living showcasing their proud heritage and culture, the young might come back."

I ask Tim if he might be guilty of some sort of western elitism, wanting to preserve an exotic yet moribund culture as a living museum for his own romantic sensibilities; if perhaps the natural course of events is for Lukomir to empty, for the villagers to move on to better lives where there are classrooms, hospitals, jobs, and choice.

"'Choice' is the operative word," he counters. Tim believes that we never fall far from the apple tree, and that if Lukomir could become economically viable, then those whose roots are here would return, as their choice. Tim asserts that he is certain he's doing the right thing trying to help these people and their singular culture, this unequaled environment, and that while the rest of the world has made irrevocable mistakes, Bosnia is at a magical inflection point, a crossroads, where it has the opportunity to be a model for the planet or fall into the same trench out of which so many are now trying to crawl.

"If there is a path of pure intent, it leads in the right direction," Tim sums his private ontology. Then he sits on a log with several of his Lukomir friends and sips substantial coffee and shares a view across a chasm that seems to transcend time.

4

THE PICTURE OF JOHN GRAY, SEA GYPSY

Thailand

AND THE

Andaman Islands

> *The most spiritual human beings, assuming they are the most courageous, also experience by far the most painful tragedies: but it is precisely for this reason that they honor life, because it brings against them its most formidable weapons.*
>
> —Friedrich Nietzsche, *Twilight of the Idols*,
> "Expeditions of an Untimely Man"

It was like a first Thai morning, still and fresh with the perfume of frangipani and night-blooming jasmine. Distant layers appeared in the sky, as if glass plates separated the pink morning air on top from the indigo shadows left from night.

As John "Caveman" Gray stepped into the Toyota pickup with his wife, he reached for his mobile phone and found it wasn't there. He must have left it on the table. He thought about heading back to the house to fetch it, a house filled with thirteen dogs collected from the streets. Like his good friend and neighbor of a dozen years, New Zealander Leone Cosens, cofounder of the Phuket Animal Welfare Society, he took pity on stray dogs and brought them home, fed and nurtured them, and tried to find them homes. He needn't worry about theft at his home.

John decided against returning for the phone. It was Sunday morning, the day after Christmas 2004. It would be a quiet day, a family day for most, with little need for phone chat. John had no children, a life choice made when he was sixteen and read that the world's population had hit two billion. So he helped stray dogs instead. Today, he would use the quiet time to catch up on work at the office.

John sat down in from of his HP Vectra computer and started to answer e-mails. Since 1989, he had been running ocean kayak tours off the coast of Phuket, the paradisiacal resort island off the mainland of Thailand. He was the first ecotour operator in the region, the first to offer sea kayaking excursions, the first to discover a series of open-roofed limestone caves, called *hongs,* which have now become a major attraction for adventure-minded tourists. Where once he was the only outfitter, he now counts twenty competitors. By his own reckoning, his simple concept has spawned more than a million commercial Thailand kayak experiences and has generated more than five billion baht in revenues for the country.

At 7:58 a.m., John felt the ground shake. It was a subtle movement, unlike the jolt-style earthquakes he had experienced growing up in Southern California, and it sustained a low-frequency shudder for several minutes. John asked Ying, his assistant, to fetch a green plastic bowl and fill it with water. She set it on the ground, and they both watched the ripples.

Ying thought it an earthquake on the island and scrambled to stand under the door frame. John suspected something more ominous. There hadn't been a significant tsunami in the region since the island volcano Krakatoa, west of Java, blew in 1883, setting off waves that killed 35,000 people. But John, something of a sea gypsy, had spent most of his life roaming oceans in small plastic craft, and he knew the signs.

If ever there were a western water baby, it was John Gray. At six months, his mother had him swimming in the ocean surf. By ten years he was in a kayak. At twelve, he was a certified scuba diver. At fifteen, he was lifeguard. As a teen, he would water-ski each weekend the twenty-two miles from the mainland to Catalina Island and back. At twenty, he was bodysurfing the notorious Wedge of Newport Beach and was once pounded so hard by a giant wave, he was certain he had died. He emerged with a newfound weltanschauung: that every day hence was a free ride. Politically active, he worked on coastal campaigns and master marine plans in Hawaii, even a paper on tsunami planning. In 1960, his father brought him to the docks of Long Beach to watch the effects of a tsunami that had hit Chile twenty hours earlier. The power of the waves left him awestruck, but with a moth-to-flame attraction. For his honeymoon, he went kayaking in a hurricane.

John jumped back on the computer and began to surf the Web. At the US Geological Service site, he saw that the USGS reported an 8.3 quake on the Richter scale off the west coast of Sumatra.

The Indian Ocean doesn't have a warning system, so his next stop was the Pacific Tsunami Warning Center, which merely warned that an "event" had occurred, one predicted to have no impact on the Pacific Basin.

It was now 9 a.m. John e-mailed the Australian Bureau of Meteorology: "Any info on this morning's Sumatra quake and possible tsunami generation?"

At 9:24, he received a response: "We have received an advice from the Tsunami Warning Center in Hawaii. They opine that a tsunami threat does not exist for the Pacific. However, they do not discount the possibility of a tsunami near the epicenter, which was off the west coast of Northern Sumatra. We have no further information."

That was all the confirmation John needed. He decided to start calling those he knew to warn of an impending tidal wave. But the phone numbers of friends, including Leone, were programmed into his cell phone, left at home. So he picked up the office landline and started to call coastal hotels, figuring he could efficiently alert the most people that way, perhaps save the most lives.

At one hotel the receptionist replied she did not know what a tsunami was, even though John tried to yell an explanation through the phone. Another put him on hold. A third said the general manager was not around and she did not have authority to frighten the guests with a warning. Just as with his many environmental campaigns, John felt a voice in the wilderness.

Frustrated, John decided to act where he could make a difference. He gathered his staff and explained that if the water suddenly receded, then they should take the guests and the villagers and head to high ground. He dispatched his staff to the dock, where twenty-nine foreigners had booked a sea kayaking day trip, including an American family on reunion with its eighty-four-year-old matriarch.

As John predicted, the sea suddenly withdrew, as if someone had pulled the plug in a bathtub. John's staff urged and then ushered the guests, local shopkeepers, and residents of the traditional fishing village of Ao Po inland, up to a school high on a hillside. Then, at 10:31, the wave hit. Then the second. And the others. The massive ocean-floor earthquake had shunted more than a thousand kilometers of fault line, displacing billions of tons of seawater at the surface. In all the roiling death soup killed as many as 230,000 people in the region, including more than 8,000 in Thailand, half of them foreigners. But John figures that by understanding the signals of nature, he saved at least forty lives, perhaps as many as eighty.

Later, though, Amporn, John's wife, drove along Ya Nui Beach, by the home of their friend Leone, whose phone number was programmed in John's left-behind cell phone. Leone's home was leveled. And her body was found 200 meters farther up the beach, along with those of several of her beloved stray dogs. As John retells this story to me, he calls Leone "the Mother Teresa of stray dogs," and tears brook down his face.

Forty miles out into the Andaman Sea, on a mote called Surin, another sea gypsy sensed the tsunami and took action. Salama Glatalay is a Moken, one of a tribe of nomadic aborigines who have plied the Andaman seas for centuries. They are a culture of Austronesians who likely migrated from southern China some 4,000 years ago. Also called the Sea Gypsies, the Mokens spend up to eight months a year living on their hand-carved, low-slung dugouts, called *kabangs*. Some say they possess a spiritual connection with the sea; others that their deep marine wisdom is simply unmatched by land-based peoples.

For years, Salama Glatalay, the headman of the Surin Moken village, listened to a legend passed down among his people that if the spirits of ancestors became angry, the *laboon*, a "wave that eats people," would flood the earth with seven surges. The navel of the seas would first suck away the water, then spit it back in rolling tides that would destroy the land, then make it clean again.

On the morning of December 26, Salama noticed first that the crickets were not chirping as usual. He went to the beach and saw the seawater had receded and fish were flopping about. He knew then what was about to happen. The 175 other Mokens on the island saw the same signs and abandoned their temporary bamboo stilt huts. They gathered up some 400 tourists who had come to the island to snorkel and dive its reefs, and yelled, "Run, run, run to the mountain!" Together they tore for a high point on the island, 113 feet above the beach. Just three tourists and one Moken, a thirty-year-old cripple who could not make the climb, were killed by the tsunami on Surin Island.

The Sea Gypsies had no advanced technology, no satellite warning systems, no computers, not even electricity or books. Their forewarnings came from an ancient bond with and understanding of the sea. They heeded their antediluvian wisdom and their myths, which most of the rest of world discounts. And yet they did more than any single group to save lives.

The Mokens are a stateless people, not recognized as citizens in any country, and yet recently were forced to move off native lands converted to national park status and prevented by governments from fishing in traditional waters. John Gray has lived in Thailand for sixteen years is married to a Thai, but the government will grant him only temporary work status. He must renew his visa each year. He has no local rights as a citizen. The sea is his country.

And so it is that eleven months after the tsunami, John Gray has decided to visit the Mokens of Surin Island, fellow sea gypsies, kindred citizens of the sea, to see if the nexus he perceives is real, and, if so, how deep it runs. Even after a lifetime studying and celebrating the sea, he believes he can learn much from the Mokens. "It's important we get back to our animal humanness, and the Moken have not left."

From John Gray's middling office in southern Phuket it is a three-and-a-half-hour drive north, some 250 kilometers and across a bridge to the mainland, to Kura Buri, a village where over recent years some Sea Gypsies have forgone their wayward lives to plant roots. After the tsunami, most of the Mokens of Surin also came here as refugees, and the animist nomads lived for a time in a Buddhist temple. But now most of these families have returned to the Andaman Sea. Kura Buri is the jumping-off point for the sixty-five-kilometer crossing to the island chain used as an off-season base.

As we wend up the west coast, John Gray acts as guide and interpreter and stops to introduce us to stories that cling almost a year after the sea-change event. We first stop at the Amanpuri, an upscale eco-lodge built on a cliff. Here, we meet Bill O'Leary, who runs Amancruises, a boat service for the haut monde guests.

Bill offers to take us out in his cruiser and re-create his own survival story.

Bill was leaving Phuket to drop off some clients at the Sheraton across the bay on the mainland. He was carrying three of his four children and was just minutes into the trip when he received a call from Manfred "Richie" Neustifter, thirty, an apprentice skipper and a former surfer who quickly understood what was happening when the water suddenly recoiled eight hundred meters at Amanpuri Beach, leaving boats and a swimming raft high and dry. Richie had tried to text-message Bill, but was so nervous he couldn't punch the buttons, so instead called and screamed that he was certain a tidal wave was coming.

Bill hesitated a second. He knew that there were only two safe places to be in a tsunami—on a mountain or in deep water. He could have turned the boat around and run for the hills with his family and guests, but there was no telling how high a wave might go. So he gunned his boat and headed eighteen miles out to sea. He positioned himself in a deepwater cove and watched as the sea assumed a meniscus shape. Then he spotted the churning wave. It was approaching faster than a jet, and there was no way to outrun it, so Bill faced the beast, roared his speedboat to its fifty-knot capacity, and punched through the shoulder of the wave. All in his forty-foot speedboat survived. Back on Amanpuri Beach, Richie scrambled about and pulled and pushed the well-heeled guests off the beach and up the stairs to the hotel proper. Many were resistant, and one man walked out to the edge of the retreated sea and poked around the coral. Richie ran out and grabbed the man just as the sea began to roll back in and snarled about their ankles. One can run in ankle-deep water, but once it reaches the knees, fate takes over.

Richie and the guest raced to the steps and made it up in time. Nobody died at Amanpuri Beach that day, due largely to Richie Neustifter.

Farther up the coast, we stop at the Marriott Hotel, another that suffered no casualties, the exception along this coast. The locals call it the "lucky hotel," as it was built back from the beach, behind a coral reef, for reasons more opportunistic than related to intelligent design. The owner loved this stretch, but it lies in a national park on a strand where leatherback turtles breed, and so permissions came with the obligation that the hotel be set back one hundred meters from the beach and that no beach chairs, Jet Skis, or other potentially disruptive appointments be allowed. So when the wave struck, fewer than forty people were on the beach, and all managed to run to the upper level of the set-back hotel and survive.

Things were a quite a bit different farther north in Phang Nga Province along Khao Lak Beach, where some seventy hotels were destroyed and about five thousand people died as a ten-meter-high wave poured over roofs and palm trees. We first visit Le Meridien, just reopened, with a smattering of guests moving about the grounds, slowly, deliberately, as though walking under water. As at all the properties along this stretch, its bungalows reach to the beach, and the topography is flat. "A billiard ball would roll several kilometers inland here," John Gray offers. Or a patrol boat. About a kilometer inland, off the main road, Patrol Boat 813 lists in the mudflats, no navigable water in sight.

The owner of Le Meridien lost his daughter here, along with twenty guests and staff, but like so many he decided to rebuild and reengage with life. Tsunamis of this magnitude come along once every seven hundred years, says the general manager, Achim Brueckner, so even though the new hotel has thicker walls and better warning systems, the hope and expectations are that nobody will ever experience such a natural horror again.

Another hotel, La Flora, sits next to a stretch of beach that looks like postbombing Dresden amid a jellyfish of concrete and rebar. But La Flora too has reopened, and here we meet a young British couple, David and Caroline Witzer. They were vacationing here on December 26 last year, enjoying breakfast on the terrace, when they saw commotion on the beach. They thought it first a shark sighting, but when they saw the wave coming, they joined the throngs running inland. They were both picked up and washed inland like rag dolls in a washing machine. She was swept into a third-floor room, knocked unconscious, and almost drowned before the wave punched a hole in the back and poured her out. He grabbed the top of a tree and hung on. They lost contact with each other, and each was convinced the other had died. Days later, after David had phoned his wife's relatives to relay news of her death, as he was headed to the airport to fly home, he received word his wife was in a hospital near the Malaysian border.

Now David and Caroline have returned to the beach hotel where seventeen staff and six guests were killed, but where in some random act of nature's temperament they were spared. They cried when they entered the lobby and have spent the days facing their fears and memories and finding solace and some healing with the return. They say they know many survivors who have come back as a sort of cathartic pilgrimage, a cleansing of the waters.

Our last stop of the day is at Baan Bang Nieng, a primary school where 20 percent of the students are orphans from the tsunami. Of the sixty-seven children here, about half are mainland Mokens, former Sea Gypsies whose parents made the decision to give up the traditional nomadic life for a more modern, stable existence selling trinkets and snacks to beach tourists or working as menial labor in the hotels. Narm Kaufman, thirty, is a volunteer teacher at the school and tells us the orphans can't concentrate on learning. Some yell and curse all day long; others sulk and never say a word. Narm's face blenches and her eyes well with tears as she tells how she is worried for their future. Relief money came in after the tsunami, but that money is drying up. So many other international disasters have rerouted charity, and she fears a lack of funding will send these children to the streets. The Mokens have no official status in Thailand. They are the nonpeople.

When the Sea Gypsies sailed the seas without borders, there was nothing romantic, except perhaps in western minds, about the hard, Spartan existence. But they understood the macrocosm of their natural world and submitted to the aqua vitae and its rhythms, moods, and tempers. And those Sea Gypsies are alive today.

* * *

It was not only the day after Christmas, not only Boxing Day (the Commonwealth designation for the day gifts are boxed up), not only the full moon, not only a Sunday when all government offices were closed, but it was also a local Buddha Day, the propitious day when Buddhists are entreated to assist in the welfare of those in need.

It took twenty-four years to build Wat Pasan, the Buddhist temple in Kura Buri, about ten kilometers inland from the Andaman Sea. Phra Atchan, a former civil engineer who gave up the bullish life of a bureaucrat for enlightenment, had served as the head monk for seventeen years. And for those years only fellow monks and a few HIV-positive children lived in his temple.

But on December 26, more than a thousand refugees from the tsunami stormed into Phra Atchan's temple, many of them animist Mokens from nearby Ko Phra Thong island and from Surin, the outer island where all but one survived by recognizing nature's warnings and heading to high ground before the massive wave hit.

Some came with one piece of clothing to their names; some came bleeding and broken; some came carrying the grief of lost loved ones. Phra Atchan had room for only twenty monks in his temple, but he took them all in and began to beseech the world for assistance.

Soon a tiny town of plywood-and-tin homes sprang up on the temple grounds; gardens were planted, meals shared, and the dead dealt with. Many, including American Rebecca Clark and Brit Lisa Jones, who had been working at a local turtle conservation project, were cremated on the grounds. A community of mixed Mokens and Thais was forged, and Phra Atchan went about teaching the survivors how to build boats, how to cultivate the soil, how to work for their own future. Like John Gray, who adamantly refuses to make cash handouts, preferring to offer tools and skill trainings, Phra Atchan did not dispense money, but shelter, rice, and teachings.

Now virtually all the Mokens from Surin have returned to their island and their traditional lives as fishers. The few Mokens who remain on the temple grounds are those from nearby Ko Phra Thong, Mokens who long ago gave up their nomadic ways for the lure of civilization. And it was these Mokens who suffered most. Ten Mokens clearing a path for a resort didn't see the wave coming and drowned. Three others gathering shells to sell to tourists were swept away. And the survivors, such as fifty-nine-year-old La Morgan, are too afraid to return and prefer to continue life as inland refugees. His sons make models of traditional Sea Gypsy boats they have never sailed, and his daughters make recycled-paper cards for Christmas, a holiday they have never observed, all to sell to tourists in hotels and craft centers. Yet when I ask La what he would do if he became the king of Thailand or had ten million baht, he expresses one of the belief systems traditional Mokens are known for. He says he wouldn't change a thing, except to make a boat for everybody, and allow everyone to fish together and eat together. The Mokens, according to their own creation myth, are meant to be poor, to take only what they need, to remain outsiders.

Before the wave, La made a living catching small oysters and selling them to restaurants and stores. But rumors that marine animals ate the corpses of humans killed by the tsunami dried up that business. Now La has no work, owns no boat, and relies upon the beneficence of others to survive. But, says Phra Atchan, the donations and subventions are drying up, and he worries about how his temple can continue to support the three hundred refugees who still occupy the temple grounds almost a year after the flood.

"Our work is like a man standing on a big tiger. If you step down, the tiger will eat you," Phra Atchan apprizes while kneeling on a mat, wrapped in a saffron robe in his gold and fili-greed dagoba dome.

John Gray shares the morality but not the sorrowful philos-ophy. His tours, and life outlook, contravene suffering. And as such John arranges for a posh live-aboard dive boat, the MV *Jazz*, to make the six-hour crossing to Surin, departing at midnight.

At the cusp of dawn, John Gray, his fuscous ponytail flapping in the wind, stands on the deck and points to a series of motes silhouetted black against the sky. There are a few faint stars. And the light on the sea is a commingling of moonlight and dawn, luminous as a pale shell. "These are the Andaman Islands. To the north . . . that's Burma. Straight ahead . . . that's Surin Island, claimed by Thailand. Though the Thai government doesn't grant citizenship to the Moken born here. They are landless. They have no rights, get no education, no health care."

About four hundred meters off Surin Island, we make anchor. We are in the lower brow of the Mergui Archipelago, some eight hundred islands scattered along two hundred fifty miles of the Andaman Sea. The island is billow backed, violently green, with occasional scars of beach that seem to bleed white. Without the breeze of the moving boat, the humidity squeezes like the coils of an invisible snake, pressing the good air from our lungs.

Within minutes of our landing, a small, low-slung planked boat paddles out to meet us.

It is covered with a blue plastic tarp, and a long-tailed out-board pokes out the stern, giving the craft an insect quality. A stick of incense burns at the bow, an homage to the female spirit who looks after the craft and its occupants. A white-haired cou-ple looks up to us and asks for benzene. They are Cha Le and Ma To, true Sea Gypsies who live and sleep on their tiny boat and fish the waters for sustenance. Even though they maintain a tempo-rary hut on Surin, everything they own is in this handcrafted ves-sel. We give them petrol and bananas and ask about the tsunami. Like the other Sea Gypsies of Surin, they saw nature's gesture and ran to the hills, Cha Le grabbing his grandchildren along the way.

Ma To didn't make it before the water grabbed her and tossed her about, snapping her arm. She shows her broken limb, which is unnaturally crooked at the elbow, looking more like a dog's leg than an arm. But she can still paddle and use their three-pronged spear, and she smiles broadly as they head back out to sea.

We have a motorized dinghy to take us to shore, but John Gray is too impatient. As we gather our gear, he worms into a strawberry-colored sea kayak and starts paddling ahead by himself. I watch him splash to shore and hold his arms out as a group of Moken children run his way.

*   *   *

Her Royal Highness Princess Maha Chakri Sirindhorn is a poet, a teacher, and an outdoorswoman who likes to trek, bike, and kayak. She has gone sea kayaking with John Gray about six times, and has booked another trip with his company for next week.

And so it is with great delight that John Gray walks the white sand to the end of the Moken village and discovers the unexpected—a clinic and a school, paid for by the Thai princess. More than the Red Cross, more than any nongovernmental organization, the princess has done the most to help the Mokens, even though her own government maroons them without status, as officially there are no "indigenous" peoples in Thailand.

There are fifty-two students in the thatched-top school, with a whiteboard and a set of Mr. Orange briefcases. John, looking like a tropic Santa Claus, belly and all, has toted a large green garbage bag up the beach, and as the children gather round he pulls from the bag notebooks, pencils, crayons, and chalk (though he notes there is no place to use the chalk, as there is only the one whiteboard in the village). The children couldn't be happier if they were receiving Game Boys or Disney DVDs. It's Christmas.

Joe Keawkudang, a Thai from the mainland, is the sole teacher on this paradisiacal strand, and he too is glad for this windfall. So when a couple of monkeys swing by for a closer look, and John Gray reveals that his Thai staff calls him Ling Yai (Big Monkey), Joe gets an idea. He assigns his students their first task with their new tools. They are each to create a picture of John Gray.

At the end of the assignment, it is more Dorian than John Gray as the students hold up their vastly different versions of the human ape in red pantaloons and a baseball cap. A couple of the students have extraordinary artistic aptitude and render drawings as striking as something from a college art class.

John Gray then goes looking for Salama Glatalay, the headman for all the Mokens of Surin Island. But it turns out the headman is off in a remote bay cutting wood for a new *kabang,* one of the distinctive Sea Gypsy boats carved with what might be interpreted as a mouth and an ass, representing the human body. The headman won't be back until nightfall. So John just wanders through a place where time seems absent, bowing to the women as they chew their betel nuts, petting the dogs, and admiring the resurrected bamboo stilt village set against the bluish-greens of the primary forest. When the tsunami hit, every village, every hut on the island was obliterated. For six to eight months of the year, the Mokens live on their boats, tramping across international waters with near impunity. But during the monsoon, which turns the Andaman Sea into a furious, unnavigable potage, many of the Mokens had camped in thatched huts on the beaches of Surin, which were declared part of a marine national park in 1981, without any consult with or input from the Mokens.

So when it came time to rebuild, government officials decreed that all the Mokens of Surin had to relocate to one beach a bay away from park headquarters. And restrictions were imposed that would impact livelihoods. The Mokens could fish the island reefs for their own sustenance, but not for commerce. They could construct huts, but only in the traditional style, so as to be a tourist attraction. They could work for the park, but not for pay, as it is illegal to hire the nationless Mokens.

The mandates presented new problems for the Mokens. Commercial Thai fishermen with vast nets have fished out the closer reefs, so the Mokens need to travel farther to sea to fish. For that they need diesel fuel for their long-tail outboards, which can be acquired only with cash. They also need to buy rice to see them through the monsoons. It was not long ago that the Moken women would make the daylong trip to the mainland in mid-April, at the start of the monsoons, and literally sing for their suppers. They would go door-to-door and croon a tune imploring the more fortunate to put, in a bucket they carried, rice, onions, and garlic—dry foods that would see them through the rainy season. Two of the elder women of the village, Jampa and Zorpa, sit in a common area of the village and sing the ditty and then translate the words: "The monsoons are coming. We will die of hunger. So please help us."

The younger Moken women no longer sing this song. Instead, they have found other ways to generate money to buy staples. They weave pandanus baskets, make models of their traditional houseboats, and collect shells and stingray teeth, all of which they sell to tourists. Once a month or so, they make the trip to the mainland and come back with goods, including these days packaged junk food, tobacco, alcohol, even drugs. There is now a black and white TV in the village, powered by car batteries charged with solar panels. There are several radios. The Mokens are not allowed bank accounts, so there is a stash of gold for a rainy day. And the beach is littered with plastic and Styrofoam and broken soda pop bottles. I watch as John goes about the village randomly picking up the trash and placing it in a pile, as though by instinct. But the sun is burning the last remnants of the day, and it's time to head back to our live-aboard. John has been a student of the sea his entire life, but he believes the Mokens, who have spent generations on the sea, may have some wisdom to impart to him. It's why he's made this pilgrimage. Tomorrow, John will return and meet the headman of the Sea Gypsies.

* * *

It is the meeting of two big men, though one is two feet taller than the other. John Gray folds his hand as though in prayer and bows down to Salama Glatalay, while the headman of the Sea Gypsies thrusts up his overly long arm for a handshake.

Salama then leads us to his little, nipa palm–thatched roofed hut, where he invites us to climb the ladder and squeeze in while he changes from a tattered plaid shirt to a more statesmanlike sash. Salama, we learn, is not just the headman, but is also a teacher, and the spiritual leader for his people. There are fifty-six family houses along this beach, each looking something like a western architect's rendition of an eco-lodge bungalow without the flush toilets, thread-count sheets, little shampoo bottles, or really any trappings. He says four people live in his hut, which is little more than the size of a motel room, including his wife and two grandchildren. He thinks he is about sixty-two years old, but really doesn't know. He had nine children, but only five survive. Four died of malaria before the clinic was opened on the island after the tsunami this year.

John and Salama then walk to the edge of the sea and sit on a fat beach hibiscus root. Behind is a half-sunken *kabang,* a remnant of the tsunami. And John begins the conversation telling Salama about his own experiences with the wave, how he understood the earthquake and tried to alert as many as possible, and took actions that saved lives, but not as many as he had hoped, as not all who heard his messaging believed.

John then asks Salama of his own experiences a near year ago. Salama pauses, then describes a series of dreams he had before the *laboon,* as the Mokens call the tsunami. Three nights before, he had his first dream, in which he saw the sea turn blood red and watched a western woman struggle in the waves. When he woke, he turned and prayed to the sea that it not be too harsh.

The second night, the dream repeated, and when he told his

wife she dismissed his premonition, saying he had had too much to eat and drink.

The third night, the dream happened again, and Salama was convinced nature was angry. The Moken legends tell that the sea sends in a *laboon* every once in a great while to clean up what has become dirty, and Salama knew his village was not clean. He lamented that the young people had been leaving the island for the mainland allures and returning with trash, which was littering the once-pristine beach. He said he knew that morning that the sea was coming to wash up his village.

He first noticed that the fish in his bay were unusually roused, frisking out of the water as though in alarm. Then the sea took its big breath and sucked the water away, and Salama knew the *laboon* was coming.

He had twenty minutes to alert his people, and such was his respect and power that everyone listened. All raced to the highlands, and all but one Moken on the Andaman island of Surin survived.

John and Salama talk and laugh for a couple of hours, trading stories of the sea, recipes for raw shellfish, and tales of their long lives, as they believe they are about the same age. Salama gives John some practical advice on jellyfish stings (wash with freshwater as soon as possible); John gives Salama a loving description of the princess, who has yet to travel to Surin, though her helping hand is felt throughout. A photo of the princess hangs in the open-sided schoolroom and in many of the bamboo huts.

Then Salama invites John to take a ride in his *kabang,* in which he is taking some of his grandkids out to the reef to dive for clams and shells. The Mokens are legendary for being some of the deepest free divers in the world. They carve goggles out of wood and insert glass from washed-ashore bottles as the eyepieces. Since he is the headman, his is the only boat that has not one but two long-tail diesel engines, and we are out above the reef's edge in minutes.

Salama and the kids don their goggles and dive in, dropping

down the reef face some ten meters without a flinch. One of the dive instructors on the MV *Jazz* putts over in the dinghy with a set of scuba gear and offers to let Salama use the second regulator as he makes a twenty-five-meter dive. Without hesitation Salama pops the regulator into his mouth and follows the professional diver to the depths with the ease of a kipper, plucking a conch from the floor. He later explains another Moken legend, that when a Moken dies, he ascends to a sort of purgatory to await sentencing. If his life has not been good enough, his head is whacked off, and he is tossed to the sea, where he becomes a shell of his former self. But when a Moken diver retrieves such a shell from the ocean bottom, he releases the lost soul through the opening, and it is allowed to ascend to the heavens.

After diving and buffeting about the bay in Salama's darkwood, plank-sided boat, John Gray fetches a bright banana-colored sea kayak from the live-aboard. He positions Salama in the bow, and out they go for a spirited paddle. Salama cackles with delight, as though one of John's clients, and is overwhelmed by the nimbleness, stability, and clean lines of the craft.

At the end of the ride, Salama makes an offer. He says he thinks the sea kayak would be just a wonderful craft for fishing and wants to trade his Moken *kabang* straight up. John likes the idea, as he has thought about offering tours in traditional craft to celebrate and support tradition, and yet he also would like to contribute something that might improve the lot of the Mokens.

I at first wince at this contrivance. I ask John whether the idea of bringing a kayak to this isolated bay might be like dropping the Coke bottle into the Kalahari in the film *The Gods Must Be Crazy*, wherein the foreign item introduced to a remote tribe becomes a totem that derogates the culture. With such a deep and distinct culture, might the introduction of modern kayaks accelerate the loss of unique traditions?

John lights into me for that notion, suggesting I was damning the Mokens to remain as museum pieces for my own romantic notions. He says my thinking was little different from that of the national park, which prohibited the Mokens from rebuilding with more modern, stable structures, as the image would not be as attractive to tourists.

Freedom to choose and evolve, John allows, is the most potent coin in any society, and for the privileged to wistfully wish that the less-advantaged remain so for the dreamy images of tourists, or media, is a shameful fancy.

We finish the day feeding Salama's boat with extra food and some Coke and then wave goodbye as the headman chugs back to his island. I ask John Gray if he learned anything from meeting the Sea Gypsy helmsman, and he nods. It was not what he expected. There was no arcanum for better knowing nature, no special wisdom about the sea, except perhaps for the hint on jellyfish stings.

But after some thought, John shares that he thinks the lesson is the power of acutely in-touch leadership. It is not about just being sharply sensitive to nature, but about being attuned to people in one's ken. John remembers how frustrated he was when he phoned hotels warning of the tsunami and was not taken seriously, and how that cost many, many lives. He tells how his own assistant, Ying, after seeing the water bowl ripple with the earthquake, called the police in a panic, but they accused her of being on drugs and hung up. And those calls were more than an hour before the tsunami hit.

John Gray says he really doesn't know if Salama's premonitory dreams really happened. John is a skeptic when it comes to mysticism, omens, and spirit messaging. But he thinks it doesn't really matter. Salama is the inherited spiritual leader of the Mokens, an ancient animist culture that believes there are spirits in trees and boats, and in the sea. And Salama is in keen touch with the spirit of his people, and in turn he receives esteem and credibility, more than any missionary, more than any soldier or philanthropist. So when it came time to persuade his people to run, all he had to do was say he had dreamed of the *laboon,* and up the mountain they ran.

"There are world leaders who could use these lessons," John hazards as he hauls his kayak onto the live-aboard deck for the long passage across the oyster-blue Andaman Sea back to a home on his own parallax tropic isle.

5

FIRST INTO HELL

Libya

Sunday, sitting in the Polo Lounge at the Heathrow Radisson, we're ten souls to Tripoli, *insh'Allah.* Down from sixteen just a few days ago, with a wait list. There is yet no Libyan People's Bureau (Libyan for embassy) or consulate in Washington, D.C., so to obtain the all-important entry stamp for the Great Socialist People's Libyan Arab Jamahiriya, Americans must apply through an overseas mission. After failing in other European capitals, we settled on London, where a visa expediter promised delivery for an up-front fee of $150 each. But a week after the promised authorizations, we have nothing. Our nonchangeable, nonrefundable tickets from London to Tripoli had a departure time of fourteen hours ago. We're pinning final hopes on a heteroclite Lebanese woman we met just yesterday. She took our passports early this morning and flew to Bonn, where through some mysterious connections on a weekend she claims she will return with visas duly rendered this evening. She promised to meet us here at 8:00 p.m. It's 8:45. If she doesn't show, we turn around and go home, though we'll have to get temporary passports at the U.S. Embassy.

This little convention of edge-of-seat travelers was put into motion a few weeks ago. Driving to the TED (Technology, Entertainment, Design) Conference in Monterey, California, I listened as National Public Radio reported the Bush administration was lifting the majority of its two-decade-long sanctions on Libya, including the travel ban, as a reward for Mu'ammar al-Gadhafi's pledge to scrap his nuclear arms programs and resolve outstanding claims from victims of the 1988 bombing of Pam Am Flight 103 over Lockerbie, Scotland. Since the late 1990s, Gadhafi has been reaching out to the West in an effort to rebrand Libya, Africa's second-largest oil producer after Nigeria, as an economic El Dorado. As I found once reaching an Internet connection, though, the United States continues to list Libya as a state sponsor of terrorism. Still, a wanderlust was piqued.

A quarter century ago, I was running a small adventure-travel firm that specialized in expeditions to remote corners: the Abyssinian Rift, Hunza Valley, the Zambezi basin, the Amazon, Patagonia, the Tibetan Plateau, the New Guinea highlands. Libya's swath of the Sahara, with its mountains boiled out of the earth and skein of wide wadis, was on my wish list, but Billy Carter's little Libyan adventure in 1978 ("The only thing I can say is there is a hell of a lot more Arabians than there is Jews") and former CIA agent Edwin Wilson's conviction for selling twenty tons of C4 plastic explosive to Gadhafi put the destination off-limits for my modest goals.

Before rapprochement but after Ping-Pong diplomacy, through a series of sublime accidents, in 1978 I ended up with a permit to escort the first American travel delegation to mainland China. At the time, China had no external air link, no internal tourism infrastructure, but Mao Tse-tung had decided to dip toes into tourism as a possible new source of state income. Through my little adventure company, Sobek, I had been conducting raft tours down the rivers of Ethiopia since 1973, through the coup of 1974 that ousted Emperor Haile Selassie, and throughout the communist-style revolution that followed. The Chinese were assisting Mengistu Haile Mariam, the leader who was, in a fashion, modeling himself after Mao, and so they turned to Ethiopia for suggestions of a U.S. tour company that might want to organize a first tour to China. When I got a call from Ethiopian Airlines inviting Sobek to take up the mantle, I was beside myself. We were granted a permit for twenty-five tourists, and I immediately crafted a letter to past clients and inserted it in an envelope with "Red Alert" bannered across the side. The tour itself was adventurous in a way new to me, largely because it was like being dropped onto another planet. Westerners had been forbidden since 1949, and the culture had evolved separately, like the wildlife of Madagascar when it separated from continental Africa. There were no signs in English; we were forbidden to speak with or touch a nonofficial Chinese, even for a handshake. Every tour began with a lengthy propaganda lecture, and besides the classic sites—Tiananmen Square, The Great Wall, the gardens of Hangzhou, the Forbidden City—we visited cooperative farms, acupuncture clinics, and factories. It was an interface with a slice of a culture now lost to time.

I felt Libya's opening might be similar. For a moment, there could be an immersion in a very different world. But if the gates remained open, as in China, in a few years Libya would become an irredeemable blend of touro-dollared resorts, golf courses, nightclubs, and fast food.

So before the NPR broadcast was over I was on the phone trying to understand what it would take to organize the first American tour group to Libya. I brought in Mountain Travel Sobek, the merged version of my adventure company. And over the next weeks together, we underwent the process of figuring out how to conduct a tour and how to get visas. Twenty years ago, we had worked with a French concern, Hommes et Montagnes, in the Algerian Sahara. So we contacted the trekking company, which had changed owners in the interim, and indeed it was conducting occasional adventure treks in southwestern Libya. It agreed to outfit a camel safari through the Akakus Mountains, though first warning that the temperate season was over. If we insisted on going now we would be into the Saharan summer, which is not for the meek. I pushed for going forward, knowing that if we waited until fall, the landscape would already be changing, and boatloads of Americans would be scrambling to the shores of Tripoli.

Visas were a different challenge altogether. Belgium is the official intermediary between the United States and Libya, so we tried contacting the Libyan embassy in Brussels. But we could never get through. We had the same experience with Libyan embassies in Ottawa, Paris, and Malta. Finally, we found a visa company in London, Horizons UK, which promised delivery. I invited a group of friends, and Mountain Travel Sobek did the same, and within a few days we had a full complement of sixteen folks ready to join me for a first foray into Libya. Photos, passports, and visa applications were sent to London, where they were translated into Arabic. Plane tickets were procured, and we each went and purchased desert survival gear.

But a week before departure, no visas had been processed. No explanation. The paperwork had supposedly been sent to Tripoli, but approvals had not returned. We wondered if we had a plant among us, a spy or unfriendly journalist or someone on a blacklist. But pleas to Tripoli went unanswered.

So I scoured the Internet, firing pleas to every Libyan I could find with an e-mail address. (Libya is quite wired; Internet cafes abound. One of Gadhafi's favorite words is "virus," as in "Viruses today are much more stronger than cruise missiles.") Then, the day before flying to London, I received a call from a Mr. Solieman Abboud, owner of Tripoli-based Sari Travel. He said that he was also a customs official in Tripoli and that he indeed could get us into the country. All we had to do was meet his associate, Ms. Naziha Hassanyeh, in London, hand over our passports, and she would make magic.

So those of us willing to roll the dice are at Heathrow sipping gin and tonics and happily paying with credit cards, hoping these might be our last such transactions for a fortnight, as Libya enforces a permanent ban on gambling and alcohol and accepts no credit cards. Then, around 9:00 p.m., Ms. Naziha proudly sashays through the door and opens our passports to the pages with blue and red eagle-logoed stamps covered with a round, dark blue seal. We are good to go.

No American carrier is yet allowed to fly into Libyan airspace, but British Airways has launched a new Airbus A320 service, and we are at the BA counter two hours before the nine o'clock departure Monday morning, where the agent scrutinizes our passports and visas. "There is only one country that's harder to get a visa for," the BA agent says. "America." Then she waves us through, and soon we are Libya-bound.

As we begin our descent into Tripoli, the "White Bride of the Mediterranean," I watch clouds scud over the landscape and see the runway wet from a morning rain. At the warehouselike terminal, we funnel in to meet Solieman Abboud, sucking a Rothmans cigarette, on the arrival side of customs and immigration. He collects our passports and disappears between a cinema-sized poster of Gadhafi in his Aviator Ray-Bans and a sign that says "Partners Not Wage Earners," a bumper-sticker aperçu from Gadhafi's *Green Book*. A few minutes later, Solieman reappears and leads us past an empty immigration booth, and inside Libya we are at last.

* * *

We're staying at the spanking, year-old, $125-million Corinthian Bab, at the western end of Tripoli's corniche, the only five-star hotel in Libya. With two soaring crescent towers, it looks like a Buck Rogers intergalactic version of a hotel, featuring Kenny G Muzak in the elevators, Buffy on the room TV. It has all the accoutrements of a resort—heated pools, spas, vast buffets—but the glaring difference is that at the various lobby bars and restaurants you cannot order a whiskey or rye, only tea, instant coffee, soft drinks, nonalcoholic beer, and "mocktails."

The hotel is just a few yards from the Barbary Coast, where freebooters looted commercial ships in the seventeenth and eighteenth centuries. In 1805, Thomas Jefferson sent American Marines across the desert from Egypt to this coast, giving rise to the line in *The Marines' Hymn,* "From the halls of Montezuma to the shores of Tripoli."

We first explore the adjacent medina, and down a serpentine passage hissing with intrigue I exchange U.S. dollars with a gold merchant for dinars, the local currency, derived from *denarius,* the most common Roman coin. Every few minutes there is a popping sound, like gunfire, and I instinctively look for a place to duck and hide. But these are just firecrackers, set off by children at play. The prophet Muhammad's birthday is in a few days, and apparently it's like Chinese New Year in that the streets snap and smoke with fireworks. This is just a preview.

Later we make the ninety-minute bus ride east to Leptis Magna, the ancient port city that kept Rome supplied with slaves for its gladiator arenas, wild animals for circuses, and women for concubinage. Under Lucius Septimius Severus, who ruled the empire from 193 to 211, the three great cities of the Libyan coast, Leptis Magna, Oea (now Tripoli), and Sabratha to the west, rivaled Rome in splendor, architecture, wealth, and decadence. Sacked after the Romans withdrew in the seventh century, Leptis Magna was abandoned, then buried under the sands until the early part of the twentieth century.

We wind along the coast down a wide road financed by petrodollars, first passing rows of Soviet-style apartment buildings, each with an oversized satellite TV dish attached to a window or porch, then orchards of olive trees, date palms, and oranges. We're stopped a few times at security checkpoints, but once we present our heavily stamped paperwork, we're nonchalantly waved through. There are no English signs; Gadhafi banned such in 1970, along with all Italians, Jews, and the American Wheelus Air Base, then largest in the world outside of the United States. We see only one western logo in the journey: the red-white-and-blue Pepsi swirl, but without a word of English.

At an inconspicuous driveway, we turn in, park, and file

into the largest and best-preserved Roman ruins outside of Italy, perhaps most remarkable for its absence of hawkers, freelance guides, beggars, and American cruise ship tourists. Leptis Magna lived under the shadow of Carthage until the Romans transformed the modest trading port into a site of imperial magnificence, prodigiously endowing the city with steam baths, forums, theaters, villas, basilicas, lighthouses, markets, marble toilets, triumphal arches, and an amphitheater that could seat 20,000 folks. One colonnaded street, marked by an etched penis, even led to the Roman version of the red light district. As we wander the cobbled streets and pose by marble monuments, we revel in the Trumpness of it all.

For dinner we head to Al Murjan (Red Coral), themed with anchors and sails and an oil of Gadhafi dressed in white captain's uniform. Between courses of schwarmas and squid, we swill Beck's nonalcoholic beer and bitters, toasting Solieman for his visa sorcery. We end with rich espressos, legacies of a colonial misadventure which began in 1911 when Italy "liberated" Libya from Ottoman rule and ended with the liberators' defeat by the Allied forces in 1943. During the occupation, almost half the indigenous population was killed, including Gadhafi's grandfather, as Italy attempted to tame its "fourth shore."

We make the long walk back to the hotel after dinner, through the night market, past hundreds of vendors along a crowded Omar al-Mukhtar Street. Outside speakers blare 50 Cent and Sting, and the contents of the great garage of Libya are for sale, from Gadhafi watches to little live gazelles to prestrung polyvinyl chloride Christmas trees. A series of tiny shops are selling foot-high hamburgers, and when a couple of meat vendors discover I'm an American, they give thumbs-up, a far cry from the moment in 1986 after the United States bombed Gadhafi's residence, killing his infant daughter, when he declared it was legal to eat American soldiers since they had been revealed to be animals. Last year, Libya chaired the UN Commission on Human Rights.

The next morning, in the volant lobby, readying for the

airport transfer, we meet our lead French guide, Bastien Stieltjes, a ringer for Hank Azaria as Claude in *Along Came Polly*. Bastien sports sun-streaked hair down to his shoulders, a Hawaiian shirt fashionably ripped across the back, and a desert finish from a season guiding in Algeria. But as we learn, this is his first time to Libya. His assistant guide, Ludovic Bousquet, has been to Libya before but never on this itinerary, so indeed this is an exploratory, as nobody has seen this route through the Akakus Massif. We're also joined by Al-Mabrouk Ali-Alzalet, thirty-six, a taciturn shadow from the Department of Security. We're not sure if he is with us to ensure our safety or to spy on us.

On a venerable Libyan Arab Airlines Fokker F27 we swoop southwest, into the Fezzan, Libya's great desert province, down toward the ancient entrepôt of Ghat, near the Algerian border. Ghat (pronounced "rat" by Bastien) was a trading center for the great camel caravans of lore, bringing ivory, gold, salt, and slaves from the sub-Sahara, and rumors abound it still traffics in human contraband. It's a long flight, almost three hours; Libya is larger than Alaska. As we begin the descent, I can see the sea of sand out the window, long ridges that butt and intersect and overlap in complex patterns, a network of ridges and dips, crescents and curls, that from above resemble the whorls of gigantic fingertips. In the distance are the Akakus Mountains, which seem to have punctured the planet's skin, leaving giant scars; and then there are the wadis, stony gashes snaking into hidden vaults.

At Ghat International, we step off the plane into the Saharan sun. It is not as hot as anticipated, and a few in our group comment they can easily handle this temperature. To the south we see the palisades of blue, blunt mountains, our destination. Certainly it will be cooler inside their rocky chambers.

In Ghat, a desultory and dusty way station, we pause for a brief wander of its labyrinthine medina, where in a mud-and-dung alcove souq merchants are hawking perfume, heavy, filigreed silver jewelry, and genuine desert tapestries with designs of grizzly bears and poker-playing dogs. I buy a pair of lightweight

Tuareg pantaloon-type pants with brocaded hems *(akerbai)*, thinking these must be the right desert attire, even if they are a tad on the small side.

At the Anay campsite just out of town, we slip under a tent and sit cross-legged on Berber rugs. We sip mint tea from shooter glasses and munch on olives, dates, and tuna salad Niçoise, all under the watchful gaze of a watercolored Gadhafi in a camel-hair sash and oversized sunglasses. Here, the Tuareg host hands out long turbans, or *sheshes,* and shows us how to wrap them securely around our heads. Centuries ago, according to lore, the Tuareg tribesmen donned veils to trick enemies into thinking they were women. Today, we're told, the Tuareg women, unlike other Muslims who generally cover their heads in public, do not wear sheshes, though we can't confirm as we never see any local women. The other, more believable theory is that the shesh humidifies the mouth and nose in the dry desert air and filters blowing sand. Then we pile into four Toyota Land Cruisers, one with Barbary sheep horns strapped to the front, two with goatskin bags, called *guerbas,* filled with freshwater hanging from the roof racks, and head into the heart of the world's biggest desert toward a 120-mile-long basalt maze, the Jebel Akakus. When we reach our first sand dune, a sensually shaped, honey-colored ridge, we pile out and leap around in sand soft as talcum, as though in our first snow. The Tuareg scratch their sheshes in amusement.

At the eastern end of a giant, crescent-shaped sand dune, in the belly of the Tadhintour Wadi, the Land Cruisers halt and Bastien announces camp, a sand spit called Tan Garaba. The cars will return to Ghat, leaving only camels as our conveyance for the next five days. We're just three miles from the Algerian border, some thirty miles northeast from Djanet, where thirty-two European tourists were kidnapped last year by an Islamic extremist group believed to have ties to al-Qaida. The camping gear is arranged in a giant U shape, pointing toward Algeria as though a trench against invaders, including the *ghibli,* the fierce blowing sands from the south.

Here, we meet our Tuareg guides as well: the *adogu,* or leader, Mama Eshtawy, forty-one, black as a crow and with gimlet eyes; Acrwof Adhan, fifty, head cameleer, with a jiggy personality and an Ed McMahon laugh; and Kadar, the steadfast cook, quiet as smoke in his *gandoma,* a long robe that sweeps the ground as he walks.

We have four women on the trip, yet all are faced with a challenge, as there are no trees or bushes near this camp, only the ruffles and flutes of sand dunes, and there is no toilet tent. Bastien warns that the Tuareg are extremely conservative in regard to showing skin, especially arms and legs, and as such we should avoid revealing our casings beyond hands, feet, neck, and face. In the nineteenth century, a young Dutchwoman, Alexine Tinne, exposed a bit too much, had her arm hacked off by one of her Tuareg escorts, and was left to bleed to death. So the far slope of a dune marked with a water bottle becomes the sacred place. Until Mabrouk marches up the dune with his prayer rug to recite his nightly prayers.

We dine on liver wrapped around the suet of a freshly slaughtered goat cooked in its own fat, and sip sugared tea into the night. Water is scarce, so no showers, and we wash our dishes with the fine Saharan sand. The Tuareg gather round a small campfire and chatter in Tamashek, a language that sounds like the squeaking of bats. Under the moonlight, the adjacent dune looks like sleek suede, the sort of storybook scene Antoine de Saint-Exupery evoked. My altimeter shows we are at 2,913 feet, and it is still 87°F at 11:00 p.m.

* * *

We awake to the sounds of old men snorting and humphing—our camels have arrived and are grazing some sere scrub a few yards from camp. I walk over to greet our ships. They are very tall, with impossibly long and knobby legs and a cavalier look. All are male and are hobbled with thick ropes between their front legs. The Tuareg load them up with all our gear and 600 liters of water in plastic literjohns, and they take off down a long-dry watercourse.

We begin our trek with a clamber up the four-hundred-foot-high dune, rose red in the morning light. Mama slips off his camel-leather sandals and climbs barefoot, moving up the hill like a ghost. For the rest of us it is tough climbing in the deep sand, the opposite of walking on sunshine, more like walking underwater. After laboring for half an hour we edge noses over the sharp crest of the ridge and gaze down into Algeria and then back toward the vermilion cliffs of the Akakus, a tableau of frozen violence through which we are supposed to hike. It is already 90°F at 9:00 a.m. as we descend the sand billow and begin our tramp in earnest.

For several hours we trek, up over the 4,000-foot Aogeraq Pass, while the temperature wheels to 104°F. Not far from here, at Al-'Aziziyah in Libya, the highest temperature in the Sahara was recorded, 136°F. Frank Headen, a veteran adventure traveler, picks up pieces of fulgurite, fused particles, like silica glass, formed from lightning striking the sand. I pluck a pottery shard from a footprint. We pass rocks etched with fossils, left over from the shallow sea that lapped in the Sahara during the long Tertiary period (65 million to somewhere around 1.6 million years ago). Then in the distance we spy a lone acacia tree in a tongue of sand, our lunch goal. Two camels with saddles wrapped around their ungainly backs have been stepping with us, their wide, padded feet making no sound on the soft sand. Mama uses his long staff to halt the camels and offers rides to the group. Cheryl Sulima, a bank analyst for the Federal Reserve, has a swollen eye from a pesky sand particle that blew in, and Frank is suffering from an upset stomach, so they accept the offer to ride, though the camels protest with sounds like Wookies in heat as the riders mount. With saddles creaking, the two-toed animals plod off, throwing off little puffs of white sand. The camel is not native to these parts. It was introduced from Arabia probably around the third century, long before the Arab invasions, but it quickly became indispensable. In the peak of the Saharan summer, a camel can endure up to five days without drinking anything. A man, other than a Tuareg, can last but one.

Water is necessary in the Sahara, but shade is a miracle. At 1:00 p.m. we stagger into the scant shade of the thorn tree, leaves torn by camel tongues, and collapse. We're all spent and thirsty from this first hike, and spread out like dead eagles on the mats. John Canning, media Sherpa and photographer, and I unroll the Brunton flexible solar panels to charge our batteries.

For a couple of hours, we rest in the heat of the day. Then Bastien asks for volunteers to help dig a path for the camels over the sandy Tafaq Pass. Ann Duncan, a Seattle portfolio manager, and I decide to offer, and off we head with Bastien and Mama to another huge dune that divides two *oueds*. As we zigzag up the dune, we use our tin dinner plates to shovel a path the camels can step along. This is hard work in the superheated air, and I have to stop and swig from my Nalgene every few minutes.

On the far side of the pass, we face an otherworldly panorama of Gothic cathedrals, medieval castles, moon mesas, McDonald's arches, and Disneyesque spires of balancing rocks, splashed with red and ocher, all seemingly baked into the landscape. We make our way down to camp, arriving as the sun is finally setting. It has been a tough day, and my one-size-too-small Tuareg pants have been chafing my groin, which now has a painful rash.

After the mats are unrolled, John plugs his laptop into a solar-charged battery and gives a slide show of the day's photography, with a Lenny Kravitz sound track, to the Tuareg, who watch the wizardry through the gap in their sheshes, dark eyes wide. We sup on lentil soup, couscous, and goat stew, with a dollop of cool Crème Mont Blanc from Bastien's bag poured over dates. We finish the meal, as we do every repast, with Tuareg champagne—a triple serving of strong green tea boiled over a wood fire, poured from a height to make cappuccinolike foam, then reheated and poured into small glasses. After tea, we lay out our sleeping bags. It's too warm to tuck in, too warm for even a sheet, so I lay naked under the Saharan stars and slip into sleep.

Although he has never been through these mountains, never been to Libya, Bastien consults with the Tuareg and reports that today is to be an easy trek, a short hike to Oued Babou, our lunch spot, where we will also camp for the night. Spirits hearten, and we take off after lingering in camp until well after the sun has punched in.

After an hour's trek, we come to our first canvas of prehistoric rock art in situ: a giraffe, a hippo, a bullock, wildlife that prospered in a greener, gentler Sahara, when the climate was kind, before it turned into the arid sandbox it is today. There are some 1,300 sites scattered through the Akakus, dating back 12,000 years. It's an astonishing book of hours.

Then out into the hard sun, rambling down Babou Wadi. We drop into a deflation basin, an oval lowland scoured by constant blowing. We wander through a forest of ventifact, rock polished by sand and carved into far-fetched shapes. Now it is really hot: my portable thermometer reads 110°F. The heat radiates back from the ground, creating little eddies of convection turbulence. It's like walking on a griddle beneath a heat lamp. We're beginning to wobble. Heinrich Barth, the German explorer who passed through here in the mid-nineteenth century, noted "it is indeed very remarkable how quickly the strength of a European is broken in these climes." At one point we stumble up to a rock ledge and take a short rest in the shade. Cheryl's left eye is swollen shut. Frank's shirt is crusty and stained white with what looks like a skin of ice. "I'm saltier than a country ham," Frank says with a grimace. After a few minutes, though, Bastien pushes us back out into the sun, saying we need to continue.

We're now into midday, and the heat seems nuclear (the French tested thirteen nuclear devices in the 1960s not far from here). We are not suffering from an overabundance of shade. All talk has dried up. Some are getting low on personal water, and the extra water is with the caravanners, who took a different route. About 1:00 p.m., we crest a ridge and see another lone acacia in a wadi . . . that must be camp. But Mama says no. We will take a right at the tree and head into a side canyon, perhaps half a mile away. The goal seems attainable. So we trip across the hyperarid landscape (Sebhah, at the other edge of the Fezzan, is credited as the most arid place on earth). We march over a level plain of lag gravel cemented by gypsum deposits and dotted with black, slablike stone. It's like skulking through a graveyard. At the head of the canyon, John Canning and I take a respite in the shade of a boulder, and I apply some aloe jelly to my groin, now ablaze in pain. I have to walk like a cowboy to keep from chafing further. Then back into the full power of the sun, and we slouch deeper and deeper into the recondite canyon. My temples feel as though they've been bound with rope pulled tight; my head feels both too big and too brittle, as though it might crack open like an egg in boiling water. Sweat pours out, but my skin is dry. Finally, about 2:00 p.m., I reel into camp, utterly exhausted, in an ecstasy of thirst, with most of the group still behind. The camels are already grazing the sparse provender, having arrived via a shortcut earlier. As the last of the team collapses in the shade of an overhang, there is discontent. "More like a forced march than an adventure," someone grumbles. "Paris–Dakar without the cars," gripes another. "Marathon des Sable without water," bellyaches one more. After a partial recovery with long pulls of water and a rest, a group meeting is called. Five of the ten Americans announce they would like to abandon the trip and fly back to Tripoli. Cheryl's eye looks worse, redder and puffier, and she seems delirious from heat exhaustion. The others simply submit that this is hotter and harder than they had anticipated, and that they would prefer to exit rather than continue to suffer.

I can't argue. The Sahara is not a place for the timorous. And I am suffering my own private hell with my rash. So we pull out the Iridium satellite phone and call in a couple of vehicles that will meet us for lunch the next day, pulling out the coalition of the unwilling. The remaining five will be Frank Headen, Ann Duncan, John Canning, Hugh Westwater, another adventure travel vet, and I.

With lines redrawn in the sand, the afternoon is relaxed. We play a version of desert boccie ball, using gourds as balls, and watch as the Tuareg, puffing on Camel cigarettes donated by Hugh, play their version of checkers (*al-karhat*), using camel pellets as pieces. As we unroll our sleeping bags, Bastien warns not to camp close to rocks, as scorpions hide in their nooks and crannies during the day and come out at night and will naturally seek out the warmth of a sleeping bag. I ignore his advice and camp in the lee of a boulder to avoid the spitting sand that is beginning to whip, the lesser of the evening's evils.

LIBYARATED

I awake to a black scarab on one side of my bag, a pale locust on the other. Footprints of a Rüppell's desert fox and a Dorcas gazelle crisscross camp. John's sleeping bag, however, is encircled by the tracks of a legion of scorpions that seemed to soldier to the edge of his bag and then scurry away, perhaps, he conjectures, from the smell. As I stand up bowlegged, my inner thighs are so chafed they bleed. I consider applying the cool Crème Mont Blanc as an ointment (it's a dessert topping; it's a desert salve) but instead elect to abandon my Tuareg pants for a pair of cotton shorts. Others have gone to shorts, and the Tuareg seem to take no offense. In fact, Ann later reveals that while each of the women have received a marriage proposal, the Tuareg voted my pale, water-rich body the sort of physique they would most have admired, if only I were a woman.

It's another hot toddle, four hours under a sun hissing like a blowtorch rather than the promised two, to the lunch spot beneath a long rock brow where the vehicles are to rendezvous. We chew on Laughing Cow cheese and pâté smuggled in from France by Bastien, our own South Libyan Beach diet. We lounge, do crossword puzzles, read Jon Krakauer, and sing show tunes. Ann knits a sock. At home, we often wish for a whole afternoon with nothing to do. Now that we have it, most are restless. At 3:00 p.m. I set my thermometer in the sand in the sun just beyond our sanctuary, and when I check a few minutes later it reads 136°F.

Late in the day, two Land Cruisers come roaring over the sand. It's too late to head back to Ghat, a six-hour drive, so they instead ferry those evacuating to the next camp, while the rest of us hike across a field of black, bony rocks, a former lava flow, then down into a sand gully. We're a small group now, the sun is low, and the mood is merry. Acrwof starts singing and dances alongside the swaying camels, occasionally breaking out in cascades of silly laughter. He hardly seems a descendant of the Tuareg people who massacred Paul Xavier Flatters's French expedition not far from here in 1881.

Camp is in the middle of a wide wadi called Anteburak, spotted with scratches of grass. While Bastien rolls a cigarette, the camels roll around in the sand. When the camels unkneel and stand back up, they are so covered with Saharan sand that they blend into the dun-colored cliffs so as to almost be indistinguishable—camelflage. Mama catches a black lizard from a tuft of grass. He says the Tuareg eat it as a cure for hepatitis. He also kicks aside several tufts in his way, and challenges us with a Tuareg riddle: what wears out if you don't use it? We're stumped; he grins and points to the ground: a trail. Bastien says these tufts are favorite hangouts for deadly sand vipers, and we should avoid them. But again the susurrating wind is kicking sand, and I bunk down behind a large grass tuft, which emits some sort of clacking sound as I drift off.

After morning tea, hugs and addresses are exchanged, and the group splits as half head back to Ghat, along with Ludovic, to catch a flight back to Tripoli, then home, Libyarated at last. The five remaining start out for the next camp, but after a short way, stoic Frank begins to complain about a double pain in his side. He seems imbalanced and flushed. We put him on a camel, but he is almost delirious with pain, and Mama walks alongside to make sure he doesn't fall off.

We finally make camp, in a beautiful tributary gateway, Tin Talahat, around noon, and spread Frank out beneath a shady rock balcony. He struggles to his feet several times to slump behind a rock and vomit. I give him a painkiller, and he confesses he is convinced a kidney stone is trying to pass. This has happened to him before, once in China, and he knows the feeling too well. I call a United States–based medical evacuation service on the Iridium and speak with a doctor, who confirms it is likely a kidney stone, which is sometimes stimulated by heat and exhaustion. It also can turn deadly. So we call in another extraction vehicle and wait. A black and white mula-mula bird flitters by, which Mama says is good luck. The Land Cruiser finally arrives at sunset, too late to return tonight. We make a bed for Frank, feed him more painkillers, and hope for the best.

Frank leaves at 5:00 a.m. in a Land Cruiser, with Bastien along to assist. Of the original sixteen signed for this trip, four remain, including Ann, who to date has had *two* marriage proposals from the Tuareg. We now have no French guides, and none of us speaks Arabic or Tamashek. And Bastien has taken my satellite phone. So we are alone in the Great Nothing, the sea without water, the Libyan Sahara, with our Tuareg guides and a dozen camels.

We spend the morning exploring galleries of rock art—the amazing displays of Tin Tagaget, including ostriches, elephants, rhinos, chariots, and even Jennifer Lopez as a stick figure with a big head and giant behind. There may be truth to theories that these ancient artists were depicting visitors from outer space.

As we lumber back to camp, the wind begins to whisk the sand like flour. The sky turns a hazy yellow, blurring the sun. Suddenly sand fills ears and noses, lungs and pores. It grits teeth, turns eyes the color of fermenting beer. We are in a sandstorm. The dunes are smoking; the wind makes a scratchy drumming sound caused by the piezoelectric properties of crystalline quartz, just as early phonograph produced scratching sounds. The full Sahara seems to be shifting, migrating. The Tuareg draw their sheshes across their faces and cast eyes downward; the camels squat, backs toward the wind, and close their long-lashed and double-lidded eyes. We climb into a cave, but it is more of an eddy and the whole of the Sahara blasts through. We're finally getting, it seems, our just deserts. All we need now to complete the experience is a plague of locusts. We finally climb up the back side of an *inselberg,* an eroded pillar from the Akakus remnant bin, and find a bit of a reprieve from the storm. There, we play hearts into twilight, awaiting our own vehicles for the final return to Ghat. At sunset, Hapip Khlil Abulkharim, a radio controller at Ghat International, swings his Land Cruiser into camp. He apologizes for arriving so late, saying he took a circuitous route: "This is an open area, a dangerous area. There is a lot of smuggling through this region, arms to Algeria, and people from Niger and Mali." In 2001, a lorry broke down in untracked sand carrying illegal immigrants from the south. Ninety-six passengers were found dead. "It's a big problem here, so I took the safe route."

For six hours we grind toward Ghat in the midst of a harmattan, a wind the Tuareg call the hot breath of the desert. Sand beats on the car metal with a sound like heavy rain. It's too hot to close the windows, but with them open it feels like a row of hair dryers pointed at us on full blast. Along with a little teddy bear, a prayer from the Koran asking for safe travel hangs from the rearview mirror, and Hapip fingers it throughout our journey. Nevertheless, we have a flat tire, and the spark plugs begin to misfire. Finally the car conks out, and we switch to another and limp into Ghat in the late afternoon. We check into the flat-roofed Ghat Hotel, an unlovely affair with a gleaming cappuccino machine that belongs in a Paul Bowles novel. Out back is a mud-walled camel stable with a very low door, making it difficult for camels to wander out. For a thousand years, these low doors have been called needle's eyes, explaining why it is easier for a camel to go through the eye of a needle than for a rich man to enter into the kingdom of God. We first call to check on Frank and learn he had not one but two kidney stones, both of which passed without incident. So we celebrate with potato chips and guava juice. Then, after spraying our beds for bugs and kneeling to shower under feeble hoses, we head down the street to a hookah bar, where we smoke ornate, waist-high *nargilahs,* puffing fruit-flavored tobacco through long, flexible hoses, and watch *Pan Arabic Idol* on TV until 2:00 a.m.

Back in Tripoli, we are invited to a final dinner hosted by a prominent Libyan businessman. We arrive and are ushered into a living room, where a Berber band dressed in black fezzes, red sashes, and white skirts puts on a wild, dervishlike performance, spinning about the house, leaping on furniture, balancing vases, apples, and bottles on heads, and bending over guests like lap dancers so that dinars can be stuffed into their hats. One band member plays an oboelike *gheeta,* another a drum made of skin stretched over a mortar (a *tende*), a third a flute called a *nay,* and the last a reed and goatskin bagpipe called a *zukra.* The music is called *mriskaawi* and is performed mostly for weddings. This evening, our host explains, is a marriage of East and West. Then, as a plate of fried camel is passed, to our surprise our host offers us his version of home-brewed tequila, or *bokha.* This is a very dry country, and we're a bit shocked, wondering if this might be some sort of setup. But the band members are kicking back shot glasses of this juice, as are others at the party, friends of the host. So we give it try. It tastes like some combination of bad grappa, anise, and arrack. But then someone appears with a couple of bottles of Tunisian wine, and someone else produces a bottle of Beefeater gin, and then a bottle of Ballantine's whiskey. We pause when our security guy, Mabrouk, walks in . . . certainly he will arrest us *kafirs,* depraved unbelievers. But he steps over to the table with the multiplying bottles of alcohol and asks for a sip, confessing he has never tried such. He then precedes to swizzle back several glasses of wine, then some scotch, then gin . . . then he starts mixing wine and whiskey in the same glass. After a time he is up dancing around the room with the band, a college kid at his first frat party. Finally, we feed him into a taxi and send him to a hotel, not his family, where he sleeps off the night.

On our last morning, Solieman Abboud arranges for an interview with the minister of tourism, His Excellency Ammare Mabrouk Eltayef, who has been in the post for about eighteen months and is keenly concerned with protocol and sending the message that Libya is ripe for tourism investment, from hotels to golf courses to beach resorts. He blames our visa imbroglio on the U.S. government, saying if America had allowed a Libyan embassy (né people's bureau) in Washington, we would not have had our problems. And he says that the new tourism initiatives come from the top, from the Great Leader Gadhafi himself.

As we pass through customs, I'm pulled aside and asked to explain my solar panels to a group of skeptical baggage handlers. I assemble it in the baggage back room of the terminal and show diagrams of how it works, and they finally let it pass. Then as the last of us file down the walkway to the plane back to London, there is a beaming Solieman Abboud waiting, wishing us good-bye. "See if you can return the favor," he asks. "I would like to be the first Libyan tourist to America."

6

Up the Wall of Death

The *Eiger* of the *Swiss Alps*

Another soul sent to Valhalla
Another murder for the Wall
On the Eigerwand in winter
Is the hardest climb of all.
 —"The John Harlin Song,"
Tom Patey in *One Man's Mountains*

One rope length from The White Spider, the last great defiance on the mountain wall that is one of the world's deadliest, the seven-millimeter fixed line broke. John Harlin II, the first American to climb the legendary North Face of the Eiger in the Swiss Alps four years earlier, fell 4,000 feet into the void.

A short time later, his nine-year-old son, Johnny Harlin III, heard the news from his sobbing mother. It was news he couldn't fathom. His father was among the world's greatest climbers, a

101

pioneer of straight-up routes, a man almost mythopoetically at home in the vertical world.

That was 40 years ago.

Now John Harlin III, a half-year shy of his 50th birthday, has returned to attempt to climb the hard, black limestone wall that killed his father, and he has brought his own nine-year-old, Siena, who will wait with her mother at the Bellevue des Alpes Hotel at the base of the spear-shaped mount. There is here in the air that indefinable smell of tension that precedes a storm. Even the mountain seems to have cried with this concept as just days ago it filled the Lutschine River in a hundred-year flood that tore away chalets and barns. Tears streak faces, including my own, as the deed is discussed.

I've spent the last few days with John Harlin, Siena, and his wife, Adele Hammond, and his two climbing partners for the attempt, German climbing stars Robert "Dr. Eiger" and Daniela Jasper. John and the Jaspers have spent most of their spare time training on the Leen Cliffs of Interlaken and at climbing gyms. They've also spent time with a crew from MacGillivray Freeman films, producers of *Everest* and *Mystery of the Nile,* who are here to document the climb for an IMAX movie, and the media elements, including my own presence, have added an extra degree of anxiety to what was for years thought to be a very private enterprise. But John agreed to the coverage, believing the results would honor and capture his dad's "love of the Eiger, of Switzerland, of life."

But much of the time here is spent in retrospection. The pater's shadow looms throughout the region, from maps that show the eponymous John Harlin Direct route to the old-time guides who have vivid remembrances of the American rock star, such as seventy-one-year-old Ueli Sommer, who was serving on the local mountain rescue team when the accident occurred, but didn't become involved because after a fall of such height, "there was not much left to rescue."

I'd heard stories of John Harlin II from fellow adventurers

over the years, including Royal Robbins, who had a falling-out with Harlin while blazing a direct route up the West Face of the Dru in the Alps in the mid-1960s. And I'd read John Rasmsey Ullman's hagiography, in which without a wink he says, "In a still earlier time, one feels sure, John Harlin would have been literally a knight . . . A few centuries later he might well have been a conquistador or privateer." Most climbers of the day were in awe of John Harlin II. One rope mate called him the man who "flamed up a mountain." Others called him "The Hardman," in both the flattering and deprecatory sense. His onetime student Larry Ware described him as having "a godlike physique" and "a vision and power that emanated from within," but added that his bulldozer personality turned some off, and several who had climbed with him refused to attend his funeral. But this is a time to hear the stories straight from the son.

By the mid-1960s, John Harlin had been a fighter pilot, a dress designer, a football star, a schoolteacher, an artist, and a groundbreaking rock climber. He loved intrigue and Ian Fleming, and fancied himself cloaked in mystery and adventure, sometimes alluding to an undocumented incident in Rome that involved a casualty, perhaps a sanction. John Harlin III told me that Clint Eastwood's character in the film *The Eiger Sanction* (based on the book by Trevanian), Jonathan Hemlock, a lover of art and an accomplished climber, was in part based on his dad.

In 1965, John Harlin was running his own International School of Modern Mountaineering in Leysin, Switzerland, and had been on the Eiger a dozen times, but had summited just once, up the classic route. He had become an enthusiastic proponent of the pure ascent, a plumb line from bottom to top, routes that ironed out the curves, crooks, and zags of traditional ascents on the big walls of the Alps. It was here he conceived of a first ascent of a clean line straight up the Eiger North Face, one that unbent the bows of the 1938 route that saw the first summiteers, including Heinrich Harrer, who later went on to live and write *Seven Years in Tibet*. It was, by some reckonings, the last great alpine enigma to be deciphered, a wall greater and harder than anything on Everest.

It was also here that the younger John Harlin felt the force of his father on his own life. He was aware of his father's reputation for toughness and enterprise, for being a superman of the rock. And he suffered his father's dissatisfaction with his own comparative lack of hardness. When young John fell in a ski race, the father was distressed and made it known. When young John was bested by a school bully, the father was furious. Young John dreaded his father's judgments and was ashamed he didn't measure up.

By mid-February of 1966, John Harlin II had gathered a crack team of English-speaking climbers, including American Layton Kor, the Scot Dougal Haston, and Britain's Chris Bonington, and all were readying for the attempt at the base of the mountain when Harlin dislocated his shoulder while skiing. The doctor forbade Harlin to climb for at least a fortnight, so he retreated home to Leysin, about two-and-a-half hours from the Eiger, where he hung about with his family and friends while recovering.

But then word came that a German team of eight was heading up the North Face of the Eiger in a *direttissima* attempt. It was now a race, and Harlin and team headed out. At first there was hostility. The Germans pelted Bonington with snowballs as he tried to take photos, but when a blizzard forced a retreat, a mutual respect took over, and as the teams started up again they now shared fixed ropes and coffee.

After several weeks of fixing ropes and bivouacking in precarious snow caves, the two teams were positioned for a final push to the summit, though John Harlin, believing his team the more experienced, felt confident the trophy was his. Harlin and Dougal Haston were checking gear at Death Bivouac, where the North Face froze its first two victims in 1935, when Harlin heard by radio that a German climber was above him on a small snowfield called The Fly. With the news, Harlin felt his Anglo-American prize slipping away. He decided to rush upward to try to catch the German team so at least there could be a shared victory.

Just short of the upper ice field called The White Spider there was a hundred-foot free-hanging drop from a planed wedge of rock. Dougal Haston went first, and with some difficulty he made it in about twenty minutes to the top of the pitch, where one of the Germans was also perched. Haston called down to Harlin to clip in and start jumaring up the rope.

A half hour passed, then an hour. Then thirty minutes more. Another of the Germans arrived on the platform on his way down to fetch a load, and Haston asked him to check on John Harlin. The German rappelled over the lip, but then returned a few minutes later with the news. The fixed Perlon rope had broken near the top, and John Harlin II was gone. From a telescope at Kleine Scheidegg, journalist Peter Gillman had watched the 4,000-foot fall.

Life magazine eulogized John Harlin II with a double-truck spread titled, "I'd have thought the Eiger would break before John did," a quote from John's climbing partner and friend Bev Clark.

Although five days later Dougal Haston with four Germans completed the climb and named the route The John Harlin Direct, some in the family remained bitter. Sometime after the climb, Dougal shared with Marilyn Harlin, wife of John II, mother of John III, that he had noticed the thousand-pound test rope was frayed as he made the last pitch before the break. He never called down to that effect, and with his admission a finger of blame was set.

Now John Harlin III is here at Kleine Scheidegg preparing to meet the ogre that has haunted him for forty years. He is taking time off from his job as editor of *The American Alpine Journal,* the prestigious annual where his father published accounts of his climbing exploits. The living John has had moments of doubt many times thinking of this endeavor, which he describes as a pilgrimage. The North Face has been called the *Mordwand* ("Murder Wall") and The Wall of Death, with some sixty fatalities to date, and John openly admits his fear and wonders about the probity of risk.

The weather is not good. It has been too warm, melting the high ice fields, sending frozen daggers and rock down the face like rain. But climbing this countenance is something John desperately wants to do, hopes to do this season, to make a long-sought father-son connection, to bring some sort of closure, some healing to a family wound. "My father would be proud and pleased with this," he substantiates. But he also admits his motivations are hard to understand. "If I think about it rationally, I probably shouldn't be doing this. Yet, I've always felt that there was no climb I had to do except the Eiger."

Through a telescope he examines the concave architecture and the road he intends to make, a route he has never tried but knows like his own neighborhood. "A vertical chess game," he calls it. Then he sets out to practice and to wait as a cloud pillows in from the southeast.

$$* \quad * \quad *$$

An enormous eddy of warm air has slipped into the Jungfrau. The bane of climbers on the Eiger, a *foehn* is coming in. Like a chinook, it is a coil of air that thaws ice and snow and triggers avalanches. Worse, directly after a *foehn* there is often a big chill that varnishes rock walls with a thin sheen of ice that neither ice axe nor piton can grip. That thin ice layer is called verglas. Verglas, John Harlin repeats in almost a mantralike way, is not something he wants to face on the Eiger.

And so he waits.

As we're gathered in the Victorian salon of the not-overstated-in-name Bellevue des Alpes Hotel, we take turns making introductions. We go through the film crew, the supporting climbers, the Yahoo! team, then John Harlin III, and finally his wife, Adele, who midway through describing a new school for her nine-year-old daughter, Siena, cracks her voice and struggles to hold back the tears. While not all in the room know the grim history of the North Face of the Eiger, everyone knows how risky this concept is and how terribly wrong things could go.

By the mid-1930s, every major face in the Alps had been climbed, save one. After years of consideration and covetousness, Munich-based Max Sedlmayer and Karl Mehringer made the first incursion onto the high North Face in 1935. But a storm drove in, trapping them halfway up the mountain's 13,000-foot summit, and they froze to death at a spot known since as Death Bivouac.

A year later, Germans Edi Rainer, Willy Angerer, Andreas Hinterstoisser and Toni Kurz were killed retreating from the mountain in brutal weather after a rock-fall mishap. Within earshot of the tourist railway tunnel window a third of the way up—where the caretaker had already begun to brew tea for the climbers—all except Kurz fell to their deaths. Kurz hung on for a night and a day, one arm frostbitten and useless, while local guides tried to rescue him.

Somehow he found the strength to clamber back up to Angerer's body, where he cut a length of rope, unraveled its three strands, and tied them together to make a line long enough to rappel down to his rescuers. As Kurz dangled beneath an over-hang, so close the guides could almost touch the soles of his boots, a knot jammed. He yelled down, "Ich kann nicht mehr" ("I'm finished") and then slumped over, dead.

Finally, in 1938, the year Germany annexed Austria into the Reich, Austrians Heinrich Harrer and Fritz Kasparek, along with Germans Anderl Heckmair and Ludwig Vorg, cracked the code and made the first successful ascent. But the accomplish-ment stirred its own storm after a photograph was published of the four climbers flanking Adolf Hitler at Breslau, inciting accu-sations that the climb was a Nazi propaganda effort, something denied to his last day by the last surviving member, Heinrich Harrer, who died in January 2006 at ninety-three after living out his final days in his native Austria.

Today the route that Harrer and companions blazed is known as the Classic Route, following the lines of weakness up the face, and it is the one John Harlin III hopes to attempt in a few days time, if weather permits. Twenty-five years ago John had wanted to retrace The John Harlin Direct, but something happened to change his will.

If the child is the father of the man, the six-year-old Johnny's genetic predisposition inspired his dad, as that year saw both the son's first multipitch climb in the Calanques of southern France and the father's ascent of the Eiger North Face, the first Anglophone to do so. John Harlin III continued to climb after his father's fall. At thirteen he climbed Mount Chamberlin, highest peak in Alaska's Brooks Range. In college in California, he became president of the mountaineering club, as his father had been two decades before at Stanford, and his dorm room was decorated with posters of Himalayan peaks he hoped to climb. By his early twenties, he was an extreme skier and accomplished climber and began to contemplate a path that would connect him to the climbs his dad had done. Then in 1979 he set out to Mount Robson in the Canadian Rockies with a climbing partner, Chuck Hospedales. After climbing its Wishbone Arête, they were descending in the late afternoon beneath a huge couloir, a hanging wall of ice, without being roped up. John led, and after negotiating over a knob and down a ten-foot section of vertical rock, he looked up to coach his less-experienced cohort. There was an unnaturally long pause as John waited, and so he yelled up, "Can't you feel the handhold?"

"I can't," Chuck muttered back. And he peeled off the mountain. John lunged, and felt the fabric of Chuck's jacket, but found no grip. Helplessly, John listened to a death scream and watched the sparks of Chuck's crampons as they repeatedly struck the rock through the 500-foot fall.

John scrambled down in the darkness to the hut, where he wrote in the logbook: "This mountain game isn't worth it."

The next morning, he reached the police station, and a helicopter was dispatched for the body. John couldn't bring himself to call Chuck's folks, but he did call his mom, who was overwrought with the news. John realized then how awful it would be for his mom should he die in a climbing accident, and at that moment he vowed to quit alpinism, "for my mom's sake." What he once felt was the finest expression of self-validation and freedom he now saw as a photographic negative: everything white was black.

Sitting in front of the gleaming wilderness of the North Face of the Eiger, John touches a deep spring of memory; his disinheriting countenance breaks, and he cries. Then for a moment the alpine world seems to balance on a point of silence.

John then gathers himself and looks to the middle distance. "I don't know why we deliberately put ourselves in harm's way. But some things are part of you that you can't leave behind."

John took a twelve-year interregnum from radical alpine climbing, but in its place he mastered extreme skiing, making descents of Orizaba and Popocatepetl in Mexico, the first three-pin descent of Peru's Huascaran, and the first ski descent of Boliva's Cunantincato, and performing other ski heroics in the Rockies and Alps.

But John likes to say, "The most important characteristic for an alpinist is a short memory. You forget the suffering and try again." And so in 1991 he was back, making an ascent of the Matterhorn and then other peaks throughout the Alps.

In 1999, John brought Adele and Siena, then three years old, to Leysin, where they planted flowers on his father's grave. He decided then to attempt the Eiger, but when he put his girls on the train he found himself in a spate of tears wandering about the station. "What's wrong?" he asked himself. He felt as if he were saying goodbye. And he imagined how awful it would be for his daughter to grow up without a dad.

But the Eiger was in poor condition that season, and the climb, with some relief, was aborted.

John went on to pioneer a new route up Mont Blanc, and made hard climbs in Austria, Germany, Italy, and throughout Europe. He even made an attempt on a virgin peak in Tibet. But always the dark wall of the Eiger dropped stones into the pool of his life, rippling interminably.

If for a time his spirit was skyjacked, it has now come home. And here, amid the clank of climbing gear, John Harlin III is hoping he can join the one club that has nagged him throughout his life, chalk off the one item on his life list, and reach the peerage that would make his father proud.

*   *   *

Like a massive muddy wave frozen in the midst of a squall, the Eiger seems about to crash down upon on us at its base. But then clouds mushroom in; it begins to snow, and the face is veiled. The storm is upon us, and the climb hangs.

Mountaineers are dragon seekers, bent on improbable deeds. But peel back the large codes, chip the granite faces, and you find souls chock-full of qualms and romantic terrors. Although John Harlin has been waiting his whole life for this moment, he is waiting still until conditions are just right. There is a constant tension here between the cult of daring and obligation to family; between the blistering attraction to the flame of risk, and the want for well-being and safety. "Safety is most important," Greg MacGillivray, the IMAX film producer, asserts, sharing that his partner died in a helicopter crash years ago while making a film. "The number one killer in the mountains is impatience," adds Pasquale Scaturro, the renowned expedition leader who has witnessed a share of field fatalities and who is here as the character George Kennedy played in *The Eiger Sanction,* the veteran in charge of mountain logistics and operations.

For these and other reasons, John Harlin III reached out to professional climbers Robert and Daniela Jasper to be his partners on this jagged grail. Although he has never climbed with either, John met Robert three years ago at a conference in southern France and learned of his passion for the Eiger. Known locally as Dr. Eiger, Robert has made twelve ascents up the North Face, all different routes. I watch Robert train on nearby rock, and he moves like liquid mercury pouring upward. I've never seen anything like it. John, who hasn't climbed since March, seems clunky and unsure by comparison; he doesn't dance the rock, he fights it, which is how his dad's climbing style was once described. By all other standards, though, John is indeed an exceptional athlete, and his forty-nine-year-old body is buff like a bullock's.

Robert Jasper, thirty-seven, who sports shaggy, rock-star hair and the conspiratorial grin of one who lives his passion, started climbing as a small boy up pine trees in the Black Forest. By age ten, he was scaling significant rock faces with his dad. At seventeen, he first climbed the Eiger. Now he lives in a chalet in Speiz, near Interlaken, not far from the Eiger, so he can be close to the peak he so loves. "He shares the same spirit for the Eiger as my dad," John offers. "That's why I want to climb this mountain with him."

Many issues evoke unease as the climb looms, but none more than safety. "Speed is safety," John intones several times. Daniela Jasper, thirty-four, is also part of the climb. She too is a world-class climber, with several first ascents to her name, but she is also a new mother, with a two-and-a-half-year-old boy, Stefan, and a baby girl, Amelie, just fourteen months into the world. "I climb laundry mountains these days. The Eiger will be a vacation from raising my kids," she says, cascading in laughter, belying a deep concern that others share. Earlier this week, she awoke in the middle of the night hearing her daughter cry, and as she tended her baby she cried out loud, "I can't do the Eiger." But she and Robert are partners, and he says, "The climb is a big adventure for our relationship."

In addition, Daniela must deal with the Alison Hargreaves syndrome. When ten years ago a sudden storm plucked the thirty-three-year-old Scottish mountaineering superstar off the south face of K2, leaving her two children, ages four and six, motherless, there was an international frenzy of censure, an outcry that mothers of young children should not climb dangerous mountains (Hargreaves first suffered criticism after climbing the Eiger six months pregnant). Now Daniela deflects her paradigmatic decision to climb by questioning why the same fury doesn't swirl around fathers who indulge in extreme adventures. Rob Hall of the 1996 Everest disaster famously left behind an unborn son, yet was never demonized as Hargreaves was. "What's the difference?" Daniela asks.

Families in all permutations are concerned with this climb. John's mother, Marilyn, would not come to Switzerland "for all the tea in China," according to Adele, John's wife. Adele also remarks that it is very important to Siena that her dad remain a part of her life, and that Siena was crying in bed the other night, "worried about what she would do if her daddy died." And Adele, who lost a sister some years ago, declares she is a terrible base-camp wife. "It's very difficult for me. I don't like to wait and watch," sentiments shared by John's mother forty years ago when she chose to sit out the blockbuster climb in their chalet rather than be in the audience of the Eiger's vertical stage.

But Adele, who met John at seventeen, has perspective that tends to the sanguine as well. "If John didn't do this climb in his lifetime he would think something was missing." Just as he has supported her extended equestrian expeditions to South America, she supports John in this quest unequivocally. And she sees that there is worth beyond the personal, that success will bring inspiration to many, that it will stand as a triumphal symbol of "every person's internal struggle to face demons" and the courage to overcome "challenges that seem insurmountable," no matter the terrain.

Although risk cannot be blocked, it can be managed, and John, who has no intention of letting his daughter grow up without a dad, as he did, is taking every step to ensure the dangers and pitfalls of this rotting limestone balk are considered and allayed.

"I love being with someone who is willing to be out there on the edge," Adele says, dabbing watery eyes with a tissue. "But even more, I appreciate being with someone who cares even more about coming back."

In the wake of the storm, the sun briefly peeks through the

clouds, shimmering as though dipped in a bowl of crystal. And there suddenly is the cenotaph to John Harlin II, the giant monument wall of the Eiger. Of all the celebrated climbers who have been on this famous face—Krakauer, Messner, Hargreaves, Terray, Bonatti, Buhl, Clint Eastwood—nobody is more associated with it than John Harlin II.

Word comes down that a fixed rope set by the support team a few days ago near Death Bivouac is now cut in two from a rock fall. Even with rope thicker and stronger than what was used in 1966, the objective dangers loom, and the randomness of rock still rules. The climb again is postponed.

* * *

While we sit with John Harlin in the still Billiard Room of the Bellevue des Alpes, he gets a call on his cell phone. It is Robert Jasper calling to announce that the climb will start tomorrow. The weather is provisionally merciful, cold enough to slow down the ice falls for the next couple of days, and yet clear. In three days, another front is predicted to roll in.

John hangs up and looks sheepishly toward me. "Oh, my. I have butterflies in my stomach."

If since 1979 John has lived with approach avoidance to the ogre on his back, he can no longer. After a couple of minutes' reflection, he offers: "In the words of Ed Hillary, 'I hope we knock this bastard off.'"

There is a good distraction, though, in Larry Ware, a friend and protégé of John's father, who has made the trek up from Leysin, where he teaches comparative literature at the same American college where John Harlin II once taught. John has brought a scrapbook of articles about Harlin II, and together they pore over the memories, laughing at the media circus that covered the 1966 climb and the escapades of climbers they know and knew, comparing the gear in faded newsprint photographs with that of today. Looking at a picture of the double boots John had designed expressly for the Eiger, John the son quips, "I couldn't walk in my father's boots; they're too long for me."

Then Larry, with beer mug in hand, does a lively, broguish reading of "The John Harlin Song," a sniggering poem to those who overworshipped the legend of the brightly hued American climber.

Larry also describes the similarities and differences between father and son. He says that where the father was aggressive and argumentative, the son is soft-spoken with little hubris in his pennant. They both clearly had love affairs with the mountains and found joy in being a part of nature, wanting to be accepted by nature. John the father had a dream to parachute his family into the wilds of New Guinea and start a colony. John Harlin III has taken his family to Mexico to live for months at a time. But the dissimilarity enjoyed the most here becomes clear when we all gaze at a photograph of John Harlin II taken during a climb in the year of his death. He looks north-weathered and hoary, old beyond his years. At forty-nine, John Harlin III looks younger than his dad did when he was thirty, and that gives the son a jiff of delight.

But then the mood turns a bit somber as Larry remembers that he was at this hotel during the last climb of John Harlin, and even spoke to him on the radio when John was at Death Bivouac. It was one of John's last communications. Now when I ask Larry what he thinks about John Harlin III making this attempt, he stops and seems to fight back memories. "I'm worried," he states, and then moves on to another yarn of flummery on the rocks.

At 7:15 this next morning, John and his family pick at the same hotel breakfast buffet that has been the fare for the last couple of weeks, a syrupless, alpine-style repast of dry cereal and bread, jam, cheese, lunchmeat and canned fruit, and orange juice. Siena gripes while John takes some bread, makes a couple of simple sandwiches for the climb, and stuffs them in his pack. At 7:45, John starts out the hotel door when Siena asks him to stop and stoop. He accommodates, and she stuffs a piece of paper in his pack, secret messages from his girls.

At the Kleine Scheidegg train station, the Jaspers and John Harlin III shoulder their kits, banked with the currency of climbing: carabiners, pitons, ice axes, and crampons, with which they hope to purchase this mountain. They step onto the cogwheel train that takes a half million tourists a year through a tunnel that bores through the bowels of the Eiger to "The Top of Europe," an emporium of restaurants and views. The climbing team, though, gets off at the first stop, a seasonal hostel in a meadow of gentians and purple saxifrage just between the Eiger glacier and the beginnings of the mountain wall. There, John gives Adele a kiss and Siena a tight hug, and he and the Jaspers begin hiking down a scree path toward the radiant point where they will unleash themselves from the surly bonds of the horizontal world.

Less than an hour later they pull on their harnesses and don their helmets (rigged with tiny high-definition video cameras). Robert is brimming with his usual brio and bliss; Daniela giggles nervously, and she looks tired, having barely slept the night before. John makes his awkward grin and shakes my hand, then points to the sky. With the foreshortening that happens at the base of mountains, The White Spider looks to be a few pitches away, when in fact it is a vertical mile straight up. I dodge a few rocks that come tumbling down the slope. The constant skin shedding of this pocked and icy face is perhaps the most dangerous aspect of the Eiger. In the Eastwood film, a main character is hit by a falling rock and dies on the mountain; in an elliptical narrative fit for the movies, a cameraman shooting *The Eiger Sanction* was hit by a falling rock and died. As I turn to head back down to the hotel and to our Brunton telescope, I notice the crushed plastic lining of a climbing helmet in a rock fall ten feet away. I resist the urge to pull away the rock to see if anything is beneath.

The next hours are ones of waiting and watching. Alternately, Adele, Siena, and others in the support crew peer through the telescope and see three tiny ants crawling up a refrigerator door. I take a turn and make out John in his yellow jacket bringing up the rear. It was here at Kleine Scheidegg in 1966 that journalist

Peter Gillman was watching through a scope when he followed a red-jacketed falling star down the face . . . the body of John Harlin II. "It was stretched out and was turning over slowly, gently, with awful finality," he wrote of the scene.

As John climbs he tries to tune into the mountain, to adopt a climber's mind-set. He doesn't want to think about family or friends, or things precious, or Eiger lore; he wants to leave the rest of the world behind and concentrate on the task at hand. He wants to shut out emotion and fear. He wants to be a hard man.

But despite his vows, he thinks about his father. When he passes a set of rusty pitons, he wonders if his dad had placed any of them. And he thinks that his eyes must be seeing the same views his dad saw; that the tinkling cowbells from below must be among the same sounds heard. And he feels some sort of connection through the rock.

Under a bright sky, at 2:44 p.m., John and the Jaspers reach the Japanese Bivouac, a tapering, shoulder-width ledge beneath an overhang that is the ultimate room with a view, except for the poor taste in wall decorations, a scrawl of graffiti left by residents prior. Their check-in time, though, is superb, as the sun is just striking the top of the Eiger (this will precipitate the day's foremost cascade of rock and ice falls). Slowly, carefully they prepare their vertical camp, in which they sling themselves to the wall, and slip into sleeping bags. John discovers he forgot to pack eating utensils and so must sup with his knife, a minor piece of metal cruelty compared to when his father forgot to sharpen his crampons for the Eiger forty years ago.

By 4:00 p.m., a giant cloud has wrapped itself around the Eiger North Face and plunged temperatures to below freezing. At 4:30, John radios his family. "Could you ask the sun to move around a little further please? Could you apply some heat to make the clouds dissipate?"

"How are you?" Adele asks.

"It's been a good day so far. But this is the easy part of the mountain. Hard part is tomorrow," he reports. Then Siena takes the walkie-talkie: "Did you get the note I put in your backpack?"

There is a long and uncomfortable silence on the deck of the hotel. Then the radio crackles: "I just found the note! It says, 'Dear Daddy. We're all thinking of you as you go up the mountain. Who knows, we might have something different for breakfast when you get back. Love, love, love, love, love, Siena.'"

Then John reads the words from Adele: "Dearest John: Embrace this experience. Think one step at a time and remember that we all are with you at all times. I love you, Adele."

Adele takes the radio: "Can you carry that extra bit of weight all the way up?"

"I would carry nothing else but this if I had to." He seems to twinkle through the radio.

Forty years ago, Marilyn Harlin, wife of John Harlin II, sent a letter to her husband, who was camped at Death Bivouac, readying for his final, historic push to the summit. It said: "Don't play with the gods up there. We give you all our support through this last stretch. And much much much love."

John Harlin III signs off, as the Jaspers want to call their kids and there is much prep to do before nightfall. Daniela is thinking of leaving the climb at an exit point farther up the wall, as her back is hurting, and she yearns to return to her children. This is the first night away from her children since Stefan was born more than two and a half years ago. But she will decide tomorrow. After tea and hot noodles, they will all try to sleep early, as tomorrow is a very big day, and there is a German team close on their heels. It is not a competition as it was in 1966, but there are eerily reminiscent dynamics. If the German team catches up, it will crowd the mountain, rendering extra danger. So John Harlin III wants to move quickly and stay ahead of an unexpected coefficient on this irresoluble limestone brick, until now a mislaid cornerstone to his life.

* * *

Although the Eiger has an aura of the absolute, it seems to bend this next morning as John and the Jaspers cruise upward, making better time than expected. Behind is not just one German team, but now a second, a guide-client combination. For weeks, potential climbers have been waiting for the right conditions, and now the mountain is crowded.

John and the Jaspers make the Hinterstoisser Traverse along a fixed horizontal rope. They hack up The Ice Hose. Then into The Ramp. Up they inch, Robert and John alternating the lead. Early that afternoon, the German guide-client team, which began the ascent by climbing out one of the train windows, passes John and the Jaspers and knocks off ice chunks as it picks its way upstairs. Ping, ping, ping goes the volley. "Leave a little ice for us," John yells upward.

John reaches Death Bivouac, where his father spent his final week, read his final letters from his family, and made his last radio call; and then farther up he sees the overhang, off and above to the right, where the skinny, colored rope that held his father failed. John the son doesn't stop to dwell. Emotional distance he wants. But then he wonders why there are no ghosts on this mountain. Old large houses have ghosts, and so many souls have been taken here. Yet he has never heard of a spirit on the Eiger. Nonetheless, something here delineates the ephemerides of his father's spirit, and it imbues a state of grace as upward John glides.

A bit farther up, they reach the snow-covered Brittle Ledges, narrower than the shelf they enjoyed the night before, but a port in the storm. It won't accommodate three full climbers, so Robert volunteers to be the one who will sleep with his legs dangling over the edge. As they settle in, the second German team passes them, which gives pause as with two teams above, progress will no doubt be slowed.

The next morning, they are up early, but progress is at a crawl. They find themselves stuck below the German teams, waiting for the Germans to reach points where their jetsam won't crash directly down on John's team. The sky has darkened, and a storm may be rolling in. The support team watches through the telescope, and several professional Swiss guides announce that John and the Jaspers are woefully behind schedule; that they won't make the summit today, and may find themselves enveloped in a storm. There is talk of rescue by roping down from the summit or by helicopter.

But slowly they grind on. They edge across The Traverse of the Gods, where John can look straight down 4,000 feet to the spot where his father's body hit the ground. Daniela hates this traverse, with its severe exposure. She began as a sport climber and never really took to the dizzying challenge of crossing walls that overhang infinity. Soon, though, they are on The White Spider, and then shimmying up the start of the Exit Cracks. Then one of the Germans above accidentally dislodges a football-sized rock that whizzes down a safe distance past John, flies out into space, then hits the middle of the White Spider and plunges between the two members of yet another German team on the mountain, just missing the tethering rope.

Back at the base, there is much jockeying for a spy through the one telescope at hand, and Adele snatches a moment only to watch as John's crampon slips and he makes a short fall, arrested by his rope. Her heart skips a beat. Behind her Siena scrambles up a sharp hill like a chamois, stopping at its crest, where she stares at the wall. John recovers and continues to climb, while Adele retreats to a section of the hotel without windows facing south.

By midafternoon, the climbing team seems to smell the barn and begins moving faster, and with confidence. John is leading the final pitch, and as they reach the Summit Icefield they bathe in sunshine for the first time on the climb. A wave of relief seems to wash over Adele and all at the base. The shadow of the Eiger seems to have lifted. But it's not over until it's over, of course, and a number of climbers have fallen off the knife-edge west ridge after touching the sky. So Adele, Siena, friends, and filmmakers grab the train to the Jungfraujoch and then start hiking across the snowfield toward the Monch Hut, a little shy of 12,000 feet, which John and the Jaspers hope to reach by nightfall.

There is a climbing occurrence related to post-traumatic stress syndrome, in which after a major, death-defying ascent, a bout of depression sets in, sometimes permanently, sometimes fatally. It is a sort of "what's next?" condition, as after months, perhaps years of dreaming, scheming, and preparing there seems little to fill the space that was so intensely a supreme ambition now achieved. Several Himalayan veterans have returned to low ground and turned to alcohol, drugs, and a stasis state of rueful reminiscences, unable to find a new passion or purpose. At least one Everest summiteer committed suicide. As we make the steps upward in the thin air, I ask Adele if this might be an aftereffect of John's reaching his lifetime goal.

"No!" she asserts. "The opposite. The Eiger has been a large and scary monster in his closet. He'll be liberated when this is done. He'll have a whole new lease, a new beginning."

And as she describes predictions of her husband's future, the radio sputters.

It is 4:03 p.m. It is John Harlin III standing on his dream.

"I'm on the summit, sweetheart."

"How is it?" Adele pipes back.

"Oh, just wonderful."

They talk lovingly in sound bites for a couple of minutes, and Siena has a turn, and then the radios go off, as the batteries need to be preserved in case of emergency. It is still a four-hour traverse down a flank of the mountain over to the Monch Hut in fading light. Daniela, who is near utter exhaustion and misses her children terribly, chooses not to make the trek and calls for a helicopter, which plucks her off the summit and deposits her in a field in Grindelwald, where she has to hitchhike to her car. John and Robert Jasper have that option as well, as the summit success belongs to all. But John and Robert choose to make their way down by foot to the hut, as "the top is only halfway," John likes to say. For Robert Jasper too there is special meaning in this climb. It was twenty years ago this month, at age seventeen, he made his first attempt up the Eiger, one in which he turned back. Now he wants a full rendering for his anniversary, one that includes clambering down to the first outpost of civilization.

As we trudge up the final steps to the Monch Hut, Adele grins. "I guess John's got to hold off on his AARP membership for another year."

John and Robert traverse the blade of the summit, the most spectacular place John has ever seen. Then they work down the East Ridge, making four rappels, crossing a saddle, and fudging around a steep ice field. And then they start across the last glacier. It is getting dark, so when they come to a crevasse they decide to traverse a snow bridge rather than take the time to skirt the blue fissure. Robert crosses first with no problem. But as John is halfway across, the bridge begins to crumble, and John begins to slide into the void. He falls and swims against the tide, finding enough purchase to crawl back to the arch of the disintegrating bridge and scramble across to safety. Most climbing accidents happen on the way down, when fatigue trumps judgment. John sometimes cites the maxim of Ed Viesturs, the only American to have climbed all fourteen of the world's 8,000-meter peaks: "Getting to the top is optional; getting back down is mandatory."

Just as the last licks of light are painting the surrounding peaks in alpenglow, John and Robert rise over a ridge and make the last few steps toward the Monch Hut. Adele and Siena run to them and first hug Robert, in the lead, then sprint to John. They embrace and swirl and fall into the snow in a giddy pile of euphoria.

When later John makes his way over to the others who have come to celebrate this moment, I lean to his ear and say, "John, you're a hard man."

He grins back. "Oh, I don't know about that."

Once inside the sanctity of the hut, John unwraps a moist towelette and wipes his face and hands. "I wash my hands of the Eiger," he pronounces with the gesture.

Minutes later, John Harlin III is walking down the snow path toward the Jungfraujoch, his family in hand, as the moon-washed Eiger fades away behind him.

7

THE HUNT FOR THE VIPER PIT

Panama

*In the case of pirates, say, I should like to know whether
that profession of theirs has any peculiar glory about it.
It sometimes ends in uncommon elevation, indeed; but
only at the gallows.*

—Herman Melville,
Moby-Dick, or The Whale

In the fall of 2004, a luxury liner, the *Seabourn Spirit,* carrying some three hundred passengers and crew was attacked by pirates armed with rocket-propelled grenades off the coast of East Africa. It was the twenty-fifth pirate attack in the region in six months.

In March of the same year there were three armed pirate attacks on ships passing through the Malacca Straits, the shallow passage between Sumatra and Singapore that has been a notoriously popular modern haunt for well-weaponed brigands.

One month earlier, the Australian yacht *Cardonnay* was

pursued by five pirate vessels en route from Central America to the Galapagos, a not uncommon incident in the murky waters off the coasts of the country that perhaps has contributed more to pirate heritage than any other: the accident of geography called Panama.

It might be said it all began with Balboa. On September 25, 1513, the Spaniard Vasco Núñez de Balboa became the first European to enjoy a Pacific sunset, crossing what is today the Darien region of Panama on a twenty-five-day trek. Along with a thousand Indians and a pack of dogs, Balboa brought with him Francisco Pizarro, an ambitious young conquistador.

The following year, Balboa hacked a forty-mile path across the isthmus and carried his ships from the Caribbean to the Pacific. It was these ships that Pizarro used to sail south to Peru and conquer the Incas and their mountains of gold and silver.

The dilemma was now how to get this fortune back to Spain. The water route south, around Cape Horn, wouldn't be discovered for another hundred years. The loot could be carried over the Andes to Cartagena, Colombia, but that journey was too long and treacherous. Back up the coast, though, in a fishing village called "Panama" (a Cueva Indian word meaning "place of abundant fish") there was a trail used by Indians for centuries to cross from one ocean to the next. This road was eventually widened and paved with flagstones and became the Camino Real, the Royal Road, where mules would carry up to three hundred pounds of plunder across the isthmus, the narrowest in the Americas, to natural harbors on the Caribbean, where Spanish galleons would deliver the precious metals to the king's treasuries in Madrid. By the sixteenth century, Panama had become the largest center of commerce in the New World and the fat pipeline to riches for Spain.

All this bounty bounding through the Caribbean provoked the epic era of the British, French, and Dutch privateers, buccaneers, and pirates, all of whom manifested an early schadenfreude over the monopolistic Spanish conduit to New World gold and silver. Scores of pirates roiled through these waters, taking the treasures that had crossed the Camino Real, sinking ships, creating mayhem and myths. One of these lusty scoundrels was Francis Drake, the "gentleman pirate and adventurer," who set out to "singe the beard of Spain." He made a hobby of plundering in Panama, and twice attacked the treasure trains on the Camino Real, until his own comeuppance, succumbing to dysentery on the poop deck of his flagship *Defiance* in 1596. He was buried at sea off Portobelo, Panama, in a lead coffin that treasure hunters today still seek.

Another infamous picaroon who left his lasting prints on Panama was Welsh buccaneer Henry Morgan, now known more for his rum than his swag. He crossed the Camino Real from the Caribbean side and sacked Panama City, returning to the Caribbean coast with 200 mules laden with loot. The city burned in his wake and was rebuilt down the road. And pirates of similar cloth have continued to loot this thin ribbon of land up to this day.

A few weeks ago, I was on the phone with Barry Clifford, whom *Men's Journal* recently named "The Pirate King," though not in the coastal Somalia way. He is a scholar and teacher of pirate history and has done more to explore pirate legacies and their bits and pieces than perhaps any other. I called to ask him about the pirates of Panama, as I had always wanted to singe the trail of a pirate. Barry is a font of information and ideas, though he had not been exploring in Panama for more than fifteen years, ever since he went searching for the resting place of the *Satisfaction,* one of Henry Morgan's key ships used in his invasion of Panama in 1670, and sunk somewhere near the egress of the Camino Real.

Barry calls himself an underwater archaeologist explorer, but he is more popularly known as one of America's foremost treasure hunters. In 1984, Barry discovered the shipwreck *Whydah,* lost in a storm off Cape Cod in 1717. The find yielded some 100,000 artifacts, many of which are displayed in a museum Barry created in Provincetown, Massachusetts. Barry is not a wealthy man, but rather than sell the treasures for big bucks, he felt the relics are better served and preserved in a museum, and so now he lives in a cramped apartment upstairs atop his chest of treasure. Barry went on to find treasure in the Indian Ocean, the Mediterranean, the Solomon Sea, and the Caribbean. Most recently, Barry thinks he may have identified the remains of the *Santa Maria*, the flagship of Christopher Columbus, off the coast of Haiti.

So when I queried Barry about Panama, he cited explorations to find Drake's coffin, and Morgan's shipwreck, and other sunken treasures. But then he riffed on a quest he began a decade and a half ago and never completed, for a place he calls the Viper Pit. According to legends, there is a high pass over the Continental Divide along the Camino Real. During the rainy season, the road became slippery, and sometimes mules, laden with pieces of eight and other booty, would slip and fall several hundred feet into deep watery pits, pools populated by poisonous water snakes. The slaves and Indians who accompanied these treasure trains couldn't swim, feared snakes, and so wouldn't dive into these pits. It seems there is no record of any attempt to recover these lost treasures, and the prospect has haunted Barry for a decade and a half. He even has a hand-drawn treasure map of the possible location, supplied by a friend who lived in Panama for many years.

And so Barry agrees to join me in Panama on this piratical quest, with a goal being the identification of the Viper Pit, if it does indeed exist. But Barry consents under a couple of conditions. When Barry was last there, Noriega was in power, and the country was teeming with shady characters, some of whom hunted treasure illegally and were not disinclined to do Barry harm. One planted an antique sword hilt in his baggage, hoping to get Barry arrested. Barry gives me a list of names and says we need to steer clear of these blokes, if they are still in-country. Second, Barry has worked hard to establish a reputation as a lawful and now much-honored explorer, and he wants to make it clear that on our little expedition we are not seeking treasure, only an X that marks a spot. If by accident we find anything that hints of treasure, we will touch nothing without alerting the proper authorities. Panama is justly sensitive about its treasures. The country has been raped and plundered for centuries, and many of its rightful treasures sit in museums and private collections around the world. Barry understands and respects that. "All I want to do is see if we can find where the Viper Pit might be. That in itself would be a great discovery."

I arrive in Panama City a couple of days early for our little expedition. Barry arrives later today along with his son, Brandon, an extreme adventurer in his own right, and the Seagren family from Illinois, Scott and Jo and their two teenagers, Parker and Josie Dee, who have traveled the world together seeking adventure and documenting along the way, sort of like The Wild Thornberrys in the flesh.

While I'm waiting, I poke around the beginnings of the Camino Real with Richard Cahill, a naturalist and cofounder of the company Ancon Expeditions, which is outfitting our adventure. Richard Cahill was for the first part of his career a banker. When in the 1980s someone suggested he get involved in an emerging concept called ecotourism, he jumped in, thinking it had something to do with "eco-nomic tourism." But as he delved into the conceit of traveling softly and honoring nature and indigenous cultures, he found it richly rewarding, and important to Panama and the planet, and he decided to devote his life to such. Now he is regarded as Panama's top ecotourism guide. And to prove it, on my first day he takes me off into the jungle, where I am promptly charged by a Baird's tapir, stared down by a harpy eagle, pecked at by toucans and parrots, and squeezed into a soprano by a fifteen-foot python. Okay, we are at the zoo just outside the city, but Panama is not suffering from an underabundance of dragonish perils, or wildness, just a few steps off the path.

I've yet to meet Barry Clifford. But in our many phone conversations I've come to believe he is a citizen of "the fourth world," that free-spirited territory where time has no weight, the true religion is exploration, and the inhabitants are rogues, nomads, and pioneers. Barry, I believe, is a sort of modern-day pirate with a code of celebration, not exploitation, and together we'll sail in search of the pirates of Panama and a pit filled with snakes and perhaps the doubloons of adventure.

* * *

Chains for the Admiral of the Ocean! Chains
For him who gave a new heaven, a new earth,
As holy John had prophesied of me,
Gave glory and more empire to the Kings
Of Spain than all their battles! Chains for him
Who push'd his prows into the setting sun,
And made West East, and sail'd the Dragon's Mouth,
And came upon the Mountains of the World,
And saw the rivers roll from Paradise!
                    —Alfred, Lord Tennyson, "Columbus"

Barry is shocked at how much Panama has changed in fifteen years. Where were once barrios there are glistening glass and steel towers. The Panama Rail Road, then a rusted "monkey condominium," now is a sleek transportation bullet. Every American fast-food franchise litters the streets. The thieves' market has an espresso stand.

On Barry's first day in Panama in 1989, he sat to lunch at the Panama Yacht Club. He had come to the country to look for Captain Morgan's wreck, the *Satisfaction*, which sank somewhere in the mouth of the Chagras River near the egress of the Camino Real. While poring over a map, sipping an Atlas beer, Barry looked up to see a human body wash up on the beach, crabs scurrying in and out of orifices. A hooker in the club looked up, watched the body for a beat, then went back to filing her painted nails. Panama then, during Noriega's reign, was full of "bad people," says Barry. He almost didn't come on this trip for fear that some of the rogues and smugglers he once dealt with might come gunning for him.

Not that they've all gone away. Panama still has more than its fair share of shade, from drug- and gunrunners to multilevel corruption to modern-day pirates.

Barry and I head out to Old Panama City, past the remains of the high cathedral that was all but destroyed in Captain Morgan's raid of 1671. Barry remembers that he practiced his climbing skills on the ancient coral walls here back in 1990. He was training for an expedition to find a treasure called the crystal skull, which, rumor told, was at the bottom of a hundred-foot-deep hollow he was to rappel into. Barry has an unusually high success rate in finding lost treasures for his trade, but even then most attempts fail. He never found the crystal skull.

Barry looks fifteen years younger than his sixty years, fit and unlined, wearing a Ron Howard–style baseball cap. That is until he takes it off to wipe his brow in the heat and reveals his own crystal skull, a shiny pate that gives him a regal aura as we walk over the arched King's Bridge, the start of the Camino Real. It's remarkably well preserved for a structure built in the sixteenth century, wide enough for two mule carts to pass in opposite directions, arched gracefully over a muddy river into which sailed the ships from Peru laden with the precious metals that would make the transisthmus crossing. Barry points up the ancient road, which a couple leagues inland has long ago been swallowed by the jungle, and says that somewhere therein lies the Viper Pit. "If we're lucky, we'll find it," he says with the sanguinity of any seeker of adventure.

But first we decide to trace the origins of the Camino Real and of the pirate activity it spawned. A treasure map can be colored that reaches into the riots of vegetation called the Darien, the practically impenetrable jungle that separates Colombia from Panama. It was here, in about 1510, that the first piece of gold crossed to the Caribbean bound for Spanish coffers, the nugget that begat empires and a thousand sea battles and the pirates of the Caribbean.

Rodrigo de Bastidas, a well-heeled notary public from Seville, was the first European to see Panama, in 1501 at the Gulf of Darien, where he met Indians dripping with gold: bracelets, earrings, and huge chest plates. He asked from where the gold came, and the Indians pointed to the mountains in the interior. Vasco Núñez de Balboa was a member of Bastidas's crew, and the prospect of all that gold was not lost upon him. Nine years later, Balboa stowed away on a voyage to Panama to escape creditors and ended up at Antigua del Darién, the first city constituted by the Spanish crown, where he managed to be elected comayor. From here he set out on his epic expedition that would end at the South Sea, a first European crossing that established a path to transport gold. The first Spanish mines were established in the Darien, worked by Indians and African slaves, and the first pirates showed up shortly thereafter to raid and plunder.

In a Twin Otter, we fly into a tiny dirt strip at Punta Patiño, the largest private reserve in Panama, on the Golfo de San Miguel, where Balboa first saw the Pacific. In long dugout canoes called *cayucos* we head up the Rio Mogue through a tangled fantasy of black mangrove toward an Emberá Indian village. The rain forest buzzes and vibrates as we steer up the twisting river, rolling back the centuries. Our naturalist guide, Richard Cahill, tells of the many deadly creatures along this waterway, from vipers to cats to crocodiles and caimans, even the insects. He says that in the late 1980s, a boatload of adventure tourists was attacked by African killer bees here. The boat flipped in the mayhem, and two drowned.

As we pull into an embankment at the village of Paraíso Mogue, we're greeted by an ambuscade of Emberá Indians, once warriors who painted themselves with the juice of the jagua fruit in jagged patterns meant to frighten an enemy. When their ancestors were forced to work in the Spanish gold mines of the Darien, they sometimes fought alongside British pirates, using poison-tipped blowgun darts and primitive weapons to beat back the conquistadores.

Today, the Emberá meet us with the same war paint but also music: drums, maracas, and a groovy flute in a combo that sounds like jungle jazz. The women and girls are bare-chested, wearing only palm fiber skirts and bandoliers of silver coins, U.S. quarters and balboas, the Panamanian small change. The little girls take hold of our hands as we walk the kilometer to the village center ("I feel like I'm cheating on my kids," says Scott Finley, our video guy, who has three children back home). Here, we meet the village chief, Aristides Teucama, forty-three, who sits on a colored cloth near a broken Cable & Wireless phone booth and tells a bit of his golden lore.

The Emberá, whose ancestry traces to Colombia, were nomadic through the centuries, and gold, found mostly along these rain forest rivages, was an abundant and decorative effect. The Spanish changed all that, bringing diseases that nearly wiped the Darien Indians out and enslaving survivors to mine gold and act as human mules. Aristides says that most of the gold is gone now, taken by both the Spanish and pirates, and that the new gold for them is tourism, small groups such as ours that come and buy their handicrafts, such as their signature intricately patterned baskets and elegantly chased pottery.

Barry is not sure he believes Aristides when he claims the gold is gone; Barry thinks that they have access, and a hoard, but that the chief is too savvy to volunteer such. Barry visited the Emberá region in 1991, when he flew in by Russian helicopter with the governor of Panama to investigate illegal gold mining by foreigners using mercury as a metal separator. The mercury leaches into the river and poisons the fish and those who feed on fish, including Darien Indians. The illegal mining continues to this day. The jungle is too porous and wild to police, and the health of the Indians is still affected, all because of gold.

On the boat ride back from Paraíso Mogue, we pull into a fishing village of ancestral Cimaroons (African slaves who had escaped the Spanish) called Punto Alegre (Happy Point) and find cold cervezas in a cantina featuring a poster of Balboa beer being served by two blondes in string bikinis. If Balboa only knew the legacies he begat, from eponymous schools, roads, theaters, towns, currency, and beer. We also meet Miguel Sala Alvarez, seventy-six, the village storyteller. He tells us it was Columbus who started all the piratry when he landed in Panama on his fourth voyage and saw the gold. And, he says, pirating continues to this day, only the booty now is shrimp and Yamaha fifteen-horsepower outboards. In the 1980s, Miguel's granddaughter, then eleven, barely escaped a pirate raid. And just a week ago, pirates stole a fishing boat and engine from Happy Point.

As long as there have been boats, there have been pirates. There were Greek and Roman pirates, and piracy when the Vikings and Danes were ravaging the coasts of Europe. But Panama has been the mother lode of piracy, it being the crossroads of the world. It is the nexus to four continents, the land bridge between North and South America, the link between eastern Asia and Europe. And as we sit on a hill above the Golfo de San Miguel, the sky breaks like an egg, and the water for an instant catches fire. We're watching the same sunset as Balboa; supping on corvina, the same fish that fed Drake; and swatting the same mosquitoes that plagued Morgan. In the whirring torque of last light, we watch a wooden vessel purl across the bay . . . it could be carrying fishermen, gold miners, tourists, or even perhaps pirates.

* * *

Such, however, is the illusion of antiquity and wealth, that decent and dignified men now existing boast their descent from these filthy thieves, who showed a far juster conviction of their own merits, by assuming for their types the swine, goat, jackal, leopard, wolf, and snake, which they severally resembled.
—Ralph Waldo Emerson, *English Traits*

It is a rare trick to make a discovery in this world, but Barry Clifford thinks he may have. On a densely forested, unpopulated island at the mouth of the Tuira River, the largest in Panama, there is a seventeenth-century Spanish stronghold that was stumbled upon just six years ago. No modern maps mark its location, but Richard Cahill researched historical papers and believes the stronghold is part of a fort system called San Carlos de Boca Chica on the island of El Encanto (The Lovely). Today, it is an island distinguished by the unlovely vultures that reel about above its black beaches, swooping to peck at dead catfish. As we poke about this ruin, suffocated in swooping vines and other luxuriant biomass, Barry pulls away some leaves and yells my name: "Richard, come here quick. I think I've found something."

Barry grabs a long stick in one hand, a machete in the other, and clears away the forest to reveal a pit in the middle of the broken fortification. "It's an unexcavated well! Do you know what that means?"

Barry goes on to explain that the wells around which forts were built were often where treasures were found. There was the accidental debris of bracelets and necklaces that fell when fetching water. But also the wells were where treasure was hidden when a pirate attack was imminent. The Spanish knew of Captain Morgan's raids only minutes in advance and filled the wells with gold. The last thing Columbus instructed his left-behind crew in 1493 was, "If you're under attack, throw the gold in the well." When Columbus returned a year later, all his men were dead, and the only thing he found in the well was a mixed-race, still-fleshed baby.

So, Barry thinks there may be something down this well. The stronghold, he thinks, was a depot for treasure, a bank for its time. Up the Tuira River were the Cana Mines of the Darien, which produced millions in gold, and the metals were carried down in canoes to this estuary and stockpiled. Larger ships would pick up and carry loads north to the Camino Real. These were tempting targets for pirates, and the Spanish built a series of forts along their route to protect their proceeds. This one is set back in the forest so it cannot be seen from either the river or the sea, and is pocked with slanted gun slits throughout, designed for defense.

The well hole looks like a dark eye to the past, but Barry declines to climb down and explore. "We're here to observe, not to treasure hunt. We'll leave this for certified archaeologists, maybe Panamanian students, to investigate what's here." Barry, though, is thrilled with this find. "It's what I do," he says with a grin.

We've stopped here on our serpentine journey to the Viper Pit. Our plan is to sail from the Darien through the Pearl Islands to the Panama Canal and through to the Caribbean to Portobelo, the terminus of the Camino Real, looking at pirate history along the way. From Portobelo, we'll head inland with our treasure map to see if we can find the Viper Pit.

After a night sally on a chartered dive boat, the MV *Coral Star,* we awake just off Isla San Telmo, a southern Pearl Island owned by ANCON (the National Association for the Conservation of Nature), the environmental organization that is part Nature Conservancy, part Sierra Club, and with its for-profit-arm, Ancon Expeditions, part Cook's Tours. When Balboa first made waterfall with the Pacific, he encountered Indians whose paddles were encrusted with pearls. They said they came from an archipelago to the west, which Balboa named Islas de las Perlas and claimed for Spain. Although Balboa never made it to the 220-island chain, when he told of its existence, other Spaniards, including Pizarro, made the foray, and within two years all the Pearl Island Indians were dead from disease and the sword. Ever enterprising, the Spanish dragoons replaced the Indians with African slaves, whose descendants populate the islands today. A dozen or so crank their long boat up to us and pry open a few plate-sized oysters, one of which yields a white pearl the size of this period: .

After Balboa, for the next two hundred years the string of Pearl Islands became a favorite haunt for pirates, not just for its profusion of plump pearls (Elizabeth Taylor's thirty-one-carat Peregrina was found here four hundred years ago), but also because the many coves, bights, and bays were ideal hideouts while waiting to sack cache-rich Spanish fleets.

It is here we find our first shipwreck.

Half-washed up a black-sand beach is a rusted bucket of a two-man submarine, its origins and purpose long lost to time. There are theories it was Civil War era, or that it was a Japanese vessel heading for the Panama Canal during World War II, or that it was a specially designed pearl-diving submersible. Barry dons his mask and snorkel and probes about its shell and surfaces to declare it a mystery. "It's like being on a faraway planet and discovering a spaceship. It provokes only questions. Who owned it? Who designed it? What was it used for? How did it get here? Did its sailors drown? Maybe someone on the Internet will know."

I have my own remote connection with the Pearl Islands, and a pirate of a different sort. In the early 1950s, my father was an operative in the newly formed CIA, and a first mission was a coup that reinstated the shah of Iran. In 1979, the shah, who had pirated away untold millions in national oil revenues to his own coffers, was forced to flee Iran as the Ayatollah Khomeini led a revolution. The CIA placed the shah in the Pearl Islands, not far from the American military in the Canal Zone, but as far from the Islamic world as geography allowed.

Despite all the seafaring activity, there aren't many known wrecks in the Pearl Islands. The ships were smaller on the Pacific side, ferrying gold from mines to the Camino Real, and hurricanes not prevalent. One Spanish galleon, though, the *San Jose,* lies off the island of the same name, and Barry once considered seeking it, but the competition was too fierce. Today, it remains an undiscovered vault.

No matter how you cutlass it, Panama is a culture of pirates, even of the nonhuman kind. On the north end of the Pearl Islands we pass Isla Pacheca, which on old Spanish maps is identified as Isla Pajaro, or Bird Island. It's a natural rookery of boobies, cormorants, pelicans, egrets, herons, terns, and most of all, thousands upon thousands of the magnificent frigate bird, also called the kleptoparasitic bird, as it steals food from other flying birds. It is, in a sense, a flying pirate. Hanging from the limestone walls are epiphytic cacti, plants that pirate nourishment from others. And on the ground are boa constrictors, which steal the eggs of the kleptoparasitics.

But then we're all pirates, in some fashion, as no matter how we propel our existence, it is at the expense of some other living things. And a Caribbean pirate who tortured, killed, and stole, but who practiced democracy and kept Sunday school, as did Captain Morgan, is afforded consideration as a decent soul. It is, in the end, a matter of degree, of perception, and most of all, of the hands of authors who inscribe the history, the rhymes, and the fabliaux of fortunes won and taken away.

HIDE THE WOMEN AND CHILDREN.
THE PIRATES ARE COMING.

> *You teacher used to teach about pirate Morgan*
> *And you said he was a very great man.*
> —Peter Tosh, Bob Marley and the Wailers,
> "You Can't Blame the Youth"

In the mid-1500s, when mules carrying treasure across the Camino Real were irretrievably slipping down slopes into snake-filled rivers and pits, the Spanish crown ordered surveys to ascertain the feasibility of constructing a canal. But King Phillip II killed the idea, concluding that if God had wanted a canal there, he would have built one.

Almost four hundred years later, the canal came to be. It now transships daily the treasure equivalent of a year's mule loads across the isthmus. But the passage doesn't come cheap. The largest cruise ships pay upward of $200,000 for the privilege. Our 115-foot live-aboard is paying $2,500. The least expensive toll was thirty-six cents, charged to adventurer Richard Halliburton when he swam the canal in 1928.

Barry, when last here fifteen years ago, couldn't afford the luxury of a boat passage and didn't intend to swim, so he drove from coast to coast, a journey of just ninety minutes as opposed to the nine hours it takes to cruise through the canal.

But like the Camino Real, which ran to the south to Portobelo, this route has always been a gold road. Between 1848 and 1869, during the height of the California gold rush, about 375,000 argonauts crossed the isthmus from the Atlantic to the Pacific on a railroad that roughly followed today's canal route, and they returned with more than a billion and a half dollars worth of gold.

As we're being raised by one of the three sets of locks along the canal, Richard Cahill explains that Panama, unlike most tropical countries, has long been a keen advocate of rain forest preservation, not so much because of inherent green sensibilities as for economic preservation. The locks in the canal are gravity-fed by the waters of two artificially created lakes, Miraflores and Gatun, the latter the result of damming the Chagres River. From the lakes, fifty-two million gallons of freshwater are dumped into the sea by the locks every time a ship transits the canal. If the rain forests that feed these lakes were ever felled and the perpetual cycle of water between sky and earth disrupted, the lakes would drop and the canal could not operate, and Panama would lose its key livelihood. So Richard Cahill's once-misconstrued definition of ecotourism as eco-nomic tourism in the case of Panama is right as rain.

"Welcome to the Caribbean," our captain cries as we spill from the last lock. On our right is a sixteen-foot crocodile, looking quite like Captain Hook's nemesis, bathing on a bank. On our left is Fort Sherman, recent headquarters to the Jungle Operations Training Center, the U.S. Army school that trained troops headed for Vietnam, astronauts whose capsules might fall into a jungle, allied Latin American armies and revolutionaries, and, according to Barry Clifford, friends of his who did black ops in Colombia against drug lords and their operations. The Emberá Indians of the

Darien were field instructors, as were several ex–Special Forces members. It was a Delta Force troop that called Barry in the late 1980s and asked him to come to Panama, as the Chagres River had flooded, scouring out a channel that exposed an eighteenth-century ship. Barry flew down, found boxes of Toledo-steel swords, and arranged for the government to pick them up, as Barry has an honor code to never sell the artifacts he finds. But the stash of swords somehow ended up in the markets of Colón, the seedy city on the other side of the canal. "Colón then was the most danger-ous city in the world," Barry pipes. "When I was driving through with the head of the jungle warfare school, he screamed at me for rolling down my window. He was frightened."

Much has changed since the United States turned the Pan-ama Canal over to Panama in December 1999. The School of the Americas is now a luxury hotel; Fort Sherman is an attraction. Colón, in the midst of a less-than-extreme makeover, boasts a new cruise-ship port, a new mall, and some freshly paved streets. But it is still more Mean than Main Street. It has the highest unemployment rate in Panama and is a haven for ruffians and modern-day pirates. When our skiff driver takes us to dock, he warns, "Even Bruce Lee shouldn't walk here at night."

We defy his warning, head to the Pirates Bar in the Washington Hotel, and order up dirty glasses of Captain Morgan spiced rum.

Barry Clifford has spent half a career chasing Captain Henry Morgan, the Caribbean's most successful pirate but one of the worst navigators—he lost perhaps a dozen ships in the Carib-bean, including four at the Laja Reef at the mouth of the Chagres River, where we are anchored just now. It was January 1671, and Morgan had assembled 1,800 buccaneers ("the scum of the seven seas, reckless and ruthless, hardened adventurers, a motley crew," as Morgan described them) on thirty-six ships for an attack on Panama City, the richest city on the Spanish Main. But first he had to take the Castle of San Lorenzo, built in 1597 as a fortifica-tion against pirates.

As we hike up to the cliff-hanging fortress, beneath black-mantled howler monkeys and a three-toed sloth, Barry explains why Captain Morgan was able to take what was then considered an impenetrable fortress with 314 well-armed Spanish soldiers defending its high walls. These outposts were the Siberia of the empire, and those lowest in the pecking order were often stationed there. The men suffered from the diseases of the day: malaria, yellow fever, and dengue fever, as well as boredom, tropic sloth, and low morale. They let their weapons rust and their powder get wet Morgan's men, on the other hand, joined of their own free will and were highly motivated. Morgan was in a way among the first businessman to offer stock options, as every pirate shared the booty.

Even then, Morgan was a lucky pirate. As his advance team was attacking the huge stone fort, lined with cannons and guns, one of the pirates was hit in the arm with an arrow. He yanked it from his limb, ripping away a swath of cotton shirt. He stuffed the arrow, now wrapped with cotton fabric, into his long-barreled Spanish musket and fired back at the bowman. The arrow caught fire, dropped over the parapet and set the entire contents of the fort ablaze. Morgan's men killed all but thirty of the Spanish soldiers, tossing most of them off the high cliffs into the churning sea.

With San Lorenzo captured, Morgan was able to make a sixteen-day crossing of the isthmus, and with 1,400 men he defeated the garrison of 2,600 in a pitched battle outside Panama City, which he then looted. Panama City was destroyed by fire, probably from blown-up powder stores, although the looters were blamed. After four weeks, Morgan left with 175 mule loads of loot, one of the biggest hauls in pirate history.

We decide to pick up where Barry left off fifteen years ago and dive for the *Satisfaction,* Morgan's flagship, which sank as it hit a reef in the Chagres estuary just in front of Fort San Lorenzo. Morgan had on board 140 men and a witch from his hometown in Wales, as he thought she could tell the future. She was a sort of navigational aide, but not a very good one, as she drowned when the *Satisfaction* went down.

We drop anchor over the reef, and Barry and I dive down to a turbid bottom. We can hardly see a thing, and Barry thinks these the ideal conditions for bull sharks (they love deltas, with all the added lower-food-chain creatures whirling about), so he calls for a short dive. We return to the ship unsatisfied.

So next is the final push to the Viper Pit, or where our hand-drawn map says it might be. We'll head down the coast to Porto-belo, the bay at the end of the Camino Real, and head inland from there to a trail long gulped and digested by the jungle. Whether we find it or not, the treasure is in the quest.

As J. M. Barrie, who penned *Peter Pan,* a fantasy of pirates and quests, wrote, "We are all failures—at least, all the best of us are."

X Marks the Spot

> *There couldn't be a society of people who didn't dream.*
> *They'd be dead in two weeks.*
>   —William S. Burroughs

It's hard to know history here. It's easy to fall under the sway of legends. Pirates generally didn't keep ship's logs, nor did they publish books or lecture. Most accounts of pirate activity come from court records of those on trial, including Captain Henry Morgan.

In 1668, Morgan and his men made an audacious predawn raid on the heavily fortified Portobelo, the terminus of the Camino Real and the address of the Royal Treasure House, through which fully a third of all the world's known gold passed, as well as bolts of silk, piles of spices, chocolate, tobacco, and the prized *sal* from the salt mines just outside Panama City.

Morgan took the city in just thirty minutes but didn't find all the treasure, so his men took to torture, searing flesh with hot irons or "woodling": tying a band around a forehead and tight-ening with a stick until the eyes popped out. The leading lady of

Portobelo was stripped naked and placed in an empty wine barrel filled with gunpowder, with a match then held to her face.

But here's where history muddies. Most accounts today go on to say that Morgan's band plundered, brutally raped the women, murdered indiscriminately, burned the city, and spiked the cannons. Morgan himself, however, during his trial reported that he accepted 100,000 pesos as ransom to *not* destroy Portobelo: "We sent the hostages on shoare, leaving both towne and castles entirely, and as good a condition as we found them." Morgan was known for his brilliant battle strategies, his charisma, and his liberalness with the fortunes of his men, and with the truth. He was convicted in his trial and sent to England to be jailed, but he talked his way out of his predicament and ended up being knighted and appointed governor of Jamaica.

Today, Portobelo is a sleepy shantytown of some four thousand, mostly descendants of the slaves Morgan didn't take. And they are almost antipiratical in nature. At the local bar, it's three Panama beers for a buck. A large bottle of rum is five dollars. Ice cream is twenty cents. And advice is dispensed for free.

When we mention to some folks we're seeking a place called the Viper Pit, one of the curators of the museum, Betto Barrera, volunteers that it is not deep in the interior but just a short trek up the mountain into the jungle. It was there the Spanish mules fell off the steep path, he says. And of course several local teens volunteer to show us the way.

So we trudge up the mountain, in muck and suffocating heat, along a barely recognizable path, beneath a host of white-throated capuchin monkeys (named for their semblance to the white-bearded Capuchin monks). On one side is a steep drop to a creek, and Scott Finley, our cameraman, as if to test a theory, slips and takes a nasty tumble, like Michael Douglas in *Romancing the Stone,* down the slope into the mire. With recovery, we continue up the mountain, and crest the ridge to find . . . a cow pasture. There is a rusted cannon, a field of well-munched grass, and the aftereffects of bovine browsing, but nothing to indicate this might have been the legendary Viper Pit. "I've chased a lot of wild gooses in my day," Barry sums. But also this is nowhere near where our treasure map marks the spot.

Jungle Paul Jennings was a career Panama Canal pilot who spent all his spare time looking for treasure. He met Barry fifteen years ago when they both ended up seeking Captain Morgan wrecks, and they became friends and stayed in touch. After reading the same source documents as Barry did that described the Viper Pit, Paul set about making forays into the jungle and asking locals where they thought might be a spot that matched the descriptions. That was how Paul sketched together our map, which he mailed to Barry from Kentucky, where he is now retired, but with no less ardor for the consideration of treasure.

The map shows the Viper Pit somewhere in the middle of the country, near the continental divide, above a steep-sided river. Much of the Camino Real is now flooded under an artificially created lake filled in 1935, but the map indicates the spot is just beyond its upper reaches.

So, false lead behind, we negotiate down the mountain, through a crumbled sally port where Morgan and Drake and other pirates passed, and onto the main road that connects to the Colón Free Zone, the second-largest duty-free shop in the world after Hong Kong. Where once foreigners sailed thousands of miles to Panama with dreams of cheap gold and exotic spices, now they come with dreams of tax-free gold jewelry, perfumes, flat-screen TVs (every hovel in Portobelo seems to have one), and even Casio cameras.

We ignore the scores of billboards advertising electronics and luxury goods and head into the interior. We come to Lake Madden, an artificially created lake on the upper Chagres River, and hire a long canoe to take us to an upper edge of the lake, into the Rio La Puente, a black tannic tributary that twists like a serpent through the forest. We ease up the river to a place where the Camino Real re-emerges, then clamber up a crag to find the flat, overgrown remains of the once-royal road.

Barry machetes his way down the overgrown path. The rain forest closes in with an airless gloom as we thrash through this creepered world of mottled light. An all-enclosing clamminess radiates from the damp leaves, the slippery humus, the great boles of hardwoods.

Then, at one turn, we make a narrow pass above the river. This is a candidate for mule slippage, but the place doesn't fit the description; there is no pit.

We continue to whack our way through the rank, springy vegetation. When Barry loses footing at one point, great words stretch his mouth: "This is the most dangerous jungle in the world. When you count all those who died trying to cut the canal, more people have died in the Panama jungles than in any other."

Then one more hack across the vines, and a jagged limestone hole is revealed. It is a pit that falls down to the black water. Barry picks up a rock and tosses it down. Bats scuttle out as the stone makes a plop and then a fathomable echo. "It's deep," Barry proclaims.

Then he sees a flick of motion in a small cavity within the vertical cave. "It's a snake."

"Probably a fer-de-lance," warns Richard Cahill. "They're pit vipers, and they're all over this range. They're extremely poisonous: the most dangerous snake in Central America. If you get bitten, you have two hours to get to a hospital, or you die."

Barry recoils with the description. "I hate rats and snakes!"

We didn't bring diving gear on this trek; too heavy in this heat. It seems a mistake now, though we do have snorkels, so Barry and I don masks and dive into the waters of this dark pit. It's very cold below the surface, very dark, and too deep to reach the bottom without bottled oxygen, though Barry estimates he makes it down about thirty feet. We poke around for about an hour, exploring natural flowstones and the edges of the pit, making repeated dives. We see no gold or silver, or treasures of any sort, except the extreme beauty of this cave and an empty plastic package of *Sal Solar,* Panama's favorite table salt, that floats by.

As we emerge from the darkness, Barry makes a proclamation: "I am convinced this is the Viper Pit. It matches the description in every way. It has the depth, it has the snakes, it would be easy for mules to fall down here. The original documents even talk about how the water was too cold for the few slaves that somehow did try to make retrieval. This has got to be the Viper Pit."

"If it is, then there might be quite a bit of treasure at the bottom; perhaps millions in gold and silver. Aren't you tempted?"

"Nope," Barry dismisses. "I gotta tell you, at this point in my life I'm trying not to become the Bogart character in *Treasure of the Sierra Madre*. I came here to investigate the legend, not to profit from it. I know too many treasure hunters who landed here forty years ago, got the fever, and had the life sucked out of them. A few made a million dollars, but it cost them two. Most are sitting in seedy bars, gray-haired and bitter, hoping for one last score.

"This has been a dream of mine for fifteen years. The joy for me is in the adventure, and for finding this obscure piece of history that few have ever even known or thought about. Let the government or certified professionals or archaeology students take over from here. My private quest is fulfilled."

Suddenly it seems as though the pit inhales and holds its breath. A silence sweeps in and hovers. Barry's face fills with the poetic lineaments of a pirate's life led and appeased: "I may look into buying some real estate around here, though."

8

DOWN THE RIVER JORDAN

Israel

The river is deep and the river is wide, hallelujah
Milk and honey on the other side, hallelujah
—"Michael Row the Boat Ashore"

It is a clear and tiny stream, singing to itself among the stones. As I cup my hands into the cool water, it seems hard to believe this is the source of so much—the source of life for millions of people for thousands of years, the source of the three great monotheistic religions, the source of serenity and war, of healing and mar, the sacred source of the holiest of holy rivers, the Jordan.

As I stir my hand, it blurs the solid surface of reality. I am in far northeastern Israel, just one mile from the Lebanese border, three from the Syrian, on the slopes of Mount Hermon, the 9,232-foot snow-capped peak that dominates the Golan Heights. Birds and fish, clouds and water know no boundaries, but here more intelligent beings have carved lines in ever-shifting sands. Near the base of Hermon there is a ledge of soft limestone from which efflues a font called the Dan, named for the seventh tribe of ancient Israel. It is the largest tributary of the Jordan and the beginning of a journey that has shaped the whole of the world.

I don't believe in spirits, but this place is magic. The sun's rays splash across the rippling waters, and there seems a sympathy between static and spirit, between animate and inanimate, an interchange of forms . . . a rock becomes a root, a lizard melts into a stone, effervescent water turns to sparkling wine, myth begets history, and reality forms fable. The Jordan River is cited one hundred eighty times in the Old Testament, fifteen times in the New Testament. In Genesis, Lot looked up "and saw the whole plain of the Jordan was well watered, like the garden of the Lord." When Moses led his people to the promised land, wandering forty years through the wilderness, he found its edge at the Jordan River. Joshua parted the waters, and the Israelites crossed the Jordan to the land of milk and honey. There are angels, and the people of Sodom and Gomorrah. Jesus was born in the watershed of the Jordan, he was baptized at its shores, and the spirit of God "descended like a dove" upon him. Jesus performed miracles on the Sea of Galilee, and he died near a wadi that feeds the Jordan. It is by this river the companions of the prophet Muhammad are buried.

Today, fully half the world's population, Christians, Muslims, Jews, and others, can trace their spiritual cradles, their religious cosmologies, to the sweet waters of this modest spill.

Empires have risen and fallen along the Jordan, and will again. The poplars are forever trembling here. After touching the Dan, we make our way down a trail of laurel, broad-boughed sycamores, and Syrian ash trees, past fields of yellow oleanders and yellow signs that warn not to wander off beyond a flimsy fence because of land mines. Although this land is paradisiacal, as wistful as any dream of rapture on earth, it also straddles some of the most contested and seismically active real estate in the world.

The two-hundred-mile-long Jordan rides down the top of the great Syrian-African rift valley, a geological crack on the face of the earth that is forever being pulled apart.

There are three primary sources of the Jordan, all emanating from Mount Hermon, the Dan being the largest. Another is the Hasbani, which bubbles up from the Lebanon side of the border, a perimeter currently closed. The third and easternmost source is perhaps the loveliest of all, the Banias, which issues beneath a giant limestone grotto with an arched and magnificently fluted roof, surrounded by Greek and Roman ruins. The Banias bursts from beneath the base as a full-born river, as though the earth could simply no longer contain it, and then cascades over a series of faultless waterfalls rimmed with watercress, so ideally idyllic it seems to have been designed by the profit Wynn. The spot is so seductively beautiful it is easy to see why the Greeks built a temple here to Pan—a squint creates a creature with curly hair, short horns, crinkled beard, and goat's hooves frolicking about with nymphs and dryads, or is that just Jim Slade entertaining schoolchildren here on holiday?

I've come to this fountain with my old friend Jim Slade, a man who has spent a lifetime exploring rivers and who holds the world record for the greatest number of first descents, negotiating unrun stretches of river. Together we've navigated upper pieces of the Indus, Zambezi, Chang (Yangtze), Euphrates, and Blue Nile, but Jim's special conceit is source to sea, making linear dives from the first spark to the final sigh. As the springs that form the Jordan all gush from a single snowy mount, Jim wants to climb that peak and touch the first manifested precipitation.

A Jewish legend tells that when God delivered the tablets to Moses on Mount Sinai, a hill named Hermon appeared before him and complained of favoritism, bursting into tears. As consolation, God made Hermon the tallest mountain in the land and gave it a crown of snow. Its tears became the Jordan River.

It is not necessary to climb Hermon, as after the 1967 Six Days' War, a war fought in part over water rights to the Jordan, the Israelis built a ski resort on the mountain. We take a lift to almost seven thousand feet but can't go much farther. There is an Israeli Army station, and beyond that a UN-controlled sector, and the summit belongs to Syria. Still, from the high vantage, the seams of the Sea of Galilee can be described. It is a hazy day, perhaps because dust from the Sahara, which has of late been drifting this way. On a clear day, they say, a mountaineer can see the Mediterranean, even Beirut, and the Dead Sea to the south. The sun is in spate, we are in T-shirts, but there is a smudge of snow on this flank, and Jim steps over and impresses his bare hand into its bitter surface. The oil from his palm will be carried to and down the River Jordan.

A few miles downstream from Mount Hermon, there is a constant ceremony as old as culture and time, that of marriage and nativity. The three streams of the mountain, the Dan, the Banias, and the Hasbani, wed, and together they birth the Jordan proper. It is an inauspicious confluence. There is nobody about, just a tractor in the distance, and beyond that a kibbutz, one that has found renown for a different source: it claims to be the place where the Birkenstock-style sandal was born. But by this rushing river, anxious to get to the sea, there is almost a loud lack of uproar, as though the Jordan is waiting. From an oak that looks tired from watching the crucibles of history there hangs a rope swing, inviting a splash, but our guide says it is forbidden. The river's purling feels like an invitation to something dangerous and forbidden, but it's necessary to move on.

Unlike most rivers, which serve as thoroughfares for vessels bringing people together, the Jordan has always been a traffrail, an edging that has separated. Crossing the Jordan has always been the event desired, to a better land, to a healthier time, to home.

But this time our goal is not to cross, but to descend the Jordan, as its Hebrew name implies. And if successful, we will be among the few who have made the trek from source to sea, connecting people of all stripes and environments of every kind in a single line and mission of elemental peace.

* * *

Like three convictions meeting at a single pool, the three tributaries, after twisting and spinning and racing, come together to create the Jordan River, a greater whole that then sleekly glides for some six miles until it spreads its wings in a wide basin called the Hula Valley. Until the midpoint of the twentieth century, this section contained marshland and a small lake created by a dam of natural rock, the "waters of Merom" in the Bible, a thicketed slough thick with lions and malaria-bearing mosquitoes, as well as the greatest concentration of aquatic plants in the Middle East, eighteen species of fish, and a rich flock of migratory birds.

In the name of reclamation and health, the Jewish pioneers in the newly formed state of Israel drained much of this swamp in the mid-1950s, hoping to turn 15,000 acres of fertile swampland into prime farmland. But as with many well-meaning environmental schemes of the era, unforeseen consequences turned this plot bad, and the promising land went bankrupt. Not only did the birds and wildlife leave their lush haven, but also as the once-moist peat soil dried, a series of spontaneous subterranean fires burst forth, burning bushes throughout the valley, damaging the precious topsoil. Worse, the nitrates and phosphates that were once filtered by the swamp now washed into the Sea of Galilee and began to pollute Israel's major freshwater reservoir. By the early 1990s, the Hula Valley was a full-blown environmental disaster that threatened the health and well-being of millions.

In 1994, the largest green organization in the country, the Keren Kayemeth Leisrael-Jewish National Fund (the same group that initially drained the swamp), resurrected the Hula with a series of canals that rewatered the valley and created a 250-acre, shallow lake, Hula Agmon, that in many ways seems to have not only restored a balance, but also perhaps tipped the scales in a better direction. The Jordan River has always been a major refueling stop for birds migrating up the Rift Valley from Africa to Europe and back, but now, with the new lake and repaired wetlands, an estimated five hundred million birds—that's half a billion birds, of every stripe and color, some four hundred species—make safaris through this draw of the Jordan River valley. Along with flocks of pelicans, herons, and ducks, about thirty thousand cranes arrive in the Hula Valley each autumn, and now about ten thousand have decided they like this sweet-water nature reserve and stay for the winter.

An unanticipated benefit of this rebirth has been ecotourism. Some farmers in the valley weren't thrilled with the prospect of reconverting their croplands, no matter how fallow, to protected wetlands, but many have discovered newfound economics in the ushering of bird-watchers. We visit the park headquarters, teeming with families and life-listers, curio shops, and ice-cream stands, and all manner of bird-watcher vehicles, from canoes and kayaks to golf carts and strollers to mountain bikes and pedal pushers, and of course air-conditioned buses. There are flocks of tourists here, virtually all Israelis, as this little, but profoundly important, environmental success story is so little known to the rest of the world as to almost be a secret.

Another secret of the Jordan River begins just downstream of the Hula Valley, just beyond the Daughters of Jacob bridge, near the remains of a Crusader fort. Here, the river drops below sea level and seems to suffer from the bends as it loses control of itself and goes plunging down one of the wildest sections of white water in the world, a seven-mile nonstop sluice of Class III–IV rapids.

Rafting on the Jordan is so little known to the world beyond these borders that there are no Web sites in English, or any other language save Hebrew, offering this bravura ride. For a foreigner it is a difficult exercise to book this adventure, and it took weeks of e-mails and phone calls with translators to figure it out. So Jim Slade and I pull up to the warehouse expecting to meet a guide who will have no acquaintance with wild rivers outside the Holy

Land or with our own histories of first descents. Instead we met Lahav Blouh of Neharot Expeditions, who has posted a gallery of blown-up photographs of familiar international rivers on an outside wall: Ethiopia's Omo, the Tatshenshini in Alaska, the Watut in New Guinea, the Coruh in Turkey, all rivers Jim and I ran as first descents. "I have been following in your footsteps for years," Lahav tells us, and we hug as kindred spirits of the river.

The put-in is below Meyzad Ateret, the only dam on the upper Jordan, and one that would make rafting an impossibility save for some relationship economics. For a few shekels, the hydroengineer at the dam opens the gate, and out spills about six hundred cubic feet per second, enough to lift our boats and propel us downstream.

This is the first time I have rafted below sea level, and it is dizzying. The Jordan here drops almost 100 feet per mile, steeper than almost any commercially raftable river in the United States, and we are riding liquid lightning. Jim and I alternate captaining the raft, and we find ourselves in a nonstop barrage of commands to the other paddlers: "Forward! Back-paddle! Left! No, right! Hard forward! *Really* hard forward! *Woman overboard! Pull her back in!*" We carom and pitch down the torrent, barely in control, broaching against boulders, high-siding to the razor's edge of capsize, hosing into trees and bulrushes. The river goes insane, chaos frothing, pluming, skibbling around and doubling back on itself like rogue fireworks. At one point the rapids' thunder peals up the burled gorge louder than before, and I fear a falls we can't fathom, when suddenly two Apache helicopters roar over us, so close we can feel the rotor wash. "Friends of mine on exercise," Lahav explains, and I exchange a look of astonishment with Jim. On no other river have we seen such avifauna.

A few hundred yards from the Sea of Galilee, we pull over near an abandoned Bailey bridge and make our way through a flotilla of inflatables to a ferry bus. About five thousand Israelis raft this wild section each year, and many thousands more float a gentle family stretch of the Jordan, yet a foreigner is not to be seen. Water is life in the desert, and also, these days, recreation, but this is a scene unseen to most of the world.

The Jordan we have experienced so far is wet with contour and risk, layered with resonance, affluent in its beauty, evoking temptation and trepidation at once, yet irresistibly pulling us downward, downward, into the Sea of Galilee, into swirls of history, narratives, and lore, and well beyond.

∗ ∗ ∗

> *Besides, the waters of themselves did rise,*
> *And as their land, so them did re-baptize.*
> —Andrew Marvell, "The Character of Holland"

The whirling, coiling Jordan takes a big gasp after its breathtaking fall and exhales into the Sea of Galilee. Also called Lake Tiberias, after the Roman emperor Tiberius, or Kinneret by Israelis, it is sixty-four square miles of fish-rich sweet water rimmed with papyrus and date palms, the artifacts of thousands of years of history, and stark kibbutzim and fancy resorts.

On the edge of this miracle lake, we meet Dr. Mordechai Aviam, director of the Institute for Galilean Archaeology and author of the tome *Jews, Pagans and Christians in the Galilee: 25 Years of Archaeological Excavations and Surveys: Hellenistic to Byzantine Periods.* Motti, as he prefers to be called, found his calling at age fourteen when he went to a youth camp for archaeology, and he loves nothing better than to be along these shores turning dirt. "Solving the detective stories of the small-but-mighty Jordan," he proffers.

Motti offers to be our guide as we travel down the Sea of Galilee, piecing the jigsaw puzzle of empires come and gone, interpreting the many superbly preserved antiquities, helping us read between the many lines, and dinting his own academic construals upon the landscape. "There is no archaeological proof for Jesus or Muhammad, of Abraham, Moses, or David," he submits, as we head into Capernaum, the supposed birthplace of the apostle Peter and where the Bible says Jesus performed miracles of healing.

We are at 696 feet below the level of the Mediterranean, and the weather is bright and dry. There are a few modern-day fishermen of the Sea of Galilee about, some with nets, some with poles, pulling in Saint Peter's fish. There are bathers and windsurfers and party boaters, and a number of folks on Jet Skis whizzing around, "our modern-day walking on water," suggests Issat, our Bedouin driver.

Our first stop is the Greek Orthodox Monastery of Saint Apostics in Capernaum, a pink-domed palace of worship built in 1925 with grounds housing fourteen peacocks and an orphaned donkey. We're received by Brother Erinarchos, a long-haired monk with crinkly eyes and a beatific smile that suggests he knows something good that others don't. When I ask if he is the head monk, he grins and points upward to his boss. As scientifically oriented as Motti is, Brother Erinarchos exudes belief without doubt. He describes how Jesus lived here in his final years, after his baptism, making it the base of his ministry, giving his Sermon on the Mount just up the 400-foot-high hill on the Mount of Beatitudes. Jesus, Erinarchos says, performed most of his miracles near these shores, including giving sight to blind men, multiplying the loaves and fishes, and walking on water. "There was no ice," he says with absoluteness, rebutting some scientific theories that a freak cold snap froze the Sea of Galilee, allowing the famous walk. Motti doesn't disagree, only saying in an aside, "You can't fight belief with archaeological weapons." Not one to shun the power of imagery, when we ask to photograph Brother Erinarchos, he says of course, but only if we shoot him in front of a fresco depicting paradise. Belief and image are reality here.

Next, Motti takes us to nearby Bethsaida, on a tell of centuries of ruins, and as if plucking figs beneath a ficus he reaches down and snaps up a clay shard, a piece of a cooking pot from the first century. This is an active excavation site, and there are artifacts from the Early Bronze II, Iron II, Hellenistic, and Early Roman periods. "The Jordan valley is a bridge," Motti postulates. "It is a crossroads to three continents; a meeting place for flora and fauna, for cultures, societies, religions, even climates; and it is an archaeological bridge between the epochs. Much of the book of mankind is revealed in the layers of this soil." There is even, we find, a Syrian bunker unearthed on a site just down the road, a remnant of the 1967 Six Days' War.

Then, to give yet another perspective, Motti treks us over to Horvat Minya, an eighth-century Muslim palace that is now a national park, a tourist site today with no tourists. When the Arabs conquered this region in the seventh century, they chased the Christians to what is now Turkey and Greece, and Islam ruled until the Crusaders, but then came the Ottomans, and on and on in this ever-turning carousel of eras. The Caliph Al-Walid had his primary residence in Damascus, but when it got too cold he moved down valley to the warm breezes and mineral baths of the Sea of Galilee and built this palace and mosque, with its elaborate mosaic floors in geometric designs, a spa for its time.

As we move downlake, past Mary Magdalene's birthplace, through Tiberias, one of the sacred cities of the Holy Land, past the medicinal hot springs and beachside hotels, past Mount Bernice, a Byzantine fortress, we approach the southern tip of the Sea of Galilee, where the Jordan River is reincarnated. It flows for a hundred yards as it flowed into the sea, brown and unhurried, like a psalm, but then is arrested by the Deganya Dam. Just downstream is the popular Christian pilgrimage site Yardenit, where millions have come to be baptized in the same waters as Jesus Christ. We arrive just as a group of fifty Filipinos begin their wade into the chilly river, each having rented a white robe and towel for six dollars from the visitor center. As the members of the flock gather to their knees in water, they sway into a song: "I have decided to follow Jesus; no turning back, no turning back."

There is a tale rabbis tell of a good man who knows how to take and how to give, and he is the Sea of Galilee, as he takes in the Jordan and then releases it. Water does cleanse, and whether it releases sins or washes away prejudice and pride or baptizes peace, it does forever move downstream, to a destination all travelers hope is better than whence they came.

* * *

I take it that what all men are really after is some form or perhaps only some formula of peace.
—Joseph Conrad, *Under Western Eyes*

We are three men in a boat, paddling down the beginnings of the lower Jordan, and when another canoe on this crowded watercourse accidentally strikes our midsection, we begin to wobble, almost to the tipping point, almost crashing into the convoluted vortex of this grand stream.

Jim and I are joined by Gidon Bromberg, the Israeli director of Friends of the Earth Middle East. The son of a Holocaust survivor, Gidon grew up in Australia, where he was involved in the successful effort to save the stunningly beautiful but little-known Franklin River from a dam. As he collected degrees in economics and law, though, he became more interested in the concepts and challenges of global peace. Gidon moved to Israel in 1988 to dedicate himself to the peace process and along the way determined that perhaps the best way to bridge differences was over the common concern with freshwater, specifically the Jordan River. Now FoEME is the only organization in the region that has Israeli, Jordanian, and Palestinian directors and staff , all working together to save the river that slakes their universal thirst.

While boating this section, we see little evidence the Jordan River needs saving at all. We launched just below Yardenit, and the river here is delightful, lipped with palm trees and picnickers. There are rope swings and swimmers, guitars and flutes, mountain bikers and many boaters bumping about, including a couple of Hasidic Jews who go merrily paddling by. Hebrew lore puts the Garden of Eden along the Jordan River, and it's easy to believe that here.

But it all changes abruptly. After a couple of kilometers, we come to a low earthen dam, park the canoe, and climb up over the crest. On the other side, the spirited Jordan River we have come to enjoy is gone, diverted for irrigation and freshwater needs, drinking, washing, and cooking. In the ditch that was once the Jordan now pours raw sewage, and the corridor for the next sixty miles is mostly sealed from the public, a fenced military zone on both sides of the once full-bodied, freshwater river.

There are a few access points, however, that are incipient tourism sites, and Gidon believes these sorts of attractions, and the economics they engender, may be the keys to rehabilitating the Jordan. Much of the Jordan water has been siphoned for subsidized agricultural schemes, such as the growing of tropical fruits that really don't belong in the desert, and if nature tourism can provide an economic alternative, then waters could again "fiercely flow into the Jordan." And as if in proof of concept, we head downstream to the first of the three public access points, Peace Island.

Where the Yarmouk, flowing from Syria and Jordan, joins with the Jordan, there is a grassy mote that once hosted canals to a giant, vaultlike hydroelectric dam for the British Mandated Territories. Built by Pinhas Rutenberg and completed in 1930, for eighteen years it provided much of the electricity for Transjordan and Palestine. Now a ghost of power gone, the dam sits sentry over a fluid edging that has too often run red. The island was occupied by the Israelis in the 1948 war, but returned to Jordanian sovereignty as part of the 1994 peace treaty. In a unique and ennobling example of transborder cooperation, Jordan leased the island back to Israel, and Peace Island is now a tourist destination, with its brilliant views, flyway birdlife, and graphic architectural history. It is the only place along the Jordan River where foreigners and Israelis alike can cross into Jordan without a passport, visa, payment, or even permission slip. As we ride a bus across the bridge to Peace Island, we stare down into two river basins that are just about dry. According to Gidon, prior to the diversions fifty years ago, the average amount of water that flowed down the Jordan to the Dead Sea each year was 1.3 billion cubic meters. Today it's just 100 million, and it's mostly saline water and sewage. The eucalyptuses planted here, though, seem cheerfully oblivious, their tiny leaves fluttering to both sides of the border and down to the trickling riverbeds.

As we stare downstream to a system that bends and oxbows so much it takes two hundred miles to travel what an ibis would do in sixty, Jim tells the story of one of his heroes, American naval lieutenant W. F. Lynch. Jim and I together made first descents of parts of the Euphrates and the Nile, but the river between, the Jordan, owes its first navigation to Lynch, who in 1848 boated from the Sea of Galilee to the Dead Sea. The lower Jordan was then raging with rapids, so many that most of the time was spent portaging, and one of the wooden boats was wrecked halfway through the weeklong expedition and its crew almost drowned. The river was full of fish, and wild boar, badgers, and tigers ambled along its banks. In his report to the secretary of the Navy, Lynch described the Jordan as more meandering than the Mississippi, and wrote, "The Jordan is the crookedest river what is."

Our next stop is the second of the current access points down the lower Jordan, the Three Bridges Park at old Gesher, where the remains of bombed Roman, Ottoman, and British bridges stand side by side at the nexus to what was once the major thorough-fare between the eastern Levant cities and the Mediterranean. They are bridges that no longer bridge, as the border between Jordan and Israel is now the center of the river and is closed to all cross-river traffic. On display is a pre-1948 bus with mannequins of British riders inside, a bullet-riddled quarantine station, and a couple of antique boxcars from the Turkish railroad, a train system so slow, legend has it that a man who lay down on the track to commit suicide died of starvation instead.

This is where Gidon is campaigning for a transborder ecological peace park, what he calls "a bubble," that would connect
with Peace Island to the north down to several archaeological
sites to the south, and unite kibbutzim Ashdot Ya'acov and Gesher
with the Jordanian villages of Baqura and Shuna to the east, with
bike paths and nature trails between. As we walk through the
electronic fence along a former minefield into the current park,
Jim remarks it is as pristine as any he's ever seen, a perverse benefit perhaps of the closed military zones that have prevented any
human development or interference for decades, and may help
usher a passageway of preservation in the future.

As we continue south down Highway 90, traveling parallel
to the Jordan riverbed, we enter the West Bank and the Palestinian Territory and turn west into the Judean hills, up an irrigation aqueduct called Auja. Here, we meet Mohammed Saaydeh, a
Palestinian field researcher for Friends of the Earth Middle East.
Mohammed takes us up the Auja Valley, past children sliding
down a sluiceway through citrus orchards, past banana groves
and fields of red poppies, to the headwaters of a dancing, cool,
clear-water creek rimmed with green tamarisk. This is the only
West Bank oasis with year-round water that flows to the Jordan,
and it is blissfully beautiful, a paradise now and hopefully forever.
Mohammed, in concert with Gidon and other environmentalists,
is lobbying for the Auja Valley to become a proper nature reserve,
one that would be administered by Palestinians, attract ecotourists from all nations, and provide an alternative livelihood for
the local farmers so they could give back diverted water to the
Jordan. This may be, Mohammed believes, a form for a balance
between nature and man in this region, a formula in some measure for the bracing air of peace.

* * *

The last in the trinity of public access points on the lower
Jordan River is Kaser el Yehud, just above where the Jordan

disembogues into the Dead Sea. Some believe this is where Joshua parted the waters of the Jordan and crossed over to Jericho, the oldest and lowest city on earth. Many believe also this is where Jesus was baptized by John, though there is disagreement as to which side of the river. The Jordanians claim it happened on the eastern banks, while in a rare occasion of consensus, the Israelis and the Palestinians aver it to have been on the western side. The pocketbooks of pilgrims can motivate accords.

Several hundred are gathered by the river, from Bulgaria, Canada, Ethiopia, Greece, Macedonia, Montenegro, and Serbia, a babble of languages and cultures with a river and belief in common. The Jordan here is not pure; it is mixed with sewage from upriver, yet the pilgrims have no hesitation for the dunking. When asked, one pilgrim responds, "The river is unclean because of our sins," and certainly in secular interpretations she is right.

We head south, passing a biblical tableau of donkeys, camels, and ibex by the road, and enter the shimmering basin of the lowest point on earth, the saltiest lake on earth, the terminus of the Jordan River, the Dead Sea. We're thirsty in the dry heat, so we turn into the first restaurant/hotel on the northern end of the sea, the Lido. But there is no refreshment here, no water, and no lake. All we find is a desolate ruin, the remains of a 1930s British resort. The closest thing to the Dead Sea is a fresco rendition of a Crusader map that stretches across a holey wall. The real Dead Sea is more than a mile away, a glimmering pearl in the distance. The Dead Sea is dying, and the Lido is a crumbling temple of testament.

For most of the nearly two thousand years since scrolls were stashed in a cave near here, the first biblical records of the region, the Dead Sea has little changed, with relatively minor seasonal and perennial ebbs and flows. But in the last fifty years, since the great diversions, the river flow that fed the lake has decreased to 8 percent of its former pour. The Dead Sea is dropping about a meter a year, and its surface area is just a third of what it once was. The Global Nature Fund has declared the Dead Sea the most

"Threatened Lake of the Year 2006," and standing here, squinting into the horizon, it's easy to see why.

To witness further evidence, we ease a bit down the road, past a parade of "Danger" signs, and come to a place that looks like a detonated minefield. It is actually a garden of sinkholes. As the lake has receded, it has sucked the water from the underbelly of the shoreline, and the earth is collapsing. There are more than a thousand sinkholes on the west side of the Dead Sea, and more appear every day. While planners once envisioned a string of resorts along the Dead Sea, there is a ban on development now. Sinkholes have swallowed campgrounds, a military camp closed, and a date plantation was evacuated. Route 90, the main road, will soon have to be moved up the surrounding mountains. "Sinkholes are nature's revenge to man's acts," Gidon tenders.

The mayor of the region, Dov Litvinoff, agrees. He was the manager of the popular Dead Sea Spa at Kibbutz Ein Gedi in 1991 and found himself "running after the sea." He bought a little tractor tram to ferry clients from the spa to the Dead Sea shoreline, but left the job when the commute stretched to more than a mile.

We head over to the spa and ride the little train to the salt-coated beach at 1,368 feet below ocean level, the low point of our lives. There are hundreds here, pilgrims of a different sort, seeking personal rehabilitation, solace, and therapeutic soaks, and many are wandering about slathered in the celebrated black Dead Sea mud, looking like creatures from the Black Lagoon. Cleopatra is said to have used Dead Sea muck for her beauty treatments, though there is scant evidence on this beach that the stuff works. Jim and I touch the waters, symbolically ending our descent from summit to sea, and then go for a swim—really more of a bob—in the heavy brine, ten times saltier than the oceans. Once feet are extended, it's hard to bring them back down, as if the whole body is suddenly made of cork. It's a singular sensation, one that most would love to experience, and many more would come with greater stability and infrastructure in the region.

"Tourism is the engine that will clean up the environment," Gidon proclaims, and he may be right. As with Lot's wife, who looked back and turned to a pillar of salt somewhere supposedly around these shores, if environmental stewards such as Gidon look back and not forward, the Dead Sea may transfigure into its own salt figure. Gidon and Friends of the Earth Middle East have been working on a plan to designate the Dead Sea and the Jordan River a UNESCO World Heritage Site, and Israelis, Jordanians, and Palestinians, the stakeholders, have expressed real interest. The designation would not only ensure proper environmental management and conservation, but would also attract tourists— religious, historical, and eco. These are the sorts of travelers who become emotionally invested in a visited area, especially one as mythic and beautiful as this, and become active constituents for preservation. It was ecotourists who saw the threatened Franklin River in Australia and worked diligently and successfully to save it. Gidon was one. Jim and I ushered ecotourists down the Tatshenshini River in British Columbia, which was threatened by an open-pit copper mine, and their collective protests and pressure turned the river corridor into a model transboundary park.

There are rafts of proposals to let the Dead Sea live, some incredibly ambitious and rife with unknowns, such as the Red-Dead canal, a concept to pump water from the Red Sea, resulting in a mixing of seas with two very different chemical compositions. It could alter the reputed therapeutic values of Dead Sea water, the main attraction in the first place. Worse, it would do nothing to rehabilitate the Jordan River.

That is the key to it all, Gidon believes. It's as simple as a hydrological cycle. Nature tourism depends upon a healthy environment. This type of tourism, if developed properly, cooperatively, can become an economic alternative to agriculture, which supplies just 2 percent of Israel's gross domestic product anyway. If farmers divert less, then more clean water pours down the Jordan, and the Dead Sea returns, and the whole of this storied ecosystem attracts more tourists.

Gidon and his compatriots have shepherded perceptions to a finer hue. They have helped raise global awareness, influence governments, and engage locals in their common issue. Along the way a blueprint for larger initiatives may be drawn. If peoples of different cultures and religions can come together to manage the Jordan and its lakes in a sustainable way, they just may be able to peacefully manage everything else, and the miraculous might just become the norm.

For thirty-three years, Jim Slade and I have run rivers, many source to sea. But the River Jordan has been different. No other watercourse is so extravagant in its humanity, so fierce in its history, so profligate in its desert beauty. As we leave its banks to wind over the hill to Jerusalem and beyond, the Jordan falls away, a teardrop to the soul.

9

THE HAZARDS OF OZ
Australia

Some years ago, I made a three-thousand-kilometer off-road drive from Cairns to Darwin across the outback of Australia. Somewhere in the middle of nowhere I got stuck in a patch of gummy black soil, and despite my sand ladder and Warn winch (which wouldn't reach to anything but a termite mound), I couldn't get out. Then from the distance I heard a buzzing, and out of the haze appeared a man on a motorbike chasing a lone Brahman bull. He veered over to my bog and offered to help. Together we were able to rock the car out of the rut, and when I offered him some remuneration for his help, he refused. He explained he was a jackaroo, an Australian cowboy, on a muster, a drive across a cattle station bigger than most central European countries, and he was rounding up a feral bull when he found me. He tipped his Akubra and rode off into the sunset.

Until that moment I thought my little cross-country expedition was rather extreme, but it didn't really compare to the lone Aussie chasing big-horned cattle on a motorbike. At least on a horse, I thought, half the team was looking where it was going during a stampede. But on a bike the jackaroo had to dodge not only the horns but also the ubiquitous potholes, spiky mallee scrub, and the odd boulder. I once thought that my job as being a wild-river guide was dodgy, but this was out there, way out there.

I mentioned this recently to the only other Australian I've met who dabbles in an extreme vocation, adventure photojournalist Jonathan Chester. Together we had shared a few expeditions, such as the first descent of the river that runs through the deepest canyon in Africa, a climb up the flanks of Annapurna in Nepal, and an expedition to Antarctica, all of which he covered photographically. He owns a company called Extreme Images and wrote a book called *Going to Extremes,* as well as a children's book on penguins. When, over a Cooper's Pale Ale, I described my outback encounter and marveled at the risk quotient of the modern jackaroo, Jonathan waved a dismissive hand. "Australia is the land of extreme jobs." And to prove it, Jonathan offered to be my guide.

And so it is we find ourselves in the antipodean bull dust, in the most extreme country on the planet. Not only is it a territory with severe latitude issues, but it is also the driest, flattest, hottest country on earth. It hosts the most dangerous creatures, from man-eating sharks and crocodiles to the most poisonous fish and spiders. Its weather is extreme, and getting more so: just in the last two months, two cyclones swept through and knocked two towns off its sunburned face. And of the ten deadliest snakes in the world, Australia hosts twelve.

The staff members at Wrotham Park Lodge, part of a 1.5-million-acre working cattle ranch in the outback of north Queensland, are looking pretty parched when we arrive, and several have chap-splits in their bottom lips. Turns out they have been isolated from the closest pub, one hundred thirty kilometers away in Chillagoe, for six months because of the unseasonable and most unreasonable soggy weather. Some sort of hangover from the wet season brought rain the day before, and our Cessna 404 was able to land only because the manager, Mat Daniel, went out with a tractor and personally moved the landing strip to the left, away from the mud puddles.

Now we're trundling along the Chillagoe "road," with our

activities attendant Cam Harms brawling his Toyota Land Cruiser toward the station homestead to meet the head jack, David Roberts. As we're rattling about at fifty klic's an hour, we come to a patch of muddy water in Harms's way, not unlike what bogged me down twenty years ago. "You ever get bogged?" Jonathan asks Cam. Australians are known for illustrating conversations with grand gestures, and in keeping, Cam's car sludges to a stop and starts to sink. We roll up pants legs and try to push and winch to no avail, which is quite distressing to Cam, not because of schedules or shame, but because by outback rules if you radio for help, you owe the rescuer a case of beer.

Ninety minutes later, after Mat Daniel has qualified for a slappy night of XXXX Gold, we're back on the road, grinding past goannas (the lizards of Oz), parrots, plovers, bustards, wallabies, dingoes, and broadsides of 'beasts,' as Cam calls the cattle. At the homestead, under a ninety-nine-year-old mango tree, we meet David, the station manager for the thirty-five-thousand-head ranch, who has just returned from a stockman's holiday at a cutting camp. He throws a saddle on Uluru, his black stallion, and rides around the billabong, remembering what it was like to be a jackaroo in "the good old days." A quarter century ago, they used only horses to muster the cattle, and the jackaroos would ride about for two months with nothing but the swag on their backs and the tucker in the saddlebags. Now they use motorbikes, quads (ATVs), and helicopters, which he figures increases efficiency and helps meet budgets, but he owns up that it feels a bit like cheating and is most certainly more dangerous than before. Even though he was riding from age four, he fell off his horse more times than he can count while mustering, and once broke his leg. But now, with all the machinery in the chaotic midst of moving cattle, he reckons the injury rate is higher, and jackaroos don't last as long, and it is increasingly hard to hire new ones ("they'd rather work in the mines"). When David first mustered, it was in the company of men. Now a broader net is cast, and about 30 percent of the wranglers are jillaroos.

We decide to meet one of these modern-day musterers, and so it is we ride the range with "Heliwood" Matt Wright. Matt flies a Robinson R22 helicopter, a doorless bird the size of a go-cart, and when he isn't herding cattle from the air, he engages his machine in his hobby, collecting crocodile eggs from grassy and toothily guarded nests.

Mustering is what brings Matt to Wrotham Park now, though, along with his two mutts, Diesel and Sky, who are trained to leap from the chopper on command and corner a stray bull. Then Matt lands, races to the beast, ties it to a tree, and radios the location. Many more feral cattle are found this way than in the past, but the hazards are definitely higher. Matt volunteers that the bloke with this job before him "wrote off" three helicopters in a year. The pilot before that lost seven.

The temptation is unsuccessfully resisted to go for a fly with Matt. But once aloft, it's like the realization of some sort of Nietschzean nightmare, waking up as a mosquito. We buzz and swoop, dip and dive, somersault and cartwheel, defying the laws of sanity and gravity. We vacuum by sulfur-crested cocka-toos, chase jabirus, and drop down next to a wild boar, so close I can see the sweat on his bristle. Matt sees a lone bull behind a paperbark tree and prods it out into the open savannah with the chopper's nose.

This guy is good. This guy is gutsy.

And when he shows a home video, one he hopes might be a pilot for a TV show, starring himself artfully wardrobed in ripped shirt and sweat-stained hat fending off a mother crocodile with a .357 in one hand and a flimsy eucalyptus branch in the other, I am ready to place bets Matt won't die of old age. If Wikipedia needs a picture to illustrate "macho," I volunteer Matt's split-lipped mug.

That is until our dinner of poached kangaroo at the lodge, when a guest walks by with a swaddling infant in her arms. She is proud to show off the bottle-feeding baby, which it turns out is a three-month-old red kangaroo. It seems two weeks ago Matt was flying low, looking for his usual quota of jaws and claws, when he spotted a crippled marsupial mother by the side of the road, probably hit by a truck. He reached into the pouch and pulled out a big-eyed baby, and brought her home to be raised until she might return to the wild. He named her Gucci, after his fashion-model girlfriend's favorite brand.

*   *   *

Flat as a pancake—that's how many perceive Australia, and I was as blameworthy as the next bloke for a long while. In fact, pancakes, if blown up to continent size, are much flatter, so even are jaffles, the Australia baked sandwiches with topographical ridges. Australia, especially in the northeast, is not suffering from a lack of relief. And when there is that rich combination of rainfall and elevation, there follow rivers, often steeply falling wild rivers.

Ten years ago, Jonathan Chester and I made the first descent of the Tekeze River in Ethiopia, a Nile tributary. It was an extreme adventure, full of crocodiles and cataracts, but now Jonathan offers that there are more-extreme rivers in Australia, and the North Johnstone in "Tropical Far North Queensland" tops the list.

Most raft trips start and end at a bridge, but the North Johnstone runs through the Palmerston section of Wooroonooran National Park, a nearly impenetrable tropical swath with some five hundred species of tropical trees tightly knitted and gnarled, including the painful fishtail palm and the even worse *Dendrocnide moroides,* affectionately called the stinging tree (pioneers are said to have died of shock when they accidentally used the leaves to wipe themselves). The legendary dropbears, the fierce antikoalas, are even said to inhabit these insalubrious woods. The only reasonable way to access the North Johnstone is by helicopter, and it was here the activity of heli-rafting was born. And the king of Queensland heli-rafting is John McCrossin, or "Johnny Mac," as he's known in these parts. He's been a full-time extreme raft guide for nineteen years, and at forty-five, with a wife, two kids, and a set of false teeth from too many face plants, he wants nothing more than to keep guiding. "Everyone else has either died or turned into something else," he says with a shrug. Even his e-mail address is evocative of his lifelong passion: johnnymacraft.

Sitting still, Johnny vibrates with excitement, blue eyes flashing, hands dicing the air like a Vegematic. And today he is really, really excited, because we've given him an excuse to organize and lead a historic exercise, the first one-day helicopter rafting expedition down the North Johnstone. Because of cost and variable weather, the NJ is not that often run. Johnny has paddled it only forty times in his near two decades rafting . . . and when it is attempted, the run lasts from three to five days. But Johnny thanks global warming for this propitious opportunity: Cyclone Larry busted through here a few weeks ago, filling the river and making this trial possible.

We begin our lift at Mungalli Falls, a tourist draw that spills from the Misty Mountains, about a two-hour drive from Cairns. From here, a Bell JetRanger whop-whops into view, plucks our rafting gear in a cargo net, and swoops down the Beatrice River valley. The rain forest here is so thick that when a chopper lost its load of rafts and gear ten years ago, teams with dogs whacked through the vegetation and never found a trace. To this day, enough equipment to start a small rafting company is hidden and locked in this jungle jewel case.

Viewed from the air, the North Johnstone basin seems a heaving sea of frozen, dark-green billows, with feather-white waterfalls tracing the faces of ridges and folds. The dark river bleeds with the cuts of white water, making it look suicidal, which without proper gear and talent it would be.

Within minutes of landing on a sandbar, amid an electric swirl of blue morpho butterflies, we launch two Taiwanese rafts and spatter downstream. Australians love to abbreviate, and Johnny's raft is labeled "DV8," as some sort of proud comment on either his path through life or his character.

It is a violent descent. Through the thunder of incoming water

I hear the frantic, staccato commands of Johnny, who rudders the rear next to me. The rapids are quick and sharp in an increasingly narrow columnar basalt gorge named Mordor, and even with Johnny's experience and expertise it is a feverish struggle to keep purchase on the current. There are smutty black boulders everywhere, and at several ill-placed ones it seems the raft is about to spear itself when at the last instant a flash of paddles swerves us into the rebounding water. The craft rolls left and right, pitches up and down as we hurtle through the churning water, until suddenly we spool into an eddy. We're at the top of a rapid called Mineshaft, and it gives everyone, especially Johnny, pause.

It has been eight years since Johnny has attempted Mineshaft. It is so dangerous that Johnny and most others have portaged all their gear and clients around as a matter of course, cursing it along the way. But today, thanks to the recent cyclone, the water level looks ideal, or about as ideal as riding the back of a rampaging rhino can be.

We hike along the banks to view the hydrotechnics, and once adjacent we can see the grotesque mushroom boils, the sharp falls, the keeper holes. The river seems to go insane, liquid chaos frothing, twisting, skibbling around and doubling back on itself like hunting boomerangs. We can hear the rapids' thunder pealing through the burled gorge. As the forty-five-year-old guide tries to pick out routes, I'm seized with a feeling of horripilation.

Things could go very wrong here. And as I found out moments ago, Johnny has forgotten the PIN code for the satellite phone to call the helicopter. Dyspepsia wraps around me like the python on the branch above us. And Jonathan Chester feels the same. He elects to shoot this little navigation from the shore.

After a quarter hour of scouting, we climb back into the boat and push off, sans Jonathan, who is wisely on solid ground pursuing art. The entry is perfect, and we make the tight pull past the first boulder and glissade through the top parts of the rapids. But then a rogue boil pushes us to a tilt, and the raft shatters against a wall of water. For an instant the raft thrums, as though a tree struck by an ax. Then the boat buckles in half and rears as if bent on catapulting me into the roiling soup. Against the river's will, I manage to hang on, and the boat does a fissiparous bop down into the eddy, right into the lens of Jonathan's waiting camera.

But it's not over yet. Several giant rapids later, we come to the confluence with the Beatrice River and the most notorious rapid in the Southern Hemisphere, The Junction. Johnny has capsized the last three times he's tried to negotiate this passage. He abstracts: "The Junction and I have a personal war going on," which does little to comfort me as a passenger.

The rapid looks fairly straightforward but huge, stepping down into a funnel that disappears between two volcanic boulders that turn the air between them white. The worst obstacle is a hole shaped like a peacock tail near the end of the rapid, where the current hoses into it, then plumes out like a parachute.

As we drop into this beast, the buzz of the river slices through me ear to ear. I forget about paddling and hang on as the boat skids, out of control, on a crackling surge of foam that delivers us to the tottering top of a midriver rock. As the water lashes at us from all sides we balance precariously on the pointed stone, on the razor's edge of capsize. But providence is with us, and after a few moments we slide down one side and spin into a pool that we share with a lazy platypus. We each punch the air in elation, and Johnny says, "That's what's called 'negative stress.' When the whole thing has gone pear shaped, and your brain is screaming in a hundred different languages, empty the crap out of your head and listen to the information you need to get you through."

It seemed more like luck to me. But no matter, we're safely through, and Johnny is more charged than before. "I love being on the river. I love poking people with a stick and seeing them change. Now let's go to the pub and get a bloody drink."

* * *

In the candied light of the Daintree, the world's oldest living rain forest, spreading her arms to a wispy, dreamy waterfall, Keely Naden, an Aborigine of the Kuku Yalangi tribe, says a proceleusmatic prayer in her native tongue. She asks for safe passage from her ancestors who were once trees and birds . . . and crocodiles.

After her evocation, she explains that before the white man appeared, the Aborigines were in harmony with the big reptiles, and there were a lot more of them back then. Both man and beast would regularly swim together, eat side by side, and generally coexist in peace. "We respected each other," she says.

But then the "settlers" showed, and things changed. They overfished, poisoned, trapped, and shot the traditional food sources for crocodiles. Out of desperation the saurians sampled new food sources: cows, pigs, dogs . . . and men. Now it is the Aborigines who don't swim in the Daintree River; they know better. Europeans lately have been seen waterskiing down its deceptively quiet middle. Occasionally, on dares, backpackers swim across for a case of beer. Then there was Beryl Wruck. A small-boned, forty-three-year-old local shopkeeper, she went swimming, after a few drinks during a Christmas party, in Barratt Creek, a tributary to the Daintree. There was a giant swirl. Beryl was lifted into the air, and then she was gone. No sound, no scream. Taken by a croc.

The ancient Greeks called it *krokē-drilos,* "pebble-worm"— a scaly thing that shuffled and lurked in low places. The most deadly existing reptile, the crocodile has always been on "man's worst enemies" list. It evolved two hundred million years ago as an efficient killing machine and was designed so perfectly it has seen no reason to change. The crocodile's instinct is predation: to kill any meat that happens into range, be it fish, wallaby, wombat, or human. To crocs, we are just part of the food chain. Crocodile hunters, upon cutting open stomachs of their prey, have discovered bracelets and bits of jewelry and human remains. Huge, ravening predators, armed with massive, teeth-studded jaws, strong, unrestrainable, indestructible, and destructive, crocodiles, if given the chance, eat people. It's their nature.

I know a bit about crocs. I started my career rafting African rivers in the early 1970s, and more than once my rubber boat was bitten by the yellow, chisel-sharp teeth of Nile crocodiles. But as horrifying as the Nile crocs were, they were chickenfeed to *Crocodylus porosus,* the saltwater crocodiles of Australia, crocs that could grow to more than twenty feet long and are found not only in estuaries and out to sea, but also all over the freshwater rivers of northern Australia, and too often lurking on the land between.

In 1987, I made a drive across the Australian outback, and while there the headlines were filled with the grisly saga of American model Ginger Faye Meadows. She and a companion were in their bikinis taking a swim below a feathery waterfall when a pair of turreted eyes and a long, nubbined nose started motoring toward them. The girls were waist deep on a shelf backed against a cliff when Ginger, a strong swimmer, decided to make a break for the boat. She made only a few feet before the croc grabbed her middle and pulled her down. She emerged with outstretched arms, looking into the eyes of her companion but saying nothing, then was yanked into oblivion. She was a day shy of her twenty-fifth birthday. Needless to say, on my trip I didn't go near the water.

"You gotta be crazy to be sane in Australia," says Sean Jennings, our driver. And so it is we meet two blokes with certainly among the most dangerous jobs in the world—wrestling crocs on a daily basis—and they treat their means as the sanest trade a man might muster.

David Leyden is the wildlife manager at Hartley's Crocodile Adventures, forty kilometers north of Cairns, a post he's held for thirteen and a half years. Hartley's is an old teahouse from the 1930s that discovered that when it featured a big ole captured croc for viewing, business got better. Now it breeds crocs for skins and meat, and in a swamp it takes visitors out in small boats to get close, but not too. As Jonathan points his lens over the railing, David pulls him back with his own snarl and points out scratches on the railings. A minute later, a thirteen-foot croc rockets into the air, up on its hind legs snatching a piece of chicken the boat pilot hangs from a stick. It's too easy to imagine a Nikon attached to an arm in lieu of fowl just now.

David has kept and played with reptiles since he was knee-high in Melbourne, and even today has a bedroom full of pythons at home (and he's still married, suggesting perhaps this is not some sort of compensation behavior). "Rather have a python than a cat," he says with a grin. Then adds, "I'd feed the cat to my snakes."

One of David's chores is hosting the daily Crocodile Attack Show for visitors in a small pond with Bart the croc, a ten-foot female. He rolls up his pants leg, wades in, pokes the croc with a stick, and taunts it with a tethered bag, all the while telling tales of croc attacks. On cue the saltie snaps into action, blindingly fast, clacking its jaws with a hollow thunk. David has done this show scores of times, but I can't help but imagine a Siegfried and Roy tragedy. On the way to our next stop, our driver, Sean, plays a CD by a local duo: "Come to Australia—you might accidentally get killed." I have to admit it is catchy.

In a government warehouse on the skirts of Cairns, we meet Clayton Enoch, an Aborigine who works for the Conservation Services. He is a genuine crocodile hunter, the real deal. When ten years ago a young girl was taken by a croc in the city limits, the government hired Clayton. His job is to catch and relocate crocs deemed too close or treacherous, and Clayton is not idle. He uses a thirteen-foot-long, specially designed, bat-black boat he calls "the stealth" and heads out on moonless nights to fetch troubling leviathans. He and his partner use lights to spot the red-eye shine of a target, then, Ahab-style, he fires what looks like a fork into the neck. What ensues is a classic struggle between man and beast, a tug-of-war in which the croc pulls the boat about until it tires. Then, with a "snouter pole," Clayton drops a noose around the croc, pulls it to the gunwales, tapes the jaws shut, covers the head with a hessian bag, and brings the tiny-brained dinosaur relation to a giant cage for transport. Clayton has had his share of close calls, but proudly shows off his full hands of fingers, saying not all crocodile hunters have been as fortunate.

While the government sanctions the culling of a million and a half kangaroos each year, crocodiles have been protected since the 1970s, and their numbers are increasing, as are the numbers of croc encounters. Clayton says a man was eaten just a month before our meeting. There are folks, often friends and family of victims, who cry out for the elimination of estuarine crocodiles in Australia. But Clayton, who deals with the cold-blooded reptiles every day, thinks differently: "Aboriginal people, my people, have been here for thousands and thousands and thousands of years, and the crocodiles were here before us. We learned to live with the crocs. Why can't others?"

And with that the gutsiest guy I've ever met tucks his six-foot-plus frame into his three-cylinder minicar and tootles off to danger.

*   *   *

Never have I had such food guilt.

We're at Titanic Fish & Chips in Bentleigh East, Victoria, and Jonathan orders up Flake & Chips, a favorite feast when he was growing up in southern Australia. *Flake* is Aussie for *shark*. It remains a popular batter-fried fast food today. Recent immigrants from Cambodia and Vietnam have taken over a swath of this trade, including the Titanic. Of course, one of the favorite dishes in the many Asian restaurants around Australia is shark-fin soup.

The night before, we dined at Taxi, a very fine restaurant in downtown Melbourne, and there, with a bottle of Mount Langi Shiraz, we supped on kingfish usu-zukuri, a premium sashimi, prepared by super sushi chef Ikuei Arakane.

If you detect a theme here, it is that we have been dining on fish for the past few days, and it has my knickers in a knot, as they like to say round here, because today we are going swimming

Sizing up the pyramids, while searching for the Nile crocodile.
photo courtesy of Laura Hubber

Richard Bangs searches for crocodile imagery and artifacts beneath the gaze of the great Sphinx. *photo courtesy of Laura Hubber*

Richard Bangs discussing conservation of the Nile crocodile with Dr. Sherif Baha El Din. *photo courtesy of Laura Hubber*

Richard Bangs and crew film a young Nile crocodile found for sale in a Cairo market. *photo courtesy of Laura Hubber*

This stuffed crocodile heralds the entrance to a quaint cafe. *photo courtesy of Laura Hubber*

Richard Bangs prepares to release a young croc purchased in a market bazaar back into the Nile. *photo courtesy of Laura Hubber*

Searching for clues to the ancient crocodile god Sobek. *photo courtesy of Laura Hubber*

A hopeful stare from a young mountain gorilla, Rwanda.
photo courtesy of Didrik Johnck

Richard Bangs and crew run a pristine gorge on the Neretva River, Bosnia.
photo courtesy of John Canning

A traditional Moken kabang powered, by a "long-tailed diesel engine," parts calm waters off the coast of Thailand.
photo courtesy of John Canning

A Moken fishing in shallow waters.   *photo courtesy of John Canning*

French guide, Bastien Stieltjes leads the group along a new route through the Akakus Massif, Libya. *photo courtesy of John Canning*

John Harlin's (III) wife, Adele Hammond, spots his progress up the Eiger, Switzerland. *photo courtesy of Canning*

The famed and deadly Eiger that claimed the life of John Harlin II.
photo courtesy of John Canning

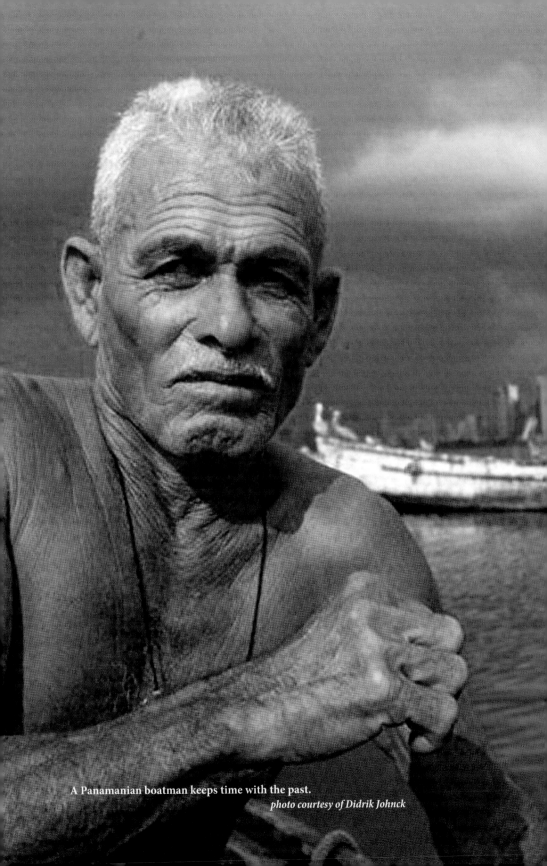

A Panamanian boatman keeps time with the past.
photo courtesy of Didrik Johnck

After running the complex and storied River Jordan, Richard Bangs' river companions take a float in the Dead Sea. *photo courtesy of John Canning*

Richard Bangs and crew run the lively North Johnstone River, Australia

photo courtesy of Didrik Johnck

Actress and conservationist Daryl Hannah along for the journey to help save the Rwandan mountain gorilla.

photo courtesy of John Canning

Elephants crossing the Luangwa River, Zambia.
photo courtesy of Paul Maritz

Showing off a champion mushroom that grows in mountainous Macedonia.

photo courtesy of Didrik Johnck

Ed Viesturs (right) and Veikka Gustafsson embarking on a high-altitude
practice run, Nepal.   *photo courtesy of Didrk Johnck*

The author, explorer, and conservationist Richard Bangs takes a cup of coffee before heading into the bush, Luangwa Valley, Zambia.

photo courtesy of Paul Maritz

with the fishes. And not just any fish. We're heading down to dive with the sharks.

While I had my unfair share of crocodile encounters while exploring African rivers—I once bashed an attacking one on the head with my paddle—Jonathan started his career diving with sharks and other sea nasties. While at university, Jonathan did a paper on sea grasses, which led to his first job as an environmental diver, collecting data on waves and tides and ocean life. He also caught lobsters underwater for a commercial operation, and if they were damaged, he had to eat them. "It's how I developed my love of seafood," Jonathan shares as he rips apart the crisped flakes of shark and dips them in tartar sauce. "I was spoiled early on."

When I imply that crocodile meat, which we enjoyed a few days ago, has a richer, sweeter taste, Jonathan sneers. When I remind him that crocodiles, as perfect killing machines, are two hundred million years old, he snickers: "Sharks go back four hundred million years." When in some sort of cognitive dissonance I hazard that at least crocs are more dangerous than sharks, he scoffs. "The tooth hurts, mate. There are at least a third more fatalities due to sharks than crocs in Australia." And I remember that when we stayed at the Wrotham Park Lodge at the beginning of this trip the staff seemed significantly more concerned over the bull sharks in the Mitchell River frontage than the crocodiles.

Jonathan's degree is in geography and psychology, and at least one part of these credentials is not being put to best use, at least if trying to comfort a colleague in culinary crime is of any import. I'm as nervous as Nemo the clownfish skirting by whatever's next up in the food chain.

And the karmic odds aren't good either. Humans kill about a hundred million sharks a year.

Sharks attack about one hundred humans annually, and of these about ten bite the dust, so to speak. These numbers are on the rise, despite the fact that as much as 80 percent of some shark species have been wiped out in the last ten years. The incident increase is blamed on everything from humans overfishing in shark waters, driving sharks to be more aggressive in carte du jour choices; to global warming, which changes the chemical balance in the seas and alters habitats and populations (as well as motivating more people to swim in those extra hot days); to tourism, such as shark dives, which habituate sharks to creatures they would normally fear. Knowing this, I hesitate when signing the comprehensive waiver. But I take the plunge.

We are hooked up with Mick Cahir, a scuba instructor for the past six years and a specialist in shark dives, though he doesn't hesitate to point out there is no "Shark Dundee" or "shark whisperer." "They can't be trusted or tamed. Sharks eat to stay alive."

Mick hands us 7.5-millimeter suits, as well as booties, gloves, and a neoprene hood, as he doesn't want our skin exposed to bites. He goes over safety procedures—mostly, avoid the sharks by staying below them—but he also suggests what to do if suddenly found in a jaw sandwich: "First of all, don't panic."

This advice seems awfully academic.

"Then push your thumbs into his eyes," Mick demonstrates in the air. "They don't have hands or feet, so their eyes are critically important to survival. Poke them, and they'll let you go." I've heard the same hypothesis about how to handle a chomping crocodile and still wonder if I would have the presence of mind to try this, yet nothing compels me to a test.

On cue, we slide into the water, cut in places with the distinctive pyramidal fins, and head straight for the sandy bottom, seven meters down. The water is clear, but every few seconds the space above dims, as if because of a passing rain cloud. I glance up and see cousins ray . . . a whole clan of rays. In fact, they are giant stingrays, four meters wide, indolently flapping inches above. I reach up and run my gloved hand down the belly of one of the beasts, and it seems to respond with a crooked gummy grin.

And then we see our first shark, a ten-foot-long grey nurse shark. Then right behind a sevengill shark. And then more, black eyes glowering, mouths gaping with sharp snaggleteeth, sleek bodies moving like torpedoes toward some indiscernible target. Humans aren't a favorite on shark menus, or so we were briefed. Most shark attacks, it is supposed, happen because the predator mistakes a swimmer or a surfer for a seal or other popular marine surface snack. So, not wanting to become a chumsicle, I kneel on the bottom, a good two meters below shark alley. Old feelings of fear fall like jellyfish as I watch the gray-denticled and triangular-toothed fish fan by above.

Australia hosts no shortage of fish stories, or maritime mysteries, when it comes to sharks. Perhaps the most infamous concerns Prime Minister Harold Holt, who disappeared just south of here when he was walking the beach and suddenly dived into the surf, never to be seen again. Some conjecture suicide, a faked death to run off with his mistress, kidnapping by the Chinese, or riptides. But the likeliest explanation for no trace is sharks.

Then there is the case of the Lonergans, made into the raw and primally chilling film *Open Water*. Americans Tom and Eileen were returning from a stint in the Peace Corps in early 1998 and stopped for a day dive at the Great Barrier Reef. Somehow the dive boat didn't head-count properly and left the couple still underwater when it motored back the 38 miles to Port Douglas. When two days later they were discovered missing, a massive search was launched, but their bodies were never found. Again, theories hotly abounded that it was murder or a double suicide, that they staged drowning and are living in paradise, or that they worked for the CIA and had their identities changed. But again, as the film suggests, the most probable end and reason for lack of bones or flesh is sharks, tiger sharks in this case.

We root about the bottom for about twenty-five minutes, and I watch as our chief videographer, Didrik Johnck, drifts upward to get some closer shots of the circling sharks. Suddenly there is a churn of water, a gray and white blur, and a turtle dives past me. Then Mick urgently tags me and motions that I, as well as Jonathan and Didrik, should follow him to the surface. Once we surface, Mick explains that Didrik got too close to a gray nurse shark, agitating it so that it took a nip at a passing turtle. He wanted us out of the water, fast.

Still, we spent almost half an hour of quality time swimming with the sharks, without a cage or chain mail, and they just left us alone. When I ask Jonathan, the veteran Aussie diver, why we didn't get chomped, he shoots his signature grin:

"Professional courtesy."

* * *

"If a cat has nine lives, then I have twelve," Jonathan Chester likes to say with just a tincture of waywardness in his eyes.

When a young man in Adelaide, Jonathan played Australian rules football, the most brutal and unprotected team sport ever concocted, and he was repeatedly crunched, one time tearing his anterior cruciate ligament. When he gave up football, he became a diver, and while underwater he had close shaves with sharks, stinging sea coral, and deadly sea snakes, and a too-close squeeze with a blue-ring octopus, which injects venom more violent than any found on land animals (and there is no known antidote). Working as a full-time diver left him wincing at the thought of pulling on a wet suit on weekend, so he picked up climbing. Before it became a tourist adventure he climbed the Sydney Harbour Bridge, illegally. Then, to help finance climbs, he taught himself the techniques and art of extreme photography. On one of his first major expeditions he survived an avalanche on Annapurna III that killed three of his mates. He was buried twice in avalanches in Alaska. He went on to lead major expeditions around the world, including more than a score to Antarctica, where he once barely survived a force 11 gale. On Mount Cook in New Zealand, he was almost crushed by a falling serac. And he began to publish books featuring his exploits and the images brought back. And he found himself drawn to wildlife. While in pursuit of creature feature pictures, he was chased in the arctic by a polar bear. In the Ross Sea, his little Zodiac was nearly capsized by a killer whale. And while he was trying to photo-graph an elephant seal in the austral summer, the one-ton beast rolled and almost flattened him. He has more scars than I do.

So as we've made this tramp through Australia, Jonathan has dangled three cameras about his neck and pursued shots of the endemic wildlife, 80 percent of which can be found nowhere else. Up north he captured wallabies, kangaroos, dingoes, feral pigs, and the giant, murderously clawed birds known as cassowaries. We also spent a day on the Daintree River, where amid the man-groves Jonathan captured adorable baby shots of those natural-born killers, estuarine crocs.

Here in the south, Jonathan spent a day poking about the fauna and returned with imagery of koalas, emus, a Tasmanian devil, and the third-deadliest snake in the world, the coastal taipan.

"So, what wildlife are you missing?" I ask when he finishes showing off his digital menagerie, imagining he is absent some-thing mammoth and unsporting, with teeth like palette knives, or bulbous with venom.

"Ahh, mate. Glad you asked. I've photographed sixteen of the seventeen penguin species in the world . . . In fact I've published five books featuring my penguin photos. But there is one that has eluded me, the one closest to where I was born: the little penguin. If I can photograph the little penguin, then I've got it all," Jona-than offers with a slightly crazed smile.

I am a bit acquainted with penguin obsession. Apsley Cherry-Garrad's classic book *The Worst Journey in the World* chronicles a maniacal winter expedition, under total darkness and minus 70°F weather, to collect an emperor penguin egg. And I once worked with Bruno Zehnder, a man so fixated with the flightless fowl he legally changed his middle name to Penguin. He died in a blizzard in 1997 while trying to photograph a penguin egg hatching.

There is but one good locality to photograph the little pen-guin parade, wherein the birds exceptional for their smallness shuffle from sea to shore to molt or nest: Phillip Island just off the southern Australian mainland. But the birds make this ritualistic march only at sunset, so Jonathan suggests we take a morning flight in a hot-air balloon.

The French, of course, invented ballooning, and so it is most often pictured as a genteel passage over vineyards and pastures while sipping champagne. But it too can be a dodgy endeavor. It was Australia in 1989 that saw the worst accident in the sport's history, when thirteen folks were killed as a balloon plunged to the ground after colliding with another during a sightseeing trip near Alice Springs.

Nonetheless, we climb into the wicker gondola and rise to the goodly height of three thousand feet. As we sail over Melbourne, the aerial views, unlike in a plane, pop with detail and relief, as our glide is so leisurely and gentle the eye has time to absorb. We gauge our pace by the heart-shaped shadow that floats across the tangled ganglia of streets and buildings. And then suddenly Jonathan starts to bounce about the basket like a rooting 'roo. "Look, there it is! It's the "G!" The "G" is short for the Melbourne Cricket Ground, the mecca for Australian rules football. Jonathan's father-in-law, Ken Melville, played in three Grand Finals in the 1950s and his 1956 team was in the Sport Australian Hall of Fame. To Jonathan, it's a pilgrimage actualized to float over this shrine.

That evening we make our way down to Summerland Beach on Phillip Island and begin to set up shop so Jonathan can get his shot. The air is filled with salt tang, and a cold breeze snaps from the southeast, alerting imminent arrivals. But as we're futzing about, the PR director for the nature park appears, regards Jonathan's pile of gear narrowly, and asks what he is doing. Jonathan is preoccupied with setting up, so when I answer for him, the PR maven sternly pronounces, "You can't photograph here! It's against the rules!" Jonathan freezes and then fixes her with the stinkiest of stink eyes. "I just came twelve thousand miles to photograph these birds. I've been waiting my whole life for this." He turns in defiance and continues to set up.

The PR person's feathers are clearly ruffled, so I try, in even tones, to explain Jonathan's background and credentials, his many books on penguins, his conservation efforts, his personal mission that culminates here. But she too is resolute and seems on the verge of calling the police. Then I throw the last morsel in my bag, "Jonathan helped produce the penguin movie *Happy Feet.*"

"Really? The one with Robin Williams? We saw it. It's great!" Hollywood here is currency, and the PR lady stands back and looks the other way.

Then, just after sunset, a couple of the bulb-shaped birds magically appear from the Bass Strait surf. They hesitate at the seam of water and land until more spill out. Soon there is a raft of penguins, maybe thirty in a group, and they dash across the fore-shore, hoping to avoid sea eagles and hawks in this brief reach of open space. Then, once to the grassy dunes, they radiate up well-worn paths to their various rookeries, where they stay until the wee hours. After that, they return to the sea for another day of floating and feeding. Now several dapper lads trudge just beneath our roost, short legs scurrying, round bodies swaying, giving us an occasional glance of yellow eyes or a snorelike call, moving up over knolls and into private seaside bungalows we perhaps covet-ously describe as burrows.

Jonathan's cameras are whirring, and he is in the zone of promise. In a little more than thirty minutes, some six hundred of the world's smallest penguins emerge and pass us by, and then evaporate into the night. Afterward, as Jonathan reviews his images, he lets loose a hoot and a Saturday night grin. He got the gold. Well, really, he got the pewter. Jonathan captured his long-sought image of a little penguin, but as it is after dark and the birds would be frightened by flash, he pushed his digital expo-sure to its limit and got just blurry images. Nonetheless, they are authored by him, and Jonathan could not be more delighted.

"Waddle we do now?" I prompt.

"I want to go climb the bloody bridge again." The once-illicit act of climbing the Sydney Harbour Bridge is now open to paying customers, and tens of thousands of tourists make the scenic ascension each year. And as always, Jonathan can't resist scaling heights, especially the iconic and evocative of his beginnings as an adventurer.

As we head back to the parking lot, Jonathan bends down and does a visual sweep beneath the car; he doesn't want to squish any wayward birds. Like virtually everyone we've met on our trek through Australia, Jonathan is plucky and tough and will face the most extreme situations, the most horrible encounters, with an airy "no worries, mate." But at the end of the day he, like his fellow Aussie adventurers, cares deeply about his place, about our environment, about the creatures with whom we share space, be they toothy predators or helpless little birds.

Like the land from which he hails, where no nontoxic or poorly dimensioned creature is uncelebrated, Jonathan Chester expresses no art, no passion, in moderation. If beauty is the mean of many extremes, then this place is the vital gallery, and Jonathan is but one of its many incandescent patrons.

10

THE DIGITAL VILLAGE

Papua New Guinea

W hen in 1540 Garcia López de Cárdenas, the first European to peer down into the Grand Canyon of the Colorado River, turned away from the spectacle, he declared it an "ugly defile." The Mursi women of southern Ethiopia cut their lips at a young age and insert plates of clay; by adulthood, the women with the largest lip plates are considered the most attractive. In the Indonesian archipelago, when the tropical sunset blazes across the sea the Balinese look the other way, gazing inland to the volcanoes for splendor.

Beauty is indeed in the eye of the beholder, and just as language and its intrinsic limitations and nuances shape perception, what our eyes see in context of culture influences our sense of wonder, of art, of awe.

While none on this expedition is a qualified anthropologist, we each conjecture how our sense of beauty has evolved, and how it is different from those immersed in vastly different settings and societies. Hence we have set out on this quest for the Digital Village, which is very much a misnomer, as we are actually seeking the Undigital Village, a place where the inhabitants have had no exposure to the digital world . . . a place where software is freshly cut arsegrass, a hard drive is a steep hike to the next valley, and bits and bytes have entirely different meanings. Deep in the far-thest reaches of the New Guinea highlands, where tribes have been separated from the leveling influence of the outside world for millennia, we hope to find a place where the villagers have yet to create or see a digital image. We hope to hand over a set of HP Photosmart digital cameras and let our hosts showcase the world as they see it, to electronically illustrate their magic, and perhaps we will each learn something in the process.

It's appropriate then that we begin our quest with the Aborig-ines of Australia. Just in the last five years, paleoarchaeologists have used mitochondrial DNA sampling to determine a prehis-toric linkage: that the Aborigines and the New Guinea High-landers were part of the same initial migration that came out of Africa, crossed Asia, and, as the first sailors, crossed several channels on bamboo rafts some fifty thousand years ago. (To put that in perspective, the oldest human remains in the Americas are seventeen thousand years old.) An ice age that sequestered ocean water in continental ice sheets set the sea three thousand feet lower then, and New Guinea and Australia were part of a single continent. But some 8,000 years ago the seas rose, New Guinea and Australia became separated by the Torres Strait, and the founding populations began a separate evolution and fate.

It wasn't until the eighteenth century, when European colo-nialists arrived, that destinies began to radically diverge. Austra-lia was ideal for imperialistic sensibilities. It was largely flat and temperate; imported livestock prospered; staple European crops took hold. The British empire's settlement was organized, aggres-sive, and armed with ordnance, and it took over the island conti-nent, reducing the population of the native, nonliterate, nomadic hunter-gatherers by 80 percent.

In nearby New Guinea, however, the precipitous terrain, impenetrable jungles, brutal climate, and tropical diseases, espe-cially malaria, kept the colonialists at bay. An attempt in 1880 to establish a French outpost with a thousand colonialists ended three years later with nine hundred thirty dead. It wasn't until

1933 that the highlands of New Guinea were even reached by outsiders, the last "first contact" recorded. And today, large populations, descendants of the original migrations, live as they have for thousands of years, using hafted stone tools, gathering food and clothing from the rain forest, living an ancient, analog life.

So in some sense, ours is a journey of devolution, dialing backward from the modern Aborigines to their early ancestors in New Guinea.

We begin our journey with a visit to the Tjapukai Aboriginal Cultural Park, just outside of Cairns. By the 1920s, the Aborigines were nearly wiped out, their numbers diminished to about sixty thousand. Through sanctioned "snipe hunts" when land was being allocated to white settlers, through government policies and laws such as the Aborigines Protection Board of 1883 that stole half-caste children and put them in missions, and through disease and displacement, the Aborigines were disenfranchised and decimated. It wasn't until 1967 that they were even counted in the Australian census and allowed to vote. Their culture was broken, unemployment was near total, their self-esteem had sunk down under, and many turned to drink and violence, validating and exacerbating the perceptions of nonindigenous Australians.

But eighteen years ago, an off-Broadway producer and his dancer wife, Don and Judy Freeman, set up a community theater operation in a basement in Kuranda, a sort of *Waiting for Guffman* performance piece that featured seven Aborigines celebrating their heritage, their dreamtime, their distinctive music, art, and language that were on the verge of extinction. It took off, and in 1996 the local tribal councils became majority shareholders in a twenty-five-acre cultural park, restaurant (the Boomerang Restaurant buffet, where you can always come back for more), and theater show that has become a world standard for indigenousness tourism. It now operates seven nights a week, year-round, and brings in about one hundred sixty thousand visitors anually, visitors who often first learn about Aborigines and their bloody history and wrecked dreams, about their walkabouts, song lines, and rich legends and traditions. The park is the largest private employer of Aborigines in Australia and serves as a vehicle for driving toward and honoring a nascent multiculturalism. And it is anything but unplugged. The Aborigines have embraced twenty-first-century technology to celebrate their past, using it to create entertainment, edification, and art, to bring economic prosperity to their community, and to rouse a generation of their own.

The centerpiece is a multimedia telling of the Aborigine creation myth in a climate-controlled two-hundred-seat theater, with a combination of live action with a front-projection video crammed with digital effects, such as holographic fire, flying spirits, and a giant crocodile biting off a man's leg. It is exhibited with a laser disc player, under a light show managed by an AMX digital system. Behind the scenes, two Windows NT servers, a dozen workstations, and five laptops loaded with Windows XP keep the operations going. The staff communicates with digital handheld radios; time is kept on digital clocks; and the lead performer, Warren Clements, applies his white ocher and chalk makeup while listening to Guns N' Roses on his iPod. The audience listens to the show through headsets that transmit in eight languages, all stored on a hard drive. And, of course, the theater is packed with visitors posing their digital cameras a couple feet or so above their laps capturing scenes from the shows. With a high-speed Internet connection, Michael Nelson, the marketing manger, promotes the messages of the park to the world, enticing more to come and appreciate a culture almost lost to dispossession and time. "Tjapukai has done more for reconciliation than any Canberra committee meeting," Michael proclaims as a group of preteen Aborigines file in to see the show. Theirs is a generation that for the first time has indigenous studies in school, a generation that just may return the pride.

"We're not savages," Warren Clements decrees after the show, still adorned in what might pass to the uninitiated as war paint, the paradox not lost on him that his access to the modern world comes from romantic presentations of his people's past primitive characteristics. "We're doing this to break down the barriers of discrimination; to give visitors a better understanding of who we are; to give our own a path back to self-respect and dignity."

On the way out, which as in all smart theme parks feeds through the gift shop, we buy a CD of didgeridoo (the oldest wind instrument in the world) and another of the players singing the park's theme song, "Proud to Be" a melodiously uplifting and catchy tune that almost drowns the stinging lyrics, such as the lines, "The white man came and pulled it (Australia) down under," and, "Spears can't fight guns and dynamite."

And now it is off to the airport, to head north to New Guinea, a step back in time, toward a less-connected but perhaps more integral state of grace, where the tyranny of the land has kept its peoples' art and beauty isolated and their own.

THE DIGITAL DIVIDE

While in transit at Port Moresby, the coastal capital of Papua New Guinea, I pick up a copy of the national rag, *The Post-Courier*, and there on page 6 is a quarter-page ad for the "IEA Photographic Essay Exhibition" this coming weekend. It seems the International Education Agency has empowered teachers, students, even preschoolers with computers and digital cameras and asked them to shoot photo essays, the best of which will be on display.

So, the digital life has come to New Guinea, though Port Moresby is the only reach on the island that might be called a city, with some three hundred fifty thousand residents. Some 85 percent of the island's six million residents still live in remote villages, most as subsistence farmers and rain-forest foragers. The interior remains largely a land apart, and there are valleys still that could be called lost worlds.

New Guinea's first recorded contact with European civilizations came during the first flush of world discovery, when the Portuguese mariner Jorge de Meneses made landfall in 1526. He called it *Ilhas dos Papuas,* the island of the fuzzy-haired men. In 1545, Ynigo Ortiz de Retes sailed by and called it *Nueva Guinea* after the colony of Portuguese Guinea in Africa. Over the next three hundred years, occasional seamen on their way to somewhere else charted the outlines of New Guinea; but cordial contact with its inhabitants was rare and penetrations into the interior unknown.

By the midnineteenth century, colonial powers began to squabble over New Guinea, and when the dust cleared, the Dutch controlled the western half of the island, now West Papua, and Britain and Germany divided up the east.

At the beginning of World War I, Australia wrested control of the German part of Papua New Guinea, and six years later, the League of Nations granted it sovereignty over the whole of the eastern part. In 1975, Australia gave Papua New Guinea its independence.

Just two generations ago, none of the million and a half people living in the Highlands had ever seen metal, the sea, or white men, and their first sight of a wheel was on an aircraft landing on a crude strip hacked out of the jungle by Australian gold prospectors. Even today life hasn't changed all that much for the Highlanders, though change is in the air.

No roads connect Port Moresby to the great mass of the interior. The only way in is to fly or hike. So we board an Air Niugini Fokker and head into the clouds.

At Mount Hagen, the main township in the Western Highlands province, we meet with Bob Bates, the Australian-born owner of Trans Niugini Tours, a resilient tour company that has been operating in-country for almost thirty years. Bob came to the then-Territory of Papua New Guinea in 1964 and for six years worked as an engineer building early tracks and bridges.

I met Bob in 1976, when I first came to New Guinea to scout for river explorations. He flew me about in his Beechcraft Baron and drove me along the washboard roads in his 1974 Range Rover, both of which he still operates today.

It is Bob who is helping us find the Digital Village. Perhaps more than any other, he has explored the backcountry of New

Guinea and has visited many extremely remote settlements and outposts. There is one village to the far west of here he thinks will suit our purposes, and with his help we hope to reach it.

Today, though, Bob introduces us to his operations manger, Mombom "Lawrence" Walep, thirty-two, who hails from a village called Wamul, down the Waghi River valley to the east of Mount Hagen. Lawrence, as he prefers to be called, is what might be called a bridge man, in that he has a foot in two very different worlds, his village, where he maintains strong ties, and the quasimodern world of the forty-thousand-strong Mount Hagen, a sort of Deadwood frontier town with a huge outdoor market where outlying villagers come to barter pigs, bird-of-paradise feathers, kina shells, brightly woven billum bags, tropical fruits and vegetables, and other jungle goods in exchange for staples such as cooking oil, salt, tobacco, pig ropes, betel nut from the coast, and used T-shirts and shorts imported by missionaries and coastal entrepreneurs.

Lawrence considers himself lucky. He was educated in a government school, spent two years in a Catholic seminary, and through hard study mastered English. He was ready, though, to settle in for village life when he heard about a sales clerk job for Trans Niugini Tours. He applied, and over three hundred other applicants he got the job.

Today, though, he is returning to his village to visit his family and *wontak* (literally, "one talk," or linguistic group), something he tries to do every month or so. He invites us along, saying we will be only the third group of "tourists" to visit his village. We throw our digital gear in the back of a Land Cruiser and start a two-hour trundle down a road outstanding in the number and quality of its ruts. Lawrence carries with him an SLR camera that was given to him by one of the company's pilots and a single roll of 24-exposure film, which costs about a day's wage. He is planning to take some photos of his family, process them, and send them back with part of his salary he regularly returns to his clan. He is the only one in the family to have ever left the village hearth, the first to ever land a job with a wage, and he feels both proud and a bit abashed.

As we park the car and begin a long, steep hike up a mountain, we pass an elderly woman tending her pigs. She sees us and begins to wail like a ghost. She's shaking and sobbing, and at first we think she is distraught, or frightened. But Lawrence explains that she is actually joyful, that this is how she expresses overwhelming happiness. Another woman approaches making ambulance sounds, and as she reaches out to shake my hand, tears run down her dark cheeks.

At the village entrance, Lawrence asks us to wait and chew some bananas as he speaks with the village chief, his uncle Mr. Bund, about our visit. We wait, and an hour later we are invited to step through a garlanded gateway, down a path lined with tulips and marigolds, into the village of Wamul. Two men in grass skirts are playing yard-long bamboo flutes, weaving a haunting tune that unfolds like a prayer. Four men dressed in brilliant plumage and hides are dancing some sort of jig as they stab spears in the air. We're witnessing, Lawrence tells us, a *sing-sing*.

Sing-sings are elaborate ceremonies performed on special occasions, such as those marking a marriage, mourning a death, honoring a tribal hero, paying homage to ancestors, beseeching spirit gods for good crops, or celebrating the arrival of special guests. The village is honored, we're told, that we chose to call, and they want to show off their best spectacle.

As we step into the village commons, about forty men, women, and children begin their elaborate show, a stomping, pounding kaleidoscope of color and sound. They parade about thumping hourglass-shaped hand drums and whooping like cassowaries; jangling necklaces, anklets, and bracelets of pig tusks, shells, and bone; bobbing headdresses made from long bird-of-paradise plumes trimmed with red parrot feathers. Off to the side, one man whets a stone adze, another tends to his pet sulfur-crested cockatoo, and a couple of elderly women blow on bamboo mouth harps.

As the pageant unfolds, Lawrence pulls out his camera to take some photos of his sisters and cousins prancing beneath the sheltering pandanus trees. But his camera doesn't work. He pushes buttons and shakes the box, but the film will not advance. He is losing the moment he had hoped to capture. Videographer Didrik Johnck notices Lawrence's frustration, pulls out one of the digital cameras we are saving for the Digital Village, and offers to let Lawrence borrow. In a trice, Lawrence is back shooting his family in motion, capturing village scenes and crafting his own art.

At the end of all the dancing, Chief Bund gathers his village around and speaks through Lawrence as the interpreter: "We are the last part of the world. We are so isolated that we are feeling a little scared and embarrassed with your visit. White visitors are new to us, and we hope you will accept us." Then he calls for a *mu-mu*, a hot-stone barbecue of sweet potatoes and chicken, and we sit down to feast.

As evening approaches, we head down the hill, and back to Mount Hagen. At the hotel, Didrik pulls out the Photosmart 375 printer we are carrying, a printer tinier than a coconut. He inserts the memory card and asks Lawrence to choose an image. He picks one of his cousin Hanna, her face swirled in brilliant colors, her nose daubed an arterial red, her hair gushing in tail feathers, her breasts covered with a mantle of possum fur. As the image prints out, Lawrence exclaims, "Wow. I don't believe this. You're doing this with such a small machine. If my family sees this, they will talk about this for the rest of their lives." Lawrence prints out several more of his family and his village, saying he will·deliver these with delight on his next trip home.

Lawrence himself is a harbinger of change in the Highlands, something about which he has mixed feelings. The village elders, he says, are concerned about losing their culture, and they call some who have left for the lights of town *long-long,* which means "crazy." Lawrence says he appreciates the tightly woven tapestry of traditions, grounded with ancient links to the land, that have remained largely intact in his village, despite the growing seductions of religion, technology, and a nearby cash-based economy. He wears shoes now, and creased trousers, and shirts with buttons. And he works in an office. But at home he keeps his plumed wigs and skins, and he brings them to the village every now and then to participate in a sing-sing. "My village is like a tree. The leaves change, but the roots of culture stay the same."

ONCE WE WERE WARRIORS

On my last trip to New Guinea, in 1990, I was riding a lorry down the Highlands Highway when suddenly we braked as a group of shrieking, feathered warriors raced across the road tossing spears at another retreating tribe to the north side. One spear hit its mark, and an older man went down. The advancing tribe moved to the downed man and finished the job. A Kiwi in the vehicle with me recorded the incident on his video camera. When we got back to the hotel, he replayed the episode, and we watched in horror. We had witnessed the age-old cultural system of payback, which has evolved and manifested itself in ghastly ways.

Today, we head east down the Highlands Highway to visit the Chimbu Mudmen, a tourist enterprise that reenacts a tribal war legend. As usual in such matters, the story begins with a bad tribe that takes over the land of a smaller village. The defeated retreat to a nearby river, cover themselves with ash-colored mud and large mud masks, and return to frighten away the raiders, who believe the mudmen are spirits of their dead ancestors returning to do justice.

While in the village of Mindima, where the mudmen show is presented, I meet a white-haired John Wamugl, who stands behind a mat displaying painted shields, spears, bows and arrows, stone battle-axes, bamboo breastplates, and penis gourds for sale. I ask in pidgin his age: "How mani Christmas belon you?" He replies that he doesn't know, but that he fought as a young man in World War II, where he took his bush knife to Japanese who parachuted into the jungle. He has fought in many tribal wars since then, and he swings his ax in a fast chop to show how he would bring down the foes. He also says he helped escort the first tourists to visit the Highlands in 1962, when they witnessed several battle reenactments in his village, including one by the mudmen. The tourists tipped the players generously for the show, a cultural purchase that could not be refunded. When the tourists showed their photos around at home, demand began to grow for the mudmen re-creations and they became a minitourist industry. When I first visited New Guinea in 1976, I saw the mudmen and was duly impressed, and so began to organize adventure tours that floated the Wahgi River and stopped to witness the mudmen. Throughout the 1980s, cultural tourism in New Guinea grew, and thousands from around the world came to the Highlands to witness vivid simulations of clan warfare. Air Niugini began direct air service from Hawaii, and chain hotels and eco-lodges cropped up. In 1990 and 1991, one of the local tour companies sponsored the "Mudmen World Tour." The villagers we were watching performed in Australia, England, France, Holland, Hong Kong, Japan, Korea, and the Philippines.

But then tourism began to crash. The intertribal violence that tourists had come to see continued, but it crossed over into the towns and cities and was undertaken not as specific revenge or payback, but for random robbery and rape. New Guinea, which had been marketed as a new paradise for world travelers, sank into apocalyptic chaos, and the tourism spigot turned down to a trickle.

As we file in to watch the mudmen, we are ushered past mats of carvings and trinkets for sale, a tribal variation of the Disney creation of making sure every ride and performance funnels through a gift shop. We sit on slim wooden benches, and the mudmen lurk out of the trees and do their ghostly show. Two women are covered in ash, dressed as war widows, who must mourn for months. In one reenactment, a boy is caught stealing some food, and a villager spears him to death, whereupon the mudmen emerge to take him away to become one of their own. We watch several ferocious battle scenes and seem to notice some glee among the players in scaring their guests by making bloodcurdling cries and hefting their minatory weapons at thin, pink skin. But when it starts to rain, the warriors hustle away, as without shelter they will quickly become the oozemen.

We also watch the nearby Chimbu Players, dressed to kill, display more mock battles, all with the same theme of a small crime of theft, such as the taking of a stalk of sugarcane, progressing into payback and then full-scale tribal war. In this culture, despite missionaries' best efforts, there is no forgiveness. If someone hits you, hit him back. It is a progressive spiral of socialized violence that once started can find no end, a crocodile eating its own tail.

With the performance done, the headman urges us to do what we can to bring more tourists. It used to be that some fifty or more foreigners a month would come to see their pageantry of interclan conflicts. Now but a fraction make the trip, repelled by the modern version of the very violence they once came in numbers to see celebrated.

As the light slants to late afternoon we're urged to head back to the hotel. Francis Ambai, the official mudmen interpreter, wears a Rebel Yell baseball cap and a T-shirt that says "I'm the boss and I don't take shit from anyone," yet he gently warns we don't want to drive the Highlands Highway at night, as that's when the rascals come out, the modern version of tribal warriors, who now use guns instead of spears and axes. So we rush back to the vehicle and roar down the rutted road, past peaceful fields of sugarcane, bananas, cabbage, coffee, and tea. The Highlanders are thought to be the world's first horticulturists, with archaeologists having discovered evidence of gardening here nine thousand years ago. But because populations grew to numbers that could not support the yields in their isolated valleys, a warrior breed developed that would raid and steal from the next valley, and the payback system emerged.

Now the payback seems to be for introducing the sins of civilization to an edenic garden. There are no rascals in the remote rain forest, only in the municipalities, such as Port Moresby and Mount Hagen, where the ancient fabric has unraveled, where unemployment is rampant and temptations plentiful.

Speeding back to our hotel, we pass vehicles completely covered in protective metal grids. Every window we drive by is barred, every cinder block building topped with razor wire and fronted with armed guards. Even our hotel, considered the most secure in the Highlands, was breached three weeks ago when a band of rascals got over the high walls and robbed the place.

But in some sense, the tables have just turned. In 1876, Italian naturalist Luigi Maria D'Albertis sailed up the Fly River, south-west of here. En route, he fired rockets at the villages he encountered. When the terrified villagers, who had never seen a white man, ran off into the jungle, D'Albertis came ashore to ransack huts and steal artifacts, including sacred objects and skeletons. D'Albertis wrote: "Exclaim if you will against my barbarity. I am too delighted with my prize to heed reproof!"

So we sip gin and tonics in the dark, dank, windowless bar, decorated with war masks, and wait for tomorrow's flight to the Sepik River, where we begin our journey upriver toward what we imagine is a softer citadel of the island that has yet to bleed the heart of darkness.

TRYING TO GET AHEAD

To hide the screams, the men play long bamboo flutes and pound lizard-skin drums. When a boy reaches manhood in the Sepik Valley, he must fast for a week, then retreat to the *haus tamburan,* the men's spirit house, where, as he sits on the back of his uncle, he is beaten with stinging nettles. Then his back and shoulders are ritualistically cut, using a bamboo razor, a freshwater mussel shell, or, often these days, a shard of broken bottle. Ash is then rubbed into the wounds until the pattern of raised welts resembles the ridges on a crocodile's back. The boy is, the ritual suggests, swallowed by a crocodile, emerging with the power of the reptilian enemy, as a man.

As he is cut, his blood pours down on his uncle, keeping a literal bloodline.

The culture of the Sepik basin is a crocodile culture. And we see hundreds. No live reptiles, but every prow of every canoe is carved to represent a *puk-puk* (crocodile); the drum handles, footstools, figurines, shields, masks, and totems feature slithering, grinning reptiles, often engaged in something indescribably erotic; and we see the orgy of scars on the bare backs of boys who have undergone initiation.

We're on the brown and serpentine Karawari River, a major tributary to the Sepik, the Congo of New Guinea. As early as 1616, Dutch sailors spotted a muddy stain on the sea and presumed it the effluent of a large river, but the mouth was not seen by blue eyes until 1885. Not until 1927, sixty-nine years after Speke stood at the source of the Nile, were the headwaters of the seven-hundred-mile-long Sepik discovered.

We turn north into a tangled, tapered passage and head up the Kangrimei Barat (a barat is narrow jungle waterway that often leads to secreted villages). As we paddle precarious dugouts against the current, the water turns black, and we flush snowy white egrets from the reeds. The rain forest is so thick, its vines so ubiquitous, it seems we're sailing through the entrails of a massive beast. Wild sugarcane nods back and forth, as though breathing. Branches and tree trunks float just below the surface of the water, like waiting crocodiles. The place feels haunted, as though spirits are watching our every move.

We glide past pitpit grass, breadfruit trees, hardwoods dripping with epiphytes, and palms of pandanus, coconut, nipa, and sago. We pass women fishing in their canoes, a smoke fire in the stern to ward off bugs; naked children swim out to greet us. Then we uncoil a corner, and the water licks the stilts of a storybook village. It is late in the day, so we pull in and park to spend the night.

But we are met with a new ritual. A line of bare-breasted women wearing grass skirts place hibiscus leis around our necks, then lie down between our moorage and the village entrance, creating a living path. This, we're told, is how the women would greet their warriors upon return from a prizewinning head-hunting raid. So we follow instructions, and step between the legs of the supine women, and make it to the high-fibered halls of the village of Kaiwaria, where the chief, blooming with cassowary feathers, calls a sing-sing.

It is a ceremony not without taint. We are actually the fourth group of travelers to come calling in the last year, and though this village is leagues from electricity, running water or anything digital, it smells the tourodollars. And so the residents paint their faces, don the kina shells and feathers, place a couple of masks and carvings out for sale, and begin to dance.

It is a welcome dance for returning warriors, adapted for pale-skinned guests, for soldiers in the tourism vanguard. The dance is simple yet expressive, dignified but provocative, a war poem of subtle arm movements, genteel turns, and graceful swoops, a ballet full of politeness to a drum that beats like a giant heart. With small, flowing movements of their spear-carrying wrists, all in synchrony, their arms rippling, their supple bodies undulating slightly, it evokes a refined and elevated art, coming from one of the most remote villages on the planet. It reminds me of a scene from the Roland Joffé film *The Mission* in which an eighteenth-century Jesuit father, in trying to convince a papal emissary that the South American Guarani Indians are more than savage heathens and deserve to have their mission preserved, has a group of naked boys perform a lyric cantata chorus with a soprano that is so clean, so celestially beautiful, that it would appear no further argument as to the elevated humanity of these people need ever be proffered.

But these traditions were almost wiped out by warriors of the cloth. The first German missionaries arrived in the early 1930s and were promptly killed and eaten. But waves more washed ashore, and by the end of the decade, the Roman Catholics had outposts throughout the Sepik region and were on a productive campaign of pacification and salvation, persuading indigenes to abandon their spirits, their rites and mystic beliefs, their head-hunting and cannibalistic ways. Even the spirit house in this village, we're told, was burned by the missionaries. But cultural tourism is creeping this direction, and for all its ills it encourages celebration of age-old traditions. Anticipating such, the villagers have rebuilt their swaybacked haus tamburan, damn the missionaries. We're thrilled by this, but as we're spending the night and want to keep our heads about it, we hope not all the discarded customs are on the return.

We have some time before dinner, so we have a look around. As within all villages in the region, life is dominated by the sago palm. The women weave skirts, baskets, rope, thatch for roof eaves, and fish traps from its fibers; they pound the pulp into *sak-sak,* the diet staple, used in pancakes and stews, and tasting to the western palate like lint.

"Let's go grab some grub" has an entirely different meaning here. A couple of the village men cut into the skin of a felled sago palm and pull out several fat, wriggling sago grubs. One man bites into one of the pudgy worms and swallows it whole, satisfied as though he has tasted ambrosia.

Several in the village look as if they drink blood. It is the unsettling effect of chewing areca palm, called betel nut. Mixed with coral lime powder and mustard pod, it stains mouths a brilliant scarlet and teeth black. One sign of the nut's narcotic effect is that devotees consider the vampire look beautiful. And when Didrik chews a plump nut and flashes a blood-red betel juice smile, the women gather around and giggle, as though in the glow of a movie star.

In the last dissolving bit of daylight, a man emerges with a big-eyed, fuzzy orange creature about his neck, a cuscus, the nocturnal marsupial rarely seen in the wild. It is cuter than a kitten, and the owner lets it crawl onto my shoulder, where it promptly wraps its long, prehensile tail around my neck and releases its bladder down my back. Didrik, his camera drawn, is quick to catch my expression, and the village children roar with laughter when he shows them the captured image on the camera monitor.

At dark, we climb the wooden ladder to a shaggy, thatched-roofed communal house, safely above the crocodiles and snakes, and sprawl along the sago-mat floor, next to a shrine to the Virgin Mary. Tomorrow we head over the sharp mountains to the cloud-wrapped Tari Valley, the hidden redoubt of the Huli wigmen, who, we hope, will lead us to a place less touched than even here, a place where time is the only thing that has changed.

OVER THE MOUNTAIN WALL

We cross over the sharp limestone pinnacles and wastes of the Muller Range and begin to drop into the Tari Valley, one of the last places on earth to record first contact. The basin itself was first breached by blue eyes in 1934, when Australian gold miners Jack Hide and Peter O'Malley crossed the great Papuan Plateau and stumbled into the land of the Huli wigmen. Remote pockets of clans were discovered over the next few decades, with the last cluster of uncontacted encountered in the early 1960s. Many believe isolated villages are yet to be found in these extreme jungle-montane reaches, and when looking at the thick, multilayered canopy of blue-green primary rain forest it is easy to believe this so.

On a forest trail we meet Paul Poki, a short, muscular man with heavy brows over deep-set eyes. He seems like a man you might meet on a tropical walk, except he sports a skirt of curled *tanket* leaves rustling over his buttocks and a knife carved from the thigh-bone of a cassowary in his belt. On his head is a wide wig of human hair extravagantly festooned with feathers from birds of paradise, looking like something from Napoleon's haberdashery. Paul is traveling with four of his cousins, similarly adorned, all Huli wigmen from the village of Tagibi, our destination. The Huli are the largest ethnic group in the Southern Highlands, smack in the center of Papua New Guinea, with a population of around fifty thousand in a fertile vale encased in eleven-thousand-foot-high, razor-ridged peaks.

Paul and his kin offer to guide us, and so along a tangled path we trek, past waterfalls that spill diamonds, across swinging rattan-cane bridges, hying by great boles of southern beech, and by wild begonias, rhododendrons, and delicate hanging orchids that look as though they have been professionally arranged. At times the rain forest closes in on us with an airless gloom as we thrash through a creepered world of endless twilight, slog across rivers, and bounce over rank, springing vegetation, all part of the oldest, richest, most stable ecosystem on earth.

The first Huli village we reach is the mile-high Benaria, where, in the cool middle-morning of a school day, we are circled and contained by a gaggle of children sucking on sugarcane stalks. Out of the flock steps Tommy Tim, thirty-six, the headmaster and sole teacher for the Benaria School, which serves grades one through six, some two hundred students from the ten closest villages. It is Tommy's eighteenth year as a teacher, and he has never been more distraught. School is out, but not for holiday.

The school, he tells us, was established in 1960 by evangelical missionaries, along with the church and clinic. The missionaries still make irregular visits, landing at the overgrown mission air strip next to the graveyard, bringing in Bibles and the latest word of God. But the money they used to bring has stopped.

Tommy takes us for a tour of the bare-bones schoolhouse, which sits on a rise above a clear-running creek. Out front is the rusted rim of a truck tire, the school bell. Inside, the walls are bare. There are no appurtenances, no lights, no charts or dioramas; no desks, tables, seats, or furniture of any kind. No digital tools, no learning tools at all. Just a single blackboard with no chalk. The children normally sit on the floor and listen as Tommy or one of his three assistants lectures. When the school is open, some of the children walk ten to twelve miles a day in each direction. Those who live in villages farther away don't make it to the classroom, as their daylight hours would be consumed in the trek.

Tommy takes us to his office, a padlocked shack near the schoolhouse. Above the entrance is a list of commandments, written in Huli, for the students: "I will not fight; I will not swear; I will not smoke; I will not gamble; I will not steal." The last is not adhered to with universal reverence, as Tommy shares that just last month some of his students broke into his office and stole all the pencils. They also stole the volleyball for recess. There are no police in Benaria; the nearest are a day's walk away. So Tommy sighs and says he needs help. "We could use eight more teachers here."

The most distinguishing feature of Tommy's office is an enormous pile of bricks of uncracked copy paper. Conspicuous in its absence is a copier, mimeograph, scanner, or any other device that might use the coated stock. He explains that evangelicals used to finance the school and other services in the village, but since 1975, when Papua New Guinea became independent, things have gone desperately downhill. It was the provincial government that supplied the copy paper, but it never found the funds to supply a copier. In fact, Tommy explains, the reason the school is closed is that the government has not sent the funds to pay his three assistants. At his own expense, still recovering from a bout of malaria, he made the two-day trip last month to provincial headquarters to see if he could receive the promised money, but he came back empty-handed and had to close the school.

"What would it cost to reopen the school?" we ask.

"It would be 300 kina [about a hundred dollars] to pay what we owe, and the assistants would come back."

So among us visitors we take a collection and ask Tommy to step outside with his students. There, Pasquale Scaturro, the renowned expedition leader and my good friend, hands over the cash and conveys gratitude for his work as a teacher.

"Thank you true," Tommy replies. "These children don't see whites very often. Why would they come here? Two years ago, a tourist walked through, but no others. The children have not seen cars, motorbikes, or cameras. They see small planes and wonder about the world beyond Benaria. My school, which teaches them about the world, will reopen because of you."

We shake hands with the teacher and his students, and then, as dark clouds shoulder up over the ridge, we set out for Paul Poki's family village, two thousand feet higher and twenty-seven valleys away.

PICTURES OF AN EXHIBITION

Paul Poki is one of three headmen for the six-hundred-person Teka clan. There are no hereditary chiefs here; rank is made upon merit. Excellence with a bow and arrow and proficiency at mediating disputes are the skill sets of a CEO. When we explain our concept of the Digital Village, he grins. Why not use his family?, he suggests.

Well, not all his family. He has two wives and eight children and an unknown number of uncles, aunts, and cousins scattered about this hanging valley. But he introduces us to his first wife, Mathar, who is forty and missing an index finger, which she cut off in spite during a dispute with her father; his uncle, Hapo, who is somewhere in his sixties, and is most distinguished by the plastic, serrated seal from a bottle of cooking oil that runs through his nose; his teenage son, James, sixteen, who has a sort of slacker slouch and a rusty key hanging from his neck; and another son, Ope, who is seven and prone to popping forest flowers into his hair.

We gather in a common area of packed dirt, and Didrik passes out the digital cameras to Paul's family. Each rolls the silver box about in his or her hands as though examining a shiny shell. None has ever held a camera before. Didrik patiently shows how to use the cameras, placing the viewfinders in front of their wide eyes, framing a shot, and demonstrating where to push to capture the image. Paul and James speak some English, and they translate to the others as Didrik explains: "It stops time . . . It's like preserving a memory."

In the astonishing documentary *First Contact*, Mick Leahy and his band of gold miners, upon entering the Highlands of New Guinea in the early 1930s, take out a gramophone and play it for their hosts, who grapple with the concept and the device in what looks to be a combination of wonder, awe, and dread. The same looks flash through Paul's family now as Didrik gently guides each one through the steps of composing and crafting an image, a piece of their lives snared as though in a trap, brought home to savor, like a lorikeet in a bamboo cage.

They each fumble around a bit with the process, placing fingers in front of the lens, moving the camera as the shutter is pushed, but after a short time they master the technique and begin firing away. Other members of the clan file out of the forest and look over the shoulders of the Teka shooters. Mathar, the mom, can't suppress a grin through the thick canary-yellow paint that cakes her face like a gaudy mud pack, and nods approval at every image she creates. This is a culture in which women are disenfranchised to the extreme; they are not allowed in the men's house, are not permitted to own property, and are relegated to tending pigs. But suddenly Mathar seems empowered, as though she were unexpectedly gifted new status, and she struts about with increasing confidence, pointing her camera in all directions.

Ope and Hapo, youngest and oldest, are more tentative and reflective. They take an image and then stare at it for a period, as though trying to absorb its meaning, before moving on to the next. James is intrigued with the various functions, and figures out how to use the video utility. And Paul, commanding in his toreador wig of human hair, arranges other clan members in a row and takes their portraits.

Several of the men in the clan decide to perform a spirit dance, a traditional ensemble piece in which painted witch doctors chant and stomp about shaking their black palm bows and arrows in a hex to rid an ailing clan member of bad spirits. As they stamp about the dirt to a somber drumbeat, waving their russet-plumed headdresses as do birds of paradise when displaying, Paul's family takes photos off to the side in a row. Only Mathar takes a Clintonesque move forward, closer to the constituency, and reaches her camera into the swirl of color. I look over her shoulder at the images she is concocting, and the head-dresses seem so brilliant they look almost as if lit from within.

When the dance is done, each person continues to shoot around the compound. When the spirit dancers line up for a group shot, Mathar moves behind them to author perhaps a more creative picture, something like the famous Babe Ruth farewell shot taken from behind the plate. Then Mathar moves to the side-lines and begins to take photos of the various young boys in atten-dance. (In this society, mothers raise their sons for only the first five years; then the boys move to the men's house, where there is little interaction with the mothers for the rest of their lives).

When each of the family has taken about fifty images, Did-rik pulls out the portable printer and one by one removes the memory cards from the individual cameras, letting each shooter choose from the monitor images he or she likes, which Didrik then prints out. Mathar's favorite is one she took of her young son, Ope, and after it is printed, she proudly holds it against her face and asks that I take a photo of her with the picture of her son. This picture within a picture is even more popular, and Mathar and Ope both want copies, which they then clutch to their chests as they move about the crowd. James looks at the family photo and says he wants to take a picture of one of his grandmothers, who is old and enfeebled, so he can remember her when she passes. Yes, Didrik promises, he can. Paul overhears and com-ments, "This is good to keep the culture."

Mathar, I must confess, reminds me of my own mother, who had a very similar beatific smile whenever she took photos of her family. I left the coop and began to travel in my early twen-ties, yet whenever I would return, she would always meet me at the airport gate and snap away as I came down the ramp. She treasured those photos like gold, like millions of mothers before and since, and now Mathar is a part of that tribe. As a last image of the day, Mathar asks that a picture be taken of the two of us together. As I write this, my own mother is quite ill in a hospice, and somehow this image seems to connect us all together. I print out three copies, one for Mathar, one for me, and one to take home for my own mother.

Although missionaries and miners have been crawling around this valley for decades, the Huli have shown scant interest in adopting outside ways. Yet at the end of the day, when we ask the family about the digital experience, each comments that the photos they took make them happy, and that they want to take more.

And we promise they will.

BEAUTY IS RELATIVES

There could scarcely be anything more beautiful than the birds of paradise of New Guinea; so says David Attenborough, the British naturalist and documentarian. The males are blooms of color, festoon, and finery, and they display and prance and preen about the branches to attract the duller-hued females. To see the Huli men dress in their wigs that bud with the brilliant, recurving filaments of bird feathers, it might seem they would exhibit the same allure, the same glamour, to their women. Yet when we give a digital camera to Mathar, Paul Poki's first wife, and ask her to go off and photograph what is beautiful in her world, she returns with no images of bright feathers, birds, decorated men, or even the luminous flowers that riot through her village. She takes pictures of her family, of the orderly women's house, of female friends harvesting coffee, corn, and pumpkins. And she takes pictures of pigs.

Paul Poki has a different take. In the soft, matutinal light of an exquisitely beautiful Highlands day, he makes pictures of wild sunflowers, hibiscus, and roses, planted as ornamentals around his sweet-potato fields. He takes a picture of a grand view from the top of a hill and of a running creek. His aesthetic sensibilities in many ways mirror those of us visiting from the outside, until he heads out for a second round. This time he returns with images of the high mud wall of his protection trench, shots of his taro crop, and a still of the grave of his mother, who died in 1988.

There is no end to the fascination on both sides of the cultural fence as Paul Poki's family goes about creating images that are beautiful, important, and even unsightly in their lives and eyes. Ope, Paul's seven-year-old son, takes fifty-seven shots of his buddies, and even has one turn the camera on him. Hapo, the sixty-something uncle, takes a still life of stones laid alongside the path, saying they are beautiful because they make the fields fertile and are the types of rocks used for cooking a mu-mu, the barbecue pig feast prepared with an earthen oven.

And James, the teen, points his lens at pandanus trees and reeds used to make men's skirts and roofs for huts. And he makes a portrait of his grandmother and two of his brothers.

A theme throughout is familial commemoration. When we ask, they photograph a person each considers beautiful; they take group portraits of their sisters, brothers, aunts, uncles, cousins, and wives, rarely distinguishing an individual. Life is communal here, with males crowding into a men's hut to eat and sleep, and women the same in their own, which from a small sampling generally seems to be tidier, even though often shared with the family pigs. When we ask why most images are of kin, each speaks about how he or she wants to hold a moment in time of those important. Mathar especially takes pictures of children and remarks that they will quickly grow up and that she wants to remember how they looked as little ones. Paul and Hapo primarily take photos of the adults and talk of how they will die at any time, and they want images to maintain the memories. In one case, Paul positions Hapo by a path and takes a photograph of his elaborate, human-hair wig, saying, "It is a beautiful wig . . . It fits, and he looks after it. Nobody else can wear that wig."

Then we turn the concept and ask that they shoot something in their environment that is unsightly, the inverse of beauty. Paul takes pictures of a broken bottle in the field, an artifact of the outside world that has made its impress just in the last half century. He explains that the glass could hurt playing children, and he hurls the ugly shards into the river. Ope shoots a pile of pig excrement. James crafts an image of sand and stones, saying they are not living things, not good for crops, therefore unattractive. Hapo records a fire pit rimmed with rubbish, saying that the ash represents to him the end of life. And Mathar first takes an artsy image of a rickety old house where a deceased woman once lived but that now houses only pigs. And then she shoots a photo of a fresh grave, where one of Paul's seven sisters, who died last Tuesday, is now buried. It is the second grave shot of the day: one by Paul of his mother, who died sixteen years ago, which he includes in the "beauty" category, and this by Mathar of a relative dead less than a week, which she cites as the contrary.

Finally, after a day of interpreting beauty and its antithesis, Paul's family members are asked to compose one last shot, a picture of something that means very much to each, a precious trace, something that will be treasured in time.

James arranges leaves in the hair of his cousin and poses him against a wooden fence, explaining that the cousin is important because he looks after the family's well-being. Ope and Mathar take shots of themselves pointing cameras at each other, they say as mementos of this special day. Hapo makes a visual report of his elder brother, saying he thinks that the brother will die soon and that he wants to remember him as he appears today. And Paul searches for his young niece, and when he can't find her he instead takes a close-up of a ten-year-old girl, the daughter of an ex-girlfriend. He says she is young, like a beautiful flower. When a forest flower withers and dies, he knows it will be replaced by another, an ever-fleeting piece in the flux of nature. Yet he knows what the young girl does not, that when she becomes old and her beauty is gone there will be no second spring. When that time comes, Paul says, he wants to show her this photograph of her shining moment of loveliness.

Like most New Guineans, the Hulis have no written language. Unlike the coastal dwellers, they do not preserve their histories, myths, and traditions in carved pieces of art. Instead, the Huli keep the legends alive with songs passed from generation to generation. "These photos are like the Huli songs," Paul says. "They will keep us alive after we are gone." Mortality and the cruel passage of time, though kept as weightless as possible, covered in masks, in the European cultures, are keenly felt here, sitting in minds like stones, revealed in the pictures the people produce.

It all seems so familiar and alien to the western eye. Flowers evoke splendor in most every culture, and indeed here. Yet in the "developed" world, the concept of human beauty is well defined, penetrating, and pervasive, and billions of dollars are spent to achieve or acquire, though as John Donne mused, "Love built on beauty, soon as beauty, dies." Here, in the Tari Valley on the island of New Guinea, a beautiful person is someone in the family, no matter the shape or size, symmetry or features. The ideal of beauty for the Hulis, in this misplaced land that has changed so little in the centuries, would seem to be immediately related to their well-being and perpetuation, and to the fadeless love of their blood relations.

And that is a beautiful thing.

PHOTO FINISH

After several days of digitally reproducing their environment and family, of capturing things and scenes these Hulis deem beautiful, the clan leader Paul Poki comes to us and asks if we want to see the most beautiful spectacle they know. He wants to throw a sing-sing for us, and have his family photograph the event.

So as the morning light clarifies the land, we gather on a ridge overlooking a barrier of steep, green mountains, where members of the Tagibi village prepare for a sing-sing.

It is a long process, about two hours' worth of primping and preening. No man can dress himself; it's a group affair, with each helping the others. First the men carefully fit their tight, wirelike wigs, adjusting the opossum fur rim. They rub ginger into the matted hair, lave it with water, tease it with sticks into its final shape. Each wig takes about eighteen months to grow, or harvest, and is colored with pork fat, charcoal, and red clay. I push my finger into one. It feels like coarse felt and resembles a seafaring bicorne worn by eighteenth-century sea captains

The wigs exist primarily as pincushions for the various fantastic feathers. The owner sticks the wig with frilly plumes of sulphur-crested cockatoos, yellow-billed lorikeets, tiger parrots, and several birds of paradise. An everlasting daisy fronts the wig like a knowing eye.

The men then push quills and pencils of black palm through the septa of their noses. They circle their necks with colorful bead and cowrie necklaces that hold pigs' tusks and kina shells, the prized half-moons cut from gold-lip mother-of-pearl that were once the trade currency of the land. They sport tight arm and leg bands of fresh pandanus leaves and aprons made from tree bark. The serrated beak of a hornbill, traded from the lowlands, hangs from the back of the neck; on the rattan-cane belt is the dagger fashioned from the thigh of a cassowary. Then, using hand mirrors where they once used glassy water, they use bamboo paintbrushes to painstakingly apply their masklike makeup, first a white base to their faces, and on top a vivid yellow clay called *ambua*. Then they complete the transformation with blood-red streaks from a local berry.

In the midst of this orgy of makeup, a very old man scuffles by the players and sits down on a log. He has the weary look of a man who has kept company with ghosts. I sit next to him, and with Paul as a translator ask him some questions. He is Joloma Angape, the oldest living Huli, who estimates his age at ninety, though he says it is a rough guess. He has come, he says, to judge the sing-sing dancers, as he has done for decades. He goes on to tell that he was in the valley when the first white men emerged from over the mountains in 1935. "We never knew there were other people in other countries," he relates. At first they thought the visitors were spirits, perhaps the souls of Hulis who had passed away and returned, and as the apparitions approached the Huli scrabbled away. Sitting on this edge of memory, Joloma recollects the white men as being generous, as they brought salt, matches, eggs, and razor blades, and gave them steel axes to replace their stone models. And they brought guns, and to show their power they shot dead several Hulis.

But Joloma recalls the time with attachment. He says the white men "tamed us" and goes on to elaborate: "We used to kill each other every day. We had payback wars all the time. We lived all the moments in fear. Now I am free, and happy the white people have come." It sounds a bit too politic from a wizened New Guinean in the company of an Anglo stranger, and as I look about at the dancers slathering their dark bodies in tigaso tree oil I see a sea of scars, all from payback battles in what they call "Highlands football." Some traditions die hard.

Bird chatter gives way to a funereal drum beat, and the dance begins, a thudding ballet of dazzling pigments and glistening muscles. Paul's family circles around the action like sports photographers and shoots the extravaganza from every angle. James the teen plays with the video function of the camera and makes several short videos of the wild colors and mean streaks, a Scorsese in the making. The warriors line up in parallel and chant and thump their snakeskin drums and do a coordinated, bouncing stomp, an exuberant bop that imitates a bird of paradise in a courting dance.

As the show is winding down, Didrik counts the number of images captured by Paul's family: 445. They are jubilant and call for group photos all around. But then I get a call on my satellite phone. My mother, a lifelong amateur photographer, with drawers and drawers stuffed with photos of her family, has passed away. Paul and Mathar can tell from my face and come over to comfort me. And the dancers do a last dance for her departed spirit.

The rich blue sky bends toward the sultry green infinity of the surrounding hills, a place where time has stood still. For us it is time now to go. I will head back and sift through the piles of photographs I am so glad my mother took over the years, a whole lifetime of memories. And I'm glad Paul and his family now have photos, too, so they can remember. As we're heading out, Paul takes a photograph of Joloma, the old man. He then turns and says, "All the Hulis who first met the Europeans are gone now. They are underground, and their bones have turned to soil. Joloma is our last connection to the past. If we had cameras like these then, we would have a better way to know what the time before was like."

And now they will. If beauty is eternity gazing at itself in the mirror, and pictures can capture pieces of eternity, then the Huli will now forever know the convulsive beauty of their living culture and vanishing past. And for that, all on this little hill in the fine heart of the island of New Guinea are thankful.

11

CURSE OF THE NAHANNI

Northwest Territories, Canada

When I grow up I will go there.
—Joseph Conrad, *Heart of Darkness*

In 1973, the axis of my identity spun on my summer job as a guide for Hatch River Expeditions on the Colorado. I was in love with fast water and felt most alive when immersed in its swirls and furbelows. Hatch was among the original rafting operations in the Grand Canyon, and as a first mover, the company relied primarily on word of mouth to fill trips, but also published a small, raw-papered black-and-white brochure, which I proudly distributed to almost everyone I met

One day, I happened across a catalog from a rival company, Grand Canyon Expeditions, owned by a former Hatch boatman. The book was like nothing I had seen before. The paper stock was thick and glossy, and the brochure was plump with lush photographs of rubber boats pitching through huge rapids. But it was the back cover that shook me to the core. There, standing on a jagged rock platform, was the owner, Ron Smith, and behind, about to devour him, was a giant misting diadem of plunging water, bigger than any cataract I had ever seen. The high-speed photograph captured tremendous columns of spindrift infused with myriads of small white comets rushing in all directions, each of which left behind a nucleus ray of foam. And all this iridescent architecture was supported by the brilliant beam of a rainbow. The falls, I learned, was called Virginia, on the Nahanni River in Canada's Northwest Territories, North America's largest wilderness waterfall, twice as high as Niagara. My hands shook with the image. I was sucked in, churned around, and I vowed at that moment to stand where Ron Smith had, on the edge of that waterfall, feeling its powerful, taunting spray. It moved to the top of my list of things to do before I died.

Thirty years later, I had ticked off many things on my list—climbed Kilimanjaro, published a book, produced a film, stood on the seven continents, jogged the Great Wall, dived the Great Barrier Reef, run with the bulls in Pamplona, rafted the Zambezi, headed a nonprofit, mentored a child. And I had felt the blustery spray of the world's most famous waterfalls: Victoria, Niagara, Iguaçú, the Blue Nile Falls. But Virginia still eluded.

Then I received an invitation to join a canoe trip down the Nahanni River. It was from John Blachford, a spiritual heir to the late Bill Mason, Canada's canoeing guru, who wrote that the Nahanni was "the greatest canoe trip in the world." John, sixty-seven, bears the scars of a happy childhood. He has been canoeing Canadian waters since he was six or seven and continues with his passion every summer. I had joined him on the Mountain River, also in the Northwest Territories, three years before, and was mightily impressed at his fluid proficiency and his spry, youthful moves. But he is bolshie in his conviction that there is no greater place to paddle than Canada. Many times I have tried to entice him with offers to boat in Africa, Europe, or Russia, but he would hear nothing of it. It is Canada utterly that pulls his heart and blade.

Of course I accepted John's invitation with alacrity. For three decades, an image had clung like a barnacle to the underside of my visual memory. But after I had made my payment, I e-mailed John with questions about the falls, and he e-mailed back that unfortunately our trip would not encounter the falls. We were starting on a tributary, the paradoxically named Flat River, and would enter the Nahanni some twelve miles below the falls.

My heart sank. "Can we hike to the falls?" I e-mailed. John didn't know, but our outfitter, Black Feather of Toronto, e-mailed back saying it was not likely in our time frame. The trip we had chartered was just ten days long, ending on a Sunday, and most participants had to be back at the office Monday next, including me. So, I lamented, I had signed for the wrong trip.

But my spirits lifted when, in preparing for the trip, I came across the May/June issue of a magazine called *Up Here,* a travel publication that features the Northwest Territories. It was a silver jubilee edition celebrating the Nahanni National Park Reserve's twenty-five years as a UNESCO World Heritage Site (it was, in fact, the first such designated site in Canada). In its pages was an interview with Chuck Blyth, superintendent of the reserve. In the interview he was asked if there were any places in the park overlooked, and he replied: "Flat River is a real jewel. And it's not flat! It's a fantastic canoe trip. People overlook it because you miss Virginia Falls and the Fourth Canyon, but you can actually hike over to take a look at them." That sounded promising; all we would have to do was pick our layover day near the route, and voilà, I could make the falls.

It's easier to get to the Nile than to the Flat. I fly first to Edmonton, overnight at the Executive Royal Inn at the airport, then catch an early morning flight north to Yellowknife, then west to the fur-trading post of Fort Simpson on the Mackenzie River, a place so high on the map that all the home television satellite dishes point not just south, but down. Then by charter de Havilland Twin Otter floatplane, we head farther west on an eighty-minute flight over miles of muskeg to meet up with John Blachford, who had flown in the day before.

An hour into the flight, the pilot dips his wings, and there, under sunlight so benign it almost seems counterfeit, is Virginia Falls. Even from a plane it is spectacular. Splicing the flow is a towering granite plug known as Mason's Rock, named after Bill Mason, paddling partner to Pierre Trudeau, a key champion for park protection. Around the sentinel rock a nearly circular rainbow hangs in the spray like a whirling firework. I can even see the stone platform at the lip of the falls where Ron Smith stood thirty years ago. And I can see the upstream dock where floatplanes landed, dropping off passengers who then hiked down to witness the falls. The pilot makes a second circle, so close I can almost feel the agitation of the falls. More than ever I want to be down alongside the great cascade. But we straighten and keep flying.

Minutes later, we land on Seaplane Lake, a mile-long teardrop adjacent to the Flat River. As we unload the canoes, I see a fading red Canadian maple leaf ambling my way. It is John Blachford in his signature patriotic shorts, and behind him in tatty and torn Frodo-like hat, his daughter, Leith, a former canoeing guide. John has a soft version of a Picasso face, with a long chin, distinguished nose, thin, unruly hair, and an impish smile. He shakes my hand and welcomes me back to one of his proud Canadian rivers. I am also greeted by Dave Shore, my old pal and fellow former guide, and two Métis park wardens, Jonathan Tsetso and Marcel Cholo, who will be joining our little expedition to better understand the Flat, which purls through their jurisdiction. Rounding out the expedition clients are friends John, Leslianne, Paul, Dan, Sean, and Erik, who is another former adventure guide and also John's son.

Our published itinerary had us heading downstream the first day, but our guides, Jamie Guptill and Jen Buck, announce we will instead practice our strokes on the clear lake and head out in the morning. This gives me pause as it might subtract our layover day, the day I hoped we might trek to the falls. But the guides rule, and we spend the shank of the afternoon spinning around the lake, John Blachford patiently going through the strokes he had performed long before our guides were born. The sun won't go down this far north; we are at sixty-two degrees north latitude, and I have handed out my selection of eyeshades to the team, forgetting to save one for myself. So at the designated time, I wrap a T-shirt round my head and try to block out the rack of light pouring into the bower of my tent, while tossing and turning, wondering if I will reach Virginia.

Next morning, clear and bright, alongside the skirling treble of loons, we paddle a few hundred yards to the northwest corner of the lake to execute a five-hundred-yard-long portage across a swampy isthmus that allows us on the Flat. With my boating partner, Dave, I struggle, hauling one of the canoes along the slippery path pocked with cloacal mud, but then I look up as someone passes us by—John Blachford, practically skipping along solo with a canoe over his head.

We load the boats, ours a green sixteen-foot Old Town, attach the splash covers, pull tight our life jackets, and point downstream to a seventy-nine-mile passage that Jen estimates fewer than one hundred fifty people have ever traversed, and those do not include our guides. This is their first run as well.

The river runs shallow and sprightly, and we crab our way through the chaos, scraping and bumping rocks along the way. A lively and fun passage it is.

Late in the afternoon, we pass a yellow sign on the western bank that shows a man carrying a canoe, the universal sign of "portage ahead." There is a second sign at the pullout, we have been told, and we need to beach there or be swept into a bedrock gorge with the decidedly Hitchcockian name the Cascade-of-the-Thirteen-Steps.

But no sign appears, and the guides become nervous as we approach a bend the map indicates is the entrance to the Steps. So the guides have us wait in an eddy as they ease down the side to locate the portage path. When it's discovered, they have us, one boat by one, paddle to them as they poise at the edge with a rope should the mark be missed and a canoe sweep toward the maelstrom.

With some close calls, we all make the pull-in and survey the beach, which is too small to house fourteen people for the night. So we trudge up the overgrown trail to a plateau littered with bear tracks and other spoor, and there pitch our tents. After dinner, the late sun heavy as molten lead, the team, sans guides, sets out to whack a way through a cheval-de-frise of boreal forest, up and down steep scree slopes, to reach the river in the midst of the Steps. It was here, in 1904, that Frank and Willie McLeod capsized their boat, made from two sluice boxes, carrying their booty after a season of gold panning, the beginnings of the curses of the Nahanni basin. The rapids look tough but navigable to me, and I wonder aloud why the half-mile portage, but the guides have made their decree. Instead of backtracking, we make a grati-fying hike along the river to the portage end, where we discover the missing yellow portage sign washed up against an island of broken logs and debris, now signaling a carry to those who might have already run the Steps. Back at camp, as we prepare for bed with the sun still hanging, John Blachford comes by and gives me an extra eyeshade he has found in his pack. I sleep like a bear.

Next morning, we make the long portage and once again launch downstream. The map shows the Flat narrowing in on the South Nahanni like one side of a V, and it appears Virginia Falls will be closest day after tomorrow, downstream of the Caribou Creek tributary. So at lunch I go over the map with the guides and ask about the hike the park superintendent had suggested. They just shake their heads, saying they have never heard of such a trail. There are a few tributaries that might be access points, but Jen does not recommend them, as "some people in the group could not make such a hard hike." I wonder whom she is refer-ring to. Certainly not John Blachford, who is the most experi-enced and one of the fittest of the group, age notwithstanding.

Everyone else in the group is quite able and fit as well, including several marathoners. Before I can protest, Jen calls to move, and we are soon weaving downstream toward the confluence.

That night, I corner our two accompanying park patrollers and ask if they can identify the passage their boss had promoted as a way to see Virginia from the Flat. In the implacable way of the North, they say they have never heard of such a thing and don't know a way. Then the guides join in the conversation, and I ask a barrage of questions. Can we hike up from the confluence?

"No. Too far."

"You said we were the first pickup of the day at our takeout. Could we use the sat phone and call the charter service and see if they might detour at trip's end and drop us above the falls for a quick hike to the viewpoint?"

"Unlikely. The Twin Otter is booked full this time of year."

"What about another air service? There were several advertising in the tourist brochures."

"Only two Fort Simpson planes have floats, the Otter and a Cessna 185, and both are booked."

"Could one pilot come early, before our scheduled pickup? I would pay extra." I am searching, a candle seeking oxygen.

"The pilots have lives; they want to sleep in their off-hours."

"But this is like hiking the Inca Trail and missing Machu Picchu," I remonstrate. "There must be a way."

They just shrug.

No matter the permutation I pitch, they come back that it is just not possible to see the falls on this trip.

"Could I hire a jet boat?"

"No, they aren't allowed, except the park service."

It is maddening, as I can see from the map we are just a few miles away. It appears there might be a route up Jorgenson Creek, named for Martin Jorgenson, found dead in his cabin by the stream in 1915, another curse victim. From there it appears it is a short tramp up over the watershed to Marengo Creek, which spills into the Nahanni near Virginia Falls. In fact, John Blachford had hiked up the Marengo on his last trip down the Nahanni in 1988, and he cottons to the idea of a reverse hike now that might get us to the falls. I beseech the guides, and at last they agree to stop at Jorgenson and evaluate the possibility. It shuts me up, and off to sleep I go.

The next day, our fourth on the Flat, we pull over for lunch and I ask about the Jorgenson tributary, which I estimate must be near.

Jamie lowers his face like a falcon swooping in on its prey: "We passed it."

"How could we pass it?"

"It was just a trickle, and we missed it." His words curve like a talon.

"Well," I continue, "there are other unnamed tributaries that might provide a route. In fact, I think we're near one . . . See this one on the map."

"It's the one right upstream,"

But I walk upstream and see it is not a tributary, but in fact just a channel of the main river exiting from an island.

"Well, it's downstream then. We'll stop," they assure.

So a while later we pull over at an overgrown gully with no water leading to an unassailable wall. By the simple expedient of standing still, the cliff dashes my hopes.

So off we push, and my mind keeps churning with endless combinations.

The final day on the Flat we pass within nine miles, as the crow flies, of Virginia Falls, and I eye potential routes, tracing paths up the hoodoos, fantastic limestone pillars fortifying the northern bank, but the guides, in contrivance with the geotyranny, nix any attempt.

At the confluence, where the deeper waters of the Nahanni swallow the Flat, I look upstream toward the Fourth Canyon. Just twelve miles to the northwest is Virginia Falls. But according to our guides, there is no path along the river or on top of the canyon, and the water is too powerful to negotiate a canoe upward.

So, the hot breath of defeat on my neck, I point the canoe down-stream. We are dropping into a land of legends and curses. One well known is the story of the two prospectors who had capsized at the Cascade-of-the-Thirteen-Steps, Willie and Frank McLeod. Their headless skeletons were found at the mouth of a small creek at the lower end of the Second Canyon. For a while, the South Nahanni River Valley became known as Headless Valley, and the incident also visited upon the geographic taxonomy the Funeral Range, Deadmen Valley, and Headless Creek.

As the fast waters of the Nahanni deliquesce into the Third Canyon, we suddenly hear a buzz, at first like an insistent mos-quito, but then it grows in volume. A plane? Then around the bend downstream it appears: a jet boat. The other canoes in our party move over to the south bank to let it pass, but I steer our canoe directly in front of its path and wave my silver aluminum paddle frantically.

The jet boat slows, and I can see the park service logo on the side and a handful of uniformed wardens inside.

"You okay?" one asks.

"Yes, fine. Are you going to Virginia Falls?" I yell.

"No. Just up to the Flat to a fuel drop, eh."

"Could I hire you guys to take me to the falls?"

"Can't hear you," the pilot yells and guns the engine to roar away upstream.

In a foul mood I float through the mixed strata of shales, sandstones, and limestones that made up the Funeral Range. I don't find solace in the belles-lettres renderings of this river: not in the grand scenery (in places the Nahanni basin combines the best of Yosemite and the Grand Canyon, without the crowds); not in the spectacular weather, which has showered us with sun for a week; not in the anodyne forests of alder, aspen, birch, fir, lodge-pole, poplar, and spruce; not in the wild strawberries, juicy blue-berries, and tart raspberries; not even in the wildlife—the moose, Dall sheep, and bears along the banks, the ospreys, hawks, and eagles in the air. At one rapid, the undernamed George's Riffle, when the guides tell us to run right, the safe route, with perfect equipoise Dave and I stitch a route down the left. When they say it is too difficult to hike up the dark slash of a slot canyon flushing with tributary water, I do anyway. When they insist we all stay together while traversing the final canyon, Dave and I hie out front, and recklessly capsize while hotdogging through an eddy fence. Then, one lunchtime, the guides gather the group to discuss logistics for the end of the trip, two days nigh. Beneath a solar flare of sweaty hair, Jamie announces he has called to South Nahanni Airways, and if weather permits, a Cessna 185 floatplane is available to pick three of us up at the takeout and drop us above the falls for a quick trip to the edge.

Hallelujah! At last. The falls are at hand. Our guides are saints. My mood leaps, and I volunteer to wash the dishes.

But that night, lenticular clouds move in, covering our camp like a marquee. At some point I hear the sharp report of a bear banger, the explosive device used to scare a too-close quadruped. But it isn't a bear banger—it's thunder. It roars and rolls all night, and with the dawn it is still raining, and clouds lock up the sky. Where for a week we had paddled in shorts and T-shirts, we now pull on wet suits and neoprene jackets and gloves, and paddle in the cold rain.

I am convinced, though, that the weather will clear, and continue to watch the pot of clouds as we channel-surf through an adagio of gravel bars and islands called the Splits. When we pull into the final camp at Nahanni Butte, at the confluence with the Liard River, the rain has stopped, and there are flashes of clear sky. I go to bed hopeful, optimistic.

Drops pelt the rain fly through the night, but by morning the skies are partially clear. Jamie had arranged to call the charter service at 9:00 a.m. to confirm it can bring the two planes in at 10:00. At 9:05, I hurry to Jamie to find what he has learned.

"The Twin Otter is on schedule. But the word is, Virginia Falls is completely socked in with fog. So the Cessna is not coming in."

These words put paid to my shot at seeing the falls. A figure that looks like a licorice stick in a rain suit approaches me. "Hey, you just gotta come back for another paddle," John Blachford says with a grin, his merry milk-blue eyes filled with the auroras of northern rivers run and the pied pipered lanterns of curses undone. I seal the goal, leaving Virginia as a manifestation of the unattainable, existing as a perpetual destination, or not at all.

When we land at Fort Simpson, I walk to the Visitor Information Centre and watch a 1962 National Film Board of Canada video of the late eremite Albert Faille hauling his homemade scow up the side of Virginia Falls. He seemed to barely notice the great falls, but instead focused on his own quest: finding gold in the Nahanni basin. He spent forty years negotiating up and down Virginia Falls and never found the gold.

The poet Bashō, in Edward Bond's play *Narrow Road to the Deep North,* returns from his dangerous northward pilgrimage in search of enlightenment, claiming to have found what he sought. And what was enlightenment? "I saw there was nothing to learn in the deep north . . . You get enlightenment where you are."

Satori seems a stretch in Fort Simpson, so to an Edmonton bar I head, to drink and play pool with John Blachford and the team, not sure if I would ever tap the spray of Virginia Falls, but then delighted with any journey that would try.

12

DOWN THE MIGHTY MO

The American West

Paint cannot touch it and words are wasted.
—Frederic Remington, describing Yellowstone

With the crinkly smile of someone cursed with an utterly satisfying career, Chester Kellen, seventy-eight, volunteers he has been "well paid. . . . in a nonmaterial sense" by his summer employer of forty-five years, the National Park Service, where he has been a Yellowstone backcountry ranger since 1960. In the winters, until retiring last year, he was a philosophy professor pondering the meaning of wilderness, which he loved and experienced deeply. He created a course, "The Philosophy of Wilderness," in which he concluded that too often we consider ecological systems in an anthropogenic way, as what happens in an environment arbitrarily defined by men, such as the boundaries of a park. And when we do such, we make incomplete decisions, such as whether and how to control wildfires, whether to reintroduce wolves and nonnative fish, whether to sanction snowmobiles, or how to determine the carrying capacity of internal-combustion-engined cars. "Until we understand the relationships between *all* ecosystems, locally and globally, inside our own human bodies, and externally, we aren't really dealing with wilderness . . . or anything else."

Then I show Chester our vehicle of conveyance to explore the park, a fresh-from-the factory Ford Escape Hybrid SUV, and he beams, as though we have moved a bit closer to achieving the ideal of an integrated ecosystem. "More than a million cars drive through Yellowstone each year," he states, standing in front of a monitor gauging air quality, "triple the number of when I started. This car" and he stoops to slide inside the hybrid, which is idling with the roar of a golf cart, "is the future."

And back to the future is this expedition. We're four on the road, looking for adventure and whatever comes our way. Our goal: to drive the length of the Missouri River, following for large portions the trail that Lewis and Clark pioneered 200 years ago, but in reverse (the Clark and Lewis Trail perhaps). And in a way we're pioneering as well, driving the first hybrid four-wheel-drive vehicle, the most ecologically friendly backcountry car in existence, down alongside America's longest river. It's a busman's holiday for this corps of rediscovery. Pasquale Scaturro recently returned from making the first full descent of the Blue Nile, from source to sea, and is intrigued with following America's counterpart, the Missouri. Didrik Johnck just got back from Tibet. Andrew Locke was covering stories in Macedonia and Vietnam. And I'm not long back from a trek in Libya the riverless, ready again for moving water. What better adventure for us than the Mighty Mo?

So, we begin our trek in Yellowstone, America's first and favorite national park, and the source of three of the primary feeder streams to the Missouri: the Gallatin, Madison, and Yellowstone. Joining us for the day is Jeremy Roberts, thirty, the staff naturalist at Papoose Creek Lodge, an upscale eco-lodge outside the park. Jeremy has been fascinated with the way Native

Americans lived in the Yellowstone region in the time of Lewis and Clark, and he carries a duffel bag of accoutrements he has fashioned from the era: a knife made of obsidian, moccasins crafted from moose hide, arrows with turkey feathers, a rock hammer held together with elk sinew and sap, and a little brain-tanned antelope-hide skirt for his twelve-week-old daughter. He is a man who celebrates the past and its more ecologically balanced life, and as we enter Yellowstone from the west entrance, he winces as we pass a line of cars parked on the side of the narrow road with a score of amateur paparazzi stepping into an adjacent field. They're pointing cameras at a bald eagle's nest about a hundred yards off the road, right beyond a large sign that says, "Don't Stop." It's a special management area, as the park doesn't want the mother eagle stressed with encroaching tourists. But a dozen or more just ignore the request and proceed in their private quest to shoot the great bird.

As it turns out, Jeremy has been taking photos for the past year of inappropriate behavior in the park, something he hopes to turn into a book. He has shots of folks dipping "chubby, Cheeto-flavored fingers" into hot springs in front of signs forbidding such. And shots of tourists stalking one-ton woolly headed, big-horned bison, who can run nearly twice as fast as a human and have been known to gore losers in such races. At the local bookstore, the salesman says the most popular tome in the park is *Death in Yellowstone: Accidents and Foolhardiness in the First National Park,* with graphic descriptions of those who fell over three-hundred-foot waterfalls, into two-hundred-degree pools, or ended up on the business end of a horn or antler.

Then on cue we round a corner and see a busload of tourists stepping through the grass toward a herd of elk. Jeremy jumps out of the hybrid and stalks the tourists, capturing more images for his book.

And fire management falls under the same hubris. On Black Saturday, August 20, 1988, red-wreathed fireballs enfiladed the lodgepole pines in one of the largest blazes in U.S. history. When the smoke settled, more than 1.4 million acres of Yellowstone country were burned. Jeremy has no love lost for Smokey Bear, blaming his "only you can prevent forest fires" mantra as a fatally incomplete consideration of interdependent ecosystems. He says the natural order in Yellowstone in the time before Lewis and Clark was high-frequency, low-intensity fires created by lightning, regularly burning small areas, fertilizing the soil, and generally keeping the land in check. But with national park designation, park officials reversed the order and decided to put a stop to most natural fires. That allowed combustible forest debris to gather in record ground layers, and when a series of bolts struck at the end of a dry summer, it set off a holocaust beyond imagining, doing more damage than all the small fires in millennia prior. But the worst "inappropriate behavior" in Jeremy's mind is that fire management policy, in the wake of the '88 fire, has not changed enough, and that the tinderbox is being fed again.

So we spend the day touring the surreal park, soaking in the splendor, looking past the blackened skeletons of lodgepoles to the high cliffs and cloud-wreathed peaks. It is the prevalent rhyolite, an eroded lava rock, that gives Yellowstone its name, though if the original trappers had seen the area after the '88 fire, it might today be called Blackwood National Park.

Yellowstone is the world's first national park, created in 1872, not many years after it was first seen by white eyes. It is land never farmed, ranched, or mined. The park's tourist potential saved it from development. Railroad executives looking for ways to expand their passenger base pressured Congress to set aside the land, arguing it useless in any other commercial way. High in the mountains, it was inaccessible and unfarmable, and no gold had been found in it. They pointed out America did not have Europe's cathedrals, castles, and cities, but it did have natural wonders, among them the geysers and "glass mountains" of Yellowstone. Congress set the land aside.

The railroad arrived eleven years later, bearing a trickle of tourists, who toured the geyser basin either on horseback or in stagecoaches. Now, 132 years later, more than 125 million people have visited Yellowstone, a rectangle of land stretching across Wyoming, Montana and Idaho. The area is sixty-three miles north to south and fifty-four miles east to west, bigger than Rhode Island and Delaware combined. And 90 percent of the three million people who enter the park each year never leave pavement or boardwalks.

We make the usual pilgrimages, to Lower Yellowstone Falls dropping into the golden Grand Canyon of the Yellowstone River; to Mammoth Hot Springs, Fort Yellowstone, Angel Terrace, Liberty Cape, Palette Springs. We hew by steaming vents, burping mud pots, bubbling fountains, and hissing fumaroles. While most parks are static gallery art—immutable mountain ranges or still lakes—Yellowstone is cinematic, ever moving, always reeling. It is one of the most geothermically active spots on earth, "a geological freak show," as Jeremy describes it—a continuing legacy of its violent volcanic origins. The most recent eruption, 640,000 years ago, spewed 240 cubic miles of debris. The park's central portion then collapsed, forming a thirty-by-forty-five-mile basin—a caldera—8,000 feet in elevation, through which we now trundle.

And along the way we find ourselves stuck in "bear jams" every mile or so as cars halt and pull over pell-mell whenever wildlife is to be seen off the road. A couple of times we inch past lines of idling cars and tourists with cameras and binoculars pointed to some middle distance, and we stretch necks and sweep the landscape for the attraction, but can see nothing. The only herds are the tourists. The nineteenth-century painter Thomas Moran said of Yellowstone, "Its beautiful tints were beyond the reach of human art," though today the candy-colored slickers and Patagucci vests contribute the primary hues dominating the roadside scenes.

At last, after a full day exploring the park, I need to heed nature's call. So we pull the hybrid over at a rare roadside quiet spot dense with vegetation, and I disappear to go see a man about a horse. When I return, a line of cars has parked in front and back of the hybrid, and crowds of people are out of their idling cars hunting for the shot of the animal I must have seen. I hop back in the car and quietly motor away to the open road.

SEEKING THE SOURCE

"Few have ever seen the true source of the Missouri, and nobody has ever filmed it." So says Tony Demetriades, the seventy-four-year-old Greek immigrant and former professor who has made a hobby of investigating the topic. That's enough to fuel our passions for a "first," so off we set out to see and videotape the utmost origins of the mighty river.

But what exactly is the source? Virtually all maps of the Missouri place the beginnings of the river at Three Forks, Montana, where three rivers conflue to create a larger stream that roils into the giant that reaches St. Louis. Lakes or bogs with central sections of nonmoving waters are generally cited, at least by engineers, as the sources of great rivers: Lake Victoria for the White Nile, the Bangweulu Swamps for the Congo, Lake Itasca for the Mississippi . . . though all have active feeder streams. Then there is the argument that the tributary with the most water should be the real source, such as the Blue Nile, which meets the White Nile in Khartoum to create the Nile proper. The Blue is the shorter stream, but it carries 80 percent of the water.

Tony gives us his take on the issue: "The length of a river is the farthest distance a molecule of water must travel to reach the river's mouth, and the source of the river is where that molecule begins its journey."

Of course, Lewis and Clark were supposed to follow the Missouri River to its source in their attempt to find an all-water route to the Pacific Ocean, but by Tony's estimation they missed it by a hundred miles. When they arrived at Three Forks in July of 1805, the Corps of Discovery correctly chose to head up the largest stream, the Jefferson. From there, they followed the Beaverhead south to its junction with two other streams, Horse Prairie Creek, coming from the west, and the Red Rock River from the south. There, Lewis made the decision that made history. Since their goal was to cross the Rockies and find the Columbia River, which then rolled west to the Pacific, they chose the western running course, Horse Prairie Creek, and hiked up toward the Continental Divide. Soon the creek became so small that Private Hugh McNeal put one foot on each side and later wrote that he "thanked God that he had lived to bestride the mighty and heretofore deemed endless Missouri." Two miles up the mountain, they came to a tiny font that was the creek's first seep, and Lewis wrote in his journal that they had reached "the most distant fountain of the waters of the mighty Missouri in surch of which we have spent so many toilsome days and wristless nights." But Lewis was wrong. The ultimate cradle of the Missouri was up the Red Rock River, which in turn is fed by Hell Roaring Creek, which issues from a hole on the subalpine flanks of Sawtell Peak. The ironic justice, though, is that had Lewis and party gone to the proper source, they might not have succeeded in their quest to reach the Pacific. As it was, they hiked up beyond Horse Prairie Creek along a Native American trail to cross Lemhi Pass, where they were able to secure Shoshone horses that allowed them to proceed through the mountains in winter. If they had gone up the southern stream, they might never have found the horses and been forced to turn back.

It was ninety-one years later that Jacob Brower, an archaeologist from Minnesota, published *The Missouri River and Its Utmost Source,* which describes how he bushwhacked up Hell Roaring Creek to the farthest point of running water from the Missouri's mouth. Beyond a small lake, he wrote, "we suddenly came in full view of a hole in the summit of the Rocky Mountains" from which issued a "little rivulet, two feet wide and scarcely two inches in depth, drawing its utmost supply from the inner walls of the mighty and towering uplifts surrounding it."

There is little record of visitation to the source for nearly a century thereafter, until in the late 1980s a couple of adventurers made the remote trek and built a rock cairn and left a glass jar with a note of their visit. The few who have followed since have also left notes in what is now known as the Sacred Jar of the Missouri.

Today Tony Demetriades lives on Hell Roaring Creek in the Centennial Valley with his wife, Donna, not far below the source, which was originally determined with tape measures, but has been confirmed now with satellite mapping and GPS. Still, some continue to argue the source is somewhere different, and Tony has made a pursuit of proving otherwise with academic precision. Most who travel to the source do so by climbing up Hell Roaring Creek, past Tony's property, but it is a tough three-mile uphill trek. As Pasquale goes over the maps with Tony, he asks about dropping down from a service road on the side of Sawtell Peak; it would be about half the distance.

So first we whisper up to the 9,866-foot-high summit of Sawtell Peak in our hybrid and step over to the edge of the Continental Divide. I take a sip of water from my bottle, and, staggering with the view, spill a few drops, half of which head down toward the Snake River, to the Columbia and the Pacific, while the other half head down the Missouri to the Gulf of Mexico and the Atlantic. Then, with a can of bear spray in a day pack, and several bottles of water, using GPS waypoints, we ambush our way down into a spruce- and pine-rimmed glacial cirque, sliding down volcanic scree of olivine basalt, scrambling over volcanic tuff, skirting past fireweed, lupine, Indian paintbrush, and Queen Anne's lace.

At 1:28 in the afternoon, after hiking for 3.99 kilometers, we drop over a burnished ledge and find a trickle oozing from the dark, igneous sand: the ultimate source of the Missouri, which combines with the Mississippi to constitute the third-longest river in the world (after the Nile and Amazon). Pasquale has now been to sources of three major rivers, the Blue Nile, the Congo, and now this; I've also been to the font of the Ganges, so I count four. But neither claims the enlightenment that some aver comes with such pilgrimages. Although others who have been here apparently have. We find the Sacred Jar, twist open its rusted top, and survey its contents. There are seven pieces inside, including one 1993 entry that declares, "This is Holy Ground." There is a prayer, and a poem about the sacredness of the spot. There is a photocopy of the map to the source from Jacob Brower's 1896 book. There is a note from John R. La Randeau of the Army Corps of Engineers that nontranscendentally states stats: the GPS coordinates, the elevation at 8,809 feet, and the elegiac phrase "source is 2619.4 miles from St. Louis."

Then there is a wallet-sized photograph of Scott Soderquist marked "my one-year-old grandson," and a pay stub for $32.58 from "Your Car Wash" in Kenosha, Wisconsin. We each sign a piece of paper, date it, and stuff it into the Sacred Jar. We then photograph and videotape the source waters, supposedly creating the first film record of such. Then Pasquale fills an empty bottle with source water, water we intend to carry to the mouth.

But as Pasquale places the jar back into the cairn, a rock slips and crashes into the glass, shattering it into pieces. Pasquale broke the Sacred Jar! Suddenly dark clouds gather, the earth begins to grumble and shake, the springs dry up, and a giant boulder perched above begins to roll toward us. Just kidding. Nothing happens but guilt. We take one of our Lexan water bottles and replace the contents in what we tell ourselves, with gallons of cognitive dissonance, is a better vessel anyway.

A few hours later, we rendezvous at Tony's home and tell him the tales. Over cheap but immensely satisfying Rhine wine he congratulates us for finding the source, but then cautions, "When you go home, tell nobody about how beautiful it is." Even though he has written persuasively that the source is just above his thousand-acre farmstead, he doesn't want hordes of amateur explorers traipsing through his little piece of Montana paradise to get there. So the word from this correspondent: Don't even think about it. It's dreadfully unattractive, and the environment is hostile. Better to go to Yellowstone. Or over the Lemhi Pass, the way Lewis and Clark went.

SEARCHING FOR SACAGAWEA

Carrying the sacred Missouri source water in a Nalgene bottle in a rucksack, we make our way to the Old Anderson Place, a modern cabin on the nine-thousand-acre J Bar L Ranch in the heart of the Centennial Valley. A river runs through it, the Red Rock, which also is carrying the source water down from Hell Roaring Creek. We're confident our water will reach the Mississippi first, though, as the Mighty Mo is now emasculated with nearly two dozen dams, and the great age of the once free-flowing river is now lost to irrigation and evaporation.

Well, maybe not. We want to label the bottle so nobody mistakenly drinks it during our journey, so Andrew pulls the bottle from the pack, as Pasquale finds a marker. But then Andrew reaches into the pack a second time, and pulls out a second, identical water bottle . . . uh-oh. One of the bottles carries water from the Papoose Creek Lodge, where we stayed the night before, and it looks exactly the same, limpid and shiny. We taste the contents of the two bottles, thinking the source might have a more mineral tang, but they are indistinguishable. We sniff the two waters, but discern no difference. Should we mix the two to ensure that at least some of the source water makes it? But then Andrew holds both bottles above his head against the sun and sees little particles of black, volcanic sand swimming at the base of one. That indeed is the source water, and we're back on mission.

We then wind our way downstream, to the Beaverhead River (Sacagawea told Lewis and Clark the Shoshone thought a promontory rock above the river looked like the head of an aquatic rodent, but to us it looks more like a giant Rodin) and onto the Jefferson, and then to where it joins the Gallatin and Madison at Three Forks, Montana, to create, without ceremony, what is officially known as the Missouri River.

It is a completely arbitrary designation set by Lewis and Clark when faced with which stream to ascend to reach the westernmost pass over the Rockies. They had encountered similar situations before, coming to forks of seemingly equal volume, such as the Yellowstone and Marias, but chose one and knighted it the Missouri. But here, knowing where their bread was buttered, they named the branches after Secretary of State James Madison, Treasury Secretary Albert Gallatin, and "the author of our enterprise," President Jefferson.

Three Forks is also noted as the spot where a prepubescent Sacagawea was kidnapped by Hidatsa warriors five years before the Corps of Discovery arrived, right across from the Sacajawea Hotel on Main Street, where patrons can imagine the ghosts of Native American wars while rocking on chairs along a white double-columned porch. The town, on the fringe of "celebrity Montana" to the south, is somewhat obsessed with Sacagawea, even promoting the Sacagawea dollar as the official currency. It seems astonishing that despite the prodigious powers of description Lewis and Clark possessed, and how critical Sacagawea was to the success of the expedition, neither ever described what the young mother looked like. So it has been up to generations since to imagine the Shoshone teenager, and when we stop into the Headwaters Heritage Museum, housed in a former bank at the southeast corner of Main and Cedar, we find dozens of creative renditions, from a Hollywood-style mannequin to dolls with chubby cheeks. However she appeared, it is widely acknowledged that her presence with her infant on the expedition signaled to wary and potentially hostile Native Americans en route that Lewis and Clark were not a war party and thus allowed safe passage.

We make a short drive to Headwaters State Park, where we watch the three rivers flow in twists and turns through a rolling, grass-covered valley. Here, we meet Larry Clark, who claims Mormon church-verified lineage to William Clark, and who in retirement casts lines every day along his favorite watershed. "I've caught my limit every day for the past month," he chimes while turning off his cell phone and readying his rod. "Best fishin' in the world." He's convincing in his enthusiasm, so we decide to go fishing.

We hook up with Montana River Outfitters and by drift boat head down the Wolf Creek Canyon section of the Missouri, legendary for its big brown and rainbow trout. The river purls past palace rocks and celebrated holes, and our guide, Neil Streeks, fifty, who has been spinning flies and lies here for twenty-five years, works the water like a concert pianist. In our two-hour float, Neil catches the only trout, an eight-inch rainbow weighing perhaps a third of a pound, but he's more sanguine than we are: "If it seems small, hold it closer to your eyes." He knows he'll be back tomorrow, yet we are heading downstream to a different Missouri.

Late in the day, we arrive at the Great Falls of the Missouri. When Lewis and Clark arrived here in mid-June 1805 they found eighteen miles of rapids with five major waterfalls. "The grandest sight I had ever beheld," Lewis wrote of his first glimpse. "When my ears were saluted with the agreeable sound of a fall of water, advancing a little further I saw the spray arise above the plain like a column of smoke which would frequently disappear again in an instant—which soon began to make a roaring too tremendous to be mistaken for any cause short of the great falls of the Missouri."

Today, the Great Falls are just a trickle a few inches wide dribbling over naked rock, as a series of hydrodams built in the early 1900s divert the water around the natural drops, robbing Montana of a world-class scenic wonder. Lewis and Clark spent a punishing month portaging around these cataracts. It takes us fifteen minutes in our hybrid.

We end the day at Fort Benton, once the most-inland port in the world, as steamboats came all the way from New Orleans to trade whiskey and tobacco for buffalo and beaver pelts and gold. The railroads, of course, turned this and other river entrepôts to shadows of their late-nineteenth-century brilliance. Its riverside hotel, the Grand Union, was once the finest between Minneapolis and Seattle, but it closed in the 1950s and was boarded up for fifteen years. It's been lovingly restored by Jim and Cheryl Gagnon

and is once again a showcase along the upper Missouri, though
it may be haunted. My room is atop the second-floor stairwell,
where a cowboy on a drunken bet rode his horse and was shot
dead by the clerk. But it's outside that I see ghosts. As the sunset paints the hills with a honey light, I squint upstream and
see a voyager canoe heading my way. It looks as though a party
of Blackfoot is paddling downriver, intentions unknown. They
could just as easily open fire as offer to trade. If only Sacagawea
were here, I fancy. But as the canoe passes, I see the happy pink
faces of tourists, who wave at me and beckon. I'm tempted to dive
in and swim over to immerse in what from the bending distance
of today seems a more romantic era, though Lewis and Clark,
hungry, fearful, and tired when they camped here, would likely
not agree.

BREAKING THE MISSOURI

Some in these parts think the most profound act of the Clinton
administration was declaring the 149 miles of the Missouri River
downstream from Fort Benton to James Kipp Park a national
monument, an act made in the second-to-last day of Clinton's
presidency, about the same time he pardoned Marc Rich, and to
some Montanans equally controversial.

But standing by the Missouri at first light, I am thankful for
this stream's protection. It is almost too beautiful to behold. The
light on the river, neither moonlight nor dawn, is a commingling
of both, luminous as a pearl. Downstream it stretches, broad and
smooth, sweeping around a vast elbow and disappearing into the
mists of history.

I can't resist the pull of this river, so off we go to canoe the
Upper Missouri National Wild and Scenic section, past the scenery that perhaps inspired Lewis and Clark more than any other.
"These hills and river cliffs exhibit the most extraordinary and
romantic appearance. They rise in most places nearly perpendic-
ular from the water, to a height of between 200 and 300 feet, and
are formed of very white sandstone into a thousand grotesque

figures, among which with a little fancy, may be discerned elegant ranges of freestone buildings, with columns variously sculptured," Lewis wrote as they pulled and poled their own canoes upriver.

We hook up with Craig Madsen, a native Montanan who has been guiding the upper Missouri since 1977. A few years before, he had returned from a stint in the military and took an Outward Bound course, where he was surprised and delighted to discover that people actually made a living as guides, and he set about that goal, then never looked back.

Craig takes us on his twenty-five-foot-long replica of a voyager canoe, a craft the Blackfoot (Black*feet* is not the plural, I'm told by historian John Lepley, the executive director of the River and Plains Society in Fort Benton) paddled two centuries ago. As we drive the broken high plains to the put-in, Craig pats his companion, Homer, a springer spaniel, who yelps with excitement with the prospect of being on the river. I feel the same way.

The Breaks and the surrounding treeless prairie were once the haunts of not only the buffalo-hunting Blackfoot, but also Assiniboin and Crow tribes, all of whom used the maze of fissures as hideouts and ambush points in the wars with the white men.

Later, this stretch of the Missouri was the water highway of the mountain men, the fur trappers who manhandled their pirogues upstream to reach the Rocky Mountain beaver country. Rustlers, whiskey traders, and notorious outlaws including Butch Cassidy, the Sundance Kid, and Kid Curry found refuge here, as do we now.

We put in to paddle the White Cliffs section and glide with the fast currents down past hoodoos and dikes, yellow cottonwoods and cacti. We flit and sally past grassy hills, wooded bottomlands, sandstone pinnacles, sere badlands, and a procession of remote Lewis and Clark campsites. A big-bodied mule deer with a broad, sweeping rack steps up a labyrinthine side canyon; a golden eagle rounds the updrafts; a rock pigeon cries down a gully. We're in the heart of the Missouri Breaks, where deep, fractured coulees snake up into the high bluffs and shattered hills beyond the riverbanks. We pass Eagle Butte, Hole-in-the-Wall, and the dark, igneous Citadel Rock, a signpost for steamboat captains in the 1860s. But though these landmarks have names, it all seems as uncharted now as then. Lewis marveled at these "scenes of visionary enchantment." And he would do the same today. While most of the Missouri would be unrecognizable to Lewis and Clark were they to reincarnate on their bicentennial—Portland, for one thing, did not exist—they would feel at era here. Nothing, not anything has changed. Wherever we look, we can see no sign of man or man's works, just wilderness as it has existed for millennia, and wilderness now preserved.

In the years just prior to World War I and continuing through the 1920s, thousands who had never handled a plow or seen the hindquarters of a horse flocked here in search of agrarian dreams. But poor soils, brutal cold, extreme heat, hail, hoppers, and drought sent the homesteaders reeling in defeat. Today, both the "wild and scenic" and "national monument" designations prevent any development along the river corridor, even in those overlooks where a scenic hotel would draw the jet set. One of the few who has private land along this stretch is Mike Arnst, whose family has scratched out a living growing wheat and barley on their 8,000-acre parcel for generations. Today, Mike runs Eagle Buttes Adventures, which takes folks hiking through the picturesque pieces of his land. He's hoping where farming has failed, tourism might succeed, especially with rising interest in following in the moccasin-steps of Lewis and Clark.

Now the canoe and its sharp bow-point bevel the river past rock polished like monument stone, past parapets, pedestals, and pyramids, past long, black rows, sometimes a hundred feet high, of horizontal rocks stacked like bricks. Steep, eroded cliffs gouged by the river plummet a thousand feet from the canyon rim, revealing 10 million years of geologic history. In places, epochs of wind and rain have washed away the sediments, exposing massive rock crags and fantastic castles of dazzling white sandstone looming high above the river. It is staggeringly beautiful. It feels as if we're in an oversized diorama, or in the middle of an IMAX film. Everything is exaggerated, the colors more brilliant than enhanced photos or HDTV.

In the midst of this revelry, there is a clap of thunder. Looking up I see the underbelly of great, gray frigate clouds, and higher still a sky nearly black, pulling into nothingness. This is indeed the Big Sky, even in the confines of this canyon.

At the takeout, the sun again peeks through, sizzling like a jacklight. As I climb back into the hybrid, I turn back to look at the river, which wools along like a slumbering mammoth. Time for a moment seems absent. Trees, grasses, white bands of high rock, warm yellow sands, the river itself are all becalmed as in the eye of a storm, living in the warmth of the sun with neither history nor tomorrows. Then suddenly a boil swirls over the quiet surface, then bursts and subsides like a sigh. It is time to move on, time to steer toward a Missouri of impoundment, of long, thin reservoirs and big schemes. Time to roll down the once mighty river once again.

CSI: Malta

On the south side of US 2 in Malta, Montana, there is a converted tire shop where the past is being unearthed. It is the Dinosaur Field Station and headquarters to the Judith River Dinosaur Institute, both brainchilds of Nate Murphy, the "people's paleontologist." Nate, who has severe dyslexia, never got his doctorate . . . nor his master's, nor bachelor's degree. And some overly degreed academics in the field look down noses at the undoctor. But he's been a fossil hound since he was ten, in 1967. He is the most unabashedly enthusiastic evangelist for the art and science of paleontology above or below this earth. And he's made some undeniably impressive and important finds.

We meet Nate Murphy in the bar of the Great Northern Hotel

in Malta, which, like some in the archaeological sciences, has an appellation bigger than its actuality. The railroad inn is really little more than a motel, but it does have the first high-speed wireless connectivity we've encountered on this trip, due, we're told, to the number of well-funded dino diggers who come to town. Before the first beer, Nate produces a long, black, serrated, scimitar-shaped potato peeler. It's a T. rex tooth, he informs, one of sixty in a typical set. Nate reports that a full-grown tyrannosaurus could swallow one hundred fifty pounds of flesh in a bite. It turns out Spielberg's Jurassic renderings were likely close to reality, with one huge error, according to Nate: "Remember when the T. rex, the greatest predator that ever lived, chomps the lawyer in two? Would never happen. Professional courtesy."

I ask the adolescent question that piques most Michael Crichton readers: Could we extract dinosaur DNA and bring them back? "Well, imagine a spiral staircase one hundred thousand miles high, and we're missing eighty thousand miles' worth. It ain't gonna happen while we're around," Nate says with a twinkle.

Like Nate, Thomas Jefferson was an avid paleontologist without formal training, and when he gave his instructions to Lewis and Clark in 1803 to explore the Missouri, he asked that they look for and bring back fossils. In the spring of 1805, they passed the tributary river Clark named Judith, after a young woman he fancied back home who happened to be his cousin and who became the future Mrs. Clark, but they never ventured up the turgid stream, passing perhaps one of the finest dinosaur fossil beds in the world.

It's here that in 2000 Nate found Leonardo, a seventy-seven-million-year-old, mummified brachylophosaurus (duckbill), entered into *Guinness World Records* as the "best-preserved dinosaur" specimen discovered to date.

The next morning, we take the block-long "trek" to Nate's Dinosaur Field Station, where he and his volunteer assistant and bone preparator, Rhonda Suggs, clean, prepare, and place pieces in giant fossil jigsaw puzzles. He first shows off Roberta, a perfectly articulated duckbill he found here in Phillips County two years ago. The key to being a good fossil, Nate shares, is being buried quickly in the right position in the right environment, such as when a creature stumbles into a tar pit. Most animals when felled are either picked apart by scavengers or cleaved and bleached away by weather and erosion, so that when unearthed after a hundred million years or so there are but pieces of the whole.

"To find one articulated specimen in an entire career is like hitting the Powerball," Nate says. "One tenth of one percent of all dinosaurs discovered are well articulated," meaning all the bones and pieces are intact and in place. "And I've found five," he boasts.

Nate gives us a tour of Roberta, pointing out her stomach. Her last meal consisted of ferns, conifers, magnolia, and thirty-six other species of plants. "The brachylophosaurus was the ultimate Cretaceous Cuisinart, a Cretaceous cow, so to speak."

Then he moves on to point out Roberta's broken bill and pronounces the likely cause of death as starvation. "How do you know the sex?" I ask, wondering why his finds have names of both genders.

"Must be a male," Rhonda calls from across the room. "Brain the size of a peanut."

"It's still a mystery," Nate gives the more scholarly answer. "We just name the fossils for the inspiration at the moment, male or female."

We spend a couple of hours wandering around rooms crammed with five hundred specimens, listening to tapes of imagined dinosaur sounds, gawking at bones and dinosaur eggs, and trying to imagine the arc of time represented. A fossil of a thirty-foot-long marine crocodile (*Terminonaris cretaceous*) is 110 million years old. Ralph, a new species of long-necked sauropod, hails from the Jurassic period, 150 million years ago or more.

One set of bones, that of a subadult hadrosaur, has a big chunk missing from his pelvis. "What happened here?" I ask.

"Attacked by a T. rex," Nate chimes back with merry eyes. "Probably tasted like chicken."

At the end of the tour, he allows us to step into his negative air chamber (basically a vacuum cleaner that sucks out the dust) and view up close and personal "the rosetta stone of paleontology": Leonardo. The twenty-two-foot-long duckbill is in perfect shape; he's all there and looks as though he's about to get up from a rest and skitter away. He's also the prime draw at the field station, and the viewing and educational fees are the prime source of income that keeps Nate's work going. Because he doesn't have a PhD, Nate says, he can't qualify for academic or public funding; he can't dig on public lands, and has to make deals with private landowners when out hunting bones. But it's almost as though a lifetime of studying extinct species has given Nate a special perspective on his own place in the cosmology of bone collectors. He tells us 99.9 percent of all things that ever lived on this earth are now extinct. "It's a natural thing, extinction." So the academic shrugs and slights in this blink of time don't seem to matter. He's happy to keep on digging, pursuing his boyhood passion along a meandering tributary of the Missouri. And as we step into the sunlight of the present, he throws on his brimmed explorer's hat, hops into a truck with the license plate "BONEMAN," and heads off toward the field for another dig.

Bully for the Badlands

When on April 12, 1805, the Corps of Discovery reached the confluence of the Missouri and the Little Missouri, William Clark shot a hare, noted that the smaller river had the same texture, color, and quality of the Big Missouri, and made a journal entry that one of his men, Baptiest, who had made an earlier forty-five-mile descent down the Little Mo, proclaimed it "not navigable." They then proceeded up the Missouri and never made mention again of the lesser stream issuing from black mountains and "a broken country."

We, however, turn our hybrid south, following the Little

Missouri upstream, and head into the heart of the North Dakota Badlands, and the Theodore Roosevelt National Park, one of the few parks in the system that tourists stay away from in droves, perhaps thankfully so.

At first the road is like a suture line dividing two dimensions and colors, brown sage flats and blue sky. But as we approach the park, the land begins to spread in shelves, in ripples, in straggling eaves. The road, no longer level, looks like an infected scratch across the weathered skin of the plateau, curvilinear in some places, sharply angled in others. It is a lacerated, folding landscape, creased with cream-colored chasms, at the bottom of which streaks of water flash—the Little Missouri River.

North Dakota is the country's least-visited state, undeservedly so, but a blessing for those who make the trek. As we drive the fourteen-mile road through Theodore Roosevelt National Park, North Unit (the two unconnected units are seventy miles apart, an unusual concept in the system), we pass a medley of multicolored buttes and twisted ravines and herds of one-ton bison that think nothing of striding right in front of the hybrid, all without the traffic jams and engine noise of Yellowstone. Lewis wrote that the buffalo of North Dakota were "so gentle that we passed near them while feeding without appearing to excite any alarm among them, and when we attract their attention they frequently approach us more nearby to discover what we are." And despite the near extinction of the bison throughout the Great Plains of America, in this park we had the same interspecies experience as Lewis and Clark.

Theodore Roosevelt found this austere and scrambled country to his liking following the deaths of his wife and mother on the same day in 1884 and fled New York for the ranching life before returning to politics. He loved the open space, the ruggedness, the remoteness. He hunted bison, learned to herd cattle through the labyrinthine terrain, and got into fisticuffs in saloons.

He told his sister Corrine he was living out a dream: "We

are so rarely able to, actually and in real life, dwell in our 'hero land.'" Roosevelt became the country's twenty-sixth chief of state in 1901 and later wrote, "I never would have been president if it had not been for my experiences in North Dakota."

Chinked by time, just like the land, we continue down the road toward the South Unit, through the Little Missouri National Grassland, a million acres of emptiness. Late in the day, just off Interstate 94, we exit to the wooden boardwalks and framed buildings of Medora, and check into the two-story Rough Riders Hotel, where supposedly Teddy himself slept. The founder of the town, the Marquis de Mores, a French nobleman seeking a New World fortune, once challenged Roosevelt to a duel, and as the Marquis was the better shot, if the challenge had been accepted history might have been written quite differently. Now Medora, tucked beneath a towering bluff and gussied in frontier dress, is owned and run by a nonprofit foundation. It's a bit like a western version of Williamsburg, or perhaps the place Patrick McGoohan was corralled in the classic TV show *The Prisoner,* with the ghost of Teddy Roosevelt looming large. It has about two hundred permanent residents, but brings in more than one hundred twenty thousand visitors each summer, mostly to see *The Medora Musical,* a costumed stage production featuring a singing Theodore Roosevelt, the single most popular tourist draw in the state. We're past the season for the famed musical, so we decide to sample the other offerings—mountain biking and golf.

We join up with Jennifer Morlock, forty-seven, co-owner with her husband of Dakota Cyclery Mountain Bike Adventures, and go rough-riding on the Maah Daah Hey Trail. In 1994, the foundation invited the Morlocks, who had a prosperous bike enterprise in Bismarck, to open shop in Medora, rent-free in the center of town. They drank the Kool-Aid, and decided to move west and make Medora home. "It's too addictive to give up," Jennifer tells us. In 1999, the Forest Service christened the 120-mile hiking, biking, and equestrian trail that runs inside, outside, and next to the two units of the park "Maah Daah Hey." The name comes from the Mandan language, meaning "an area that has been or will be around for a long time." In its short existence, the trail has already been ranked as among the top in the country.

We saddle up and ride toward the pass that George Armstrong Custer crossed on his way to Little Big Horn. He described the area we now wheel as "Hell with the fires burned out," though it seems paradisiacal to us. We spin up and down a foot-wide single track in landscapes not dissimilar to the slickrock trails outside of Moab, Utah, but without the flocks of fat tires. The early French explorers called these bewildering and seemingly endless varieties of landforms "mauvaises terres à traverser," or "bad lands to cross," but they are good to us, and we're tempted to move to Medora. Perhaps there was something in the buffalo steak last night.

We continue our undaunted bike tour to the afternoon and then check out the latest foundation offering, the Bully Pulpit Golf Course. In the midst of the bone-dry badlands, with bleached buttes and naked pinnacles that break the sky, sits a tableau of bright green grass, and eighteen holes. It's a sight as bizarre as the landscape, but in the spirit we take up seven irons and slice balls across the canyons toward the emerald island fairways. Most of our balls fall into cactus beds or dusty gulches. Perhaps we should have used the eight irons. Were Teddy Roosevelt around today, tooling softly about on an electric cart through his "hero land," he might have carried a bigger stick of a different sort.

ANY FORT IN A STORM

Lewis and Clark slept here . . . 146 times. About twelve miles upriver of what is today Bismarck, North Dakota, the Corps of Discovery spent the most time they did at any stop on their three-year expedition as they wintered, in brutally cold conditions, from October 1884 to April 1885 after the first leg of the expedition. Now between these banks runs the last original reach of the Missouri River, seventy meandering miles bookended by two dams.

It was then the end of the known world. After a frigid winter, Lewis and Clark sent their keelboat back to St. Louis and prepared to head upstream to uncharted waters in six cottonwood canoes and two pirogues. Upon leaving Fort Mandan on April 7, 1805, Lewis wrote: "We were now about to penetrate a country at least 2,000 miles in width, on which the foot of civilized man had never trodden."

We arrive at the upper end of this reach, just beneath the gates of the Garrison Dam holding back Lake Sakagawea, and make our way to the Missouri River Lodge, on a 2,000-acre ranch owned by Orville and Diane Oster. Like several along the upper Missouri River who have barely scratched a living off the land in recent years, they decided to open their modest home to tourists to supplement their income. But for Orville, it is something more as well, as he is a true Lewis and Clark history buff and can recite entire journal passages with a cue. I ask if he can find an entry from when Lewis and Clark camped by a tributary, and in an instant he's pulled the passage from his shelf and laid it on the table. He's especially proud that Lewis and Clark not only camped on his property, but also recorded three separate entries, and he's posted signposts for such. The upcoming spring will be the 200th anniversary of Lewis and Clark on Orville's property, and I ask if he is booked full, what with the countless Lewis and Clark enthusiasts retracing steps. "Nah," he comes back. "We're kinda outta the way. And April is too iffy for weather round here. It might snow. Even Stephen Ambrose didn't venture out here."

After four-wheeling about the property on one of the ranch's golf carts, I head to my room to unpack and notice a flyswatter on the desk, not something I've seen in many hotel rooms in my travels. There are no insects about, and the weather is sublime, as it has been throughout the journey. North Dakota has a reputation for severe weather, but it's been sunny and eighty-five degrees for our forays.

At dusk we're called to a home-cooked meal in the unassuming Oster dining room, and I make an error that would have deserved fifty lashes a couple of centuries ago. I leave the door to my bedroom open with the light on. When I return, there are at least five hundred flies buzzing about the bedroom. Lewis described the insects along this stretch as worse than the curses of Egypt, and my bedroom was now the synecdoche of that blight. I spend the next ninety minutes vainly trying to swat them away and finally collapse in exhaustion, the job just half done. Then a deep-throated thunder begins to peal above, and the bed begins to vibrate, like Magic Fingers. Mine was one rough night; Lewis and Clark spent five months camped in this reach.

Still scratching and reeling from too little sleep, I head out with our corps next morning for Washburn and the North Dakota Lewis & Clark Interpretive Center, featuring a reproduction of Fort Mandan in a cottonwood grove near the river. The original fort was picked apart for firewood, or burned down, or washed away. Nobody knows. But the replica, pieced together from descriptions, feels almost too real. The weather has turned, and it is pouring rain, so we seek shelter in the various fourteen-by-fourteen-foot rooms of the fort, where up to nine men slept as it got down to minus 45°F—in the winter of 1804. There are small stone fireplaces in each room, and we huddle by the flames as Kevin Kirkey, thirty-five, the interpretive coordinator for the fort, looking genuinely cold in period dress, describes the simple and severe life in the triangular-shaped fort for the thirty-three young soldiers.

He also tells us that not far from here, on the Knife River just upstream, Lewis and Clark made an encounter that may have been the most important to the success of the expedition.

When casting about for a translator, they met Toussant Charbonneau, a French Canadian trapper and trader who lived with Native Americans at what was the original Mall of America, the trading center for the major tribes of the West. When Lewis and Clark arrived, there were more Native Americans living along this stretch than people in St. Louis or Washington, DC. Charbonneau told Lewis and Clark they would need to negotiate with the Shoshones for horses to successfully cross the Rocky Mountains. He, as fortune would have it, had two Shoshone wives; one, Sacagawea, he had married only a year before when she was fourteen. Of the two, she had been captured more recently and could be of invaluable assistance in obtaining horses. Charbonneau was hired and chose Sacagawea, although large with child at the time, to accompany him.

Once selected, Sacagawea and her husband moved from the Native American village into Fort Mandan to live with the members of the corps. When the time came, Lewis became the midwife. But he had nothing among his pills for easing childbirth. A Native American told Lewis to crush the rattle of a snake and have Sacagawea drink it. Thus they did, and on February 11, 1805, the babe was born. His father named him Jean Baptiste Charbonneau, but Sacagawea called him Pomp, which meant "firstborn" in her birth language.

And so, in April, the expedition again headed upstream with a conspicuous papoose in the back, a sign to the warriors along the way: Baby on Board.

Sacagawea spoke Hidatsa and Shoshone, but not English. Her husband spoke French and Hidatsa. Between them, they were sort of a translation team. Sacagawea would negotiate with the Shoshone in their language. Then she would translate that to her husband in Hidatsa. He, in turn, would translate that into French, and convey it to expedition member Francois Labiche, who spoke French and English. Labiche would make the final translation so that the two English-speaking captains could understand.

When the Corps of Discovery returned to the Mandan villages in August 1806, William Clark asked Charbonneau to let the boy continue on to St. Louis with him. He offered to raise the boy as his own, to see that he received proper schooling and learned the white man ways. The offer was turned down because Pomp, barely eighteen months old, was still being breast-fed. But Charbonneau promised "later" and, indeed, six years later, he delivered his son to Clark, who by then had married Judith (of Judith River) and was serving as superintendent of Indian affairs for Upper Louisiana.

True to his word, Clark had Pomp educated by Catholic and Baptist missionaries. When he was eighteen, Pomp met Prince Paul Wilhelm of Württemberg, Germany, at the mouth of the Kansas River (present-day Kansas City). The German offered to become Pomp's patron. So the half-breed went to Europe and spent six years as a guest of the Royal Court.

When Pomp returned to America in 1829, at age twenty-four, he had acquired a cultural polish and spoke English, French, German, Spanish, and numerous Native American languages. He traveled extensively, hunting, trapping, trading, guiding, and exploring. He rode with infamous frontiersmen, including Jim Bridger and Kit Carson, and traveled with John C. Fremont, whom I once doubled for in a television miniseries. He served as a scout and guide in the Mexican War (1846–48), leading troops from New Mexico to California. Later, he was appointed alcalde, or mayor, of San Luis Rey Mission.

But as it was for his parents, the call of the mountains, and the mother lode, was irresistible, and Pomp resigned his post and lit out for the California gold fields. He didn't strike it rich, and in 1861 found himself working as a hotel desk clerk in the foothills of the Sierras, where I once lived and sampled drams at every old saloon and perchance touched the same oak bar as he, my closest encounter, perhaps, with the ghosts of the Lewis and Clark expedition.

DANCES WITH DESCENDANTS

The ghosts of Lewis and Clark have tapped our shoulders throughout our journey down the Missouri, but this is something else altogether.

As we check into our riverside hotel in Chamberlain, South Dakota, I look out the window and see a man with a fox fur cap and fringed buckskin sipping a beer and eating a slice of pizza on the lawn near the waterfront. Then another man in a linen shirt, a cravat, and a tricorne hat steps into view with a cell phone pressed to his ear. Then one more, looking like a post–Revolutionary War soldier, marches over, and I hear him ask, "Time for colors, Captain Lewis, sir?"

I discover these are the men of the Discovery Expedition of St. Charles, Missouri, a team of living historians who are re-creating the Lewis and Clark expedition in replica boats and costumes, trying as much as is practical to follow the same itinerary and live the same way as the original explorers 200 years ago. Today marks their four-month anniversary on the expedition, and some are looking as haggard as their honorees must have. But it may have more to do with age than conditions. While some estimate the average age on the Corps of Discovery expedition was twenty-five, here it looks closer to AARP membership. One on the roster is eighty years old. Another, Jim Rascher, has missed his wedding anniversary for the last seven years, but this coming one, his fiftieth, he says he can't miss or it will be his last. Who else can find the time to volunteer to keelboat up the Missouri for weeks or months or years but retirees?

"Captain Lewis, I presume." I extend my hand to a trim, handsome man of erect bearing wearing an early military hat with bear fur and a white deer tail. He nods back. He is Scott Mandrell, thirty-eight, a teacher at Wydown Middle School in Clayton, Missouri, and a former member of the Army's Third U.S. Infantry, "The Old Guard" fife and drum corps. He has a wife and two young children at home, whom he sees periodically when they rendezvous at certain stops en route. Scott has been reenacting history since he was nine years old and grew up just four miles from Lewis and Clark's 1803 winter in Camp Wood River, Illinois. He has been working on this re-creation mission for ten years now, and when I ask if he will submit to the same fate as Meriwether Lewis (widely thought to have committed suicide) when this challenging project is over, he grins. "I may be ahead of schedule on that one."

We also meet the bespectacled Peyton "Bud" Clark, of Dearborn, Michigan, a former Ford Motor Company engineer, who plays his great-great-great-grandfather on this journey. One of the secrets of the original expedition was that William Clark was not really a captain. His commission, as requested by his friend Meriwether Lewis, never came through, so Lewis decided to ignore the government and pretend Clark was of equal rank regardless. Now Bud had the honor of rewriting history when he met in the East Wing of the White House an administration ago and received, on behalf of his grand relative, a posthumous commission as captain from President Clinton. Bud Clark, who says he is trying to live the spirit of his ancestor, describes the man as honorable, one who lived by the creed "death before dishonor." When I ask if he'll give lashings, as his relative did, to maintain discipline, he replies, "lots of good tongue lashings." Nor will he re-create the master-servant relationship William Clark had with his black slave, York, here played by Lynn "Smokey" Hart, a half-black–half-Yankton Sioux who is also a world champion rodeo bullfighter. But he does line the men up in the morning, soldier fashion, and leads them in the martial anthem "Chester" as they raise the seventeen Stars and Stripes up the spruce-wood mast:

> *Let tyrants shake their iron rod,*
> *And slav'ry clank her galling chains,*
> *We fear them not, we trust in God,*
> *New England's God forever reigns*

Then they fire up the 150-horsepower Mercury outboard hidden beneath the western cedar hull of the fifty-five-foot-long keelboat, check the fish finder for depth, and chug out into the Fort Randall Reservoir, communicating with the two pirogues by radio. They're looking for a campsite to set up and show off the old ways to some local schoolchildren.

The great experiment of this re-creation at first puzzles me. When Thor Heyerdahl set off on *Kon-Tiki*, sailing in a replica of an ancient Polynesian boat, he was out to prove a theory. When living history buffs don Civil War costumes and chase around old battlefields, it is a weekend of grown-up hide-and-seek. But three years laboring up the Missouri in period dress, sleeping on wooden boards on cramped boats, enduring the North Dakotan winter, portaging the upper reaches, crossing the Rockies in moccasins, camping in the December rains on the Columbia, and doing it all in reverse, seems a bit barmy. But then Scott, ahem, Captain Lewis describes the educational aspect of his expedition, and the mission seems indeed noble. All the way up and back they have arranged for students who live on or near the Missouri to visit the expedition and their camps, where the crew presents life and the environment as it was and how it has changed, and the children interact with history in a way no book ever can let them. There are interactive video conferences piped to classrooms, orchestrated by Jim Sturm, a tech wizard who follows the expedition in a tricked-out mobile home pulling a trailer with a satellite dish.

Expeditionary learning, wherein a young mind is exposed in a full-bodied, sensory way to a subject, is a powerful tool, less abstract, more profound, than conventional learning.

And it is through this firsthand exposure and discovery that issues then and now can be brought to consciousness and perhaps moved in some way toward resolution. The environmental impact of the dams and weirs, of irrigation and power schemes, of urban sprawl along the river, is more keenly appreciated when riding a keelboat across a stagnant and heavy artificially created lake. At this very spot, Lewis described "immense herds of buffaloe, deer, elk and antelopes we saw in every direction feeding on the hills and plains. I do not think I exaggerate when I estimate the number of buffaloe which could be comprehended at one view to amount to 3,000." When a child hears this passage, standing where it was written, and looks about to see perhaps three thousand boats and automobiles but no wildlife whatsoever, the question of how and why this came to be must be logged.

And then there are the Native Americans. Scott is concerned about the next leg of his journey, as his forebears were. In these bicentennial years not all Americans are celebrating what Lewis and Clark did. Scott's redux exercise has received a threat from a group called The Descendants of Crazy Horse. Crazy Horse was the Oglala Lakota warrior with strong personal convictions to preserve his people's traditional way of life, and who fought against Lieutenant Colonel George Custer's Seventh Cavalry at The Battle of the Little Big Horn in 1876. Like virtually all the western tribes that Lewis and Clark shook hands with and gave Jefferson peace medals to, the Lakotas were overwhelmed by the encroaching white race and ultimately robbed of a way of life and consigned to some of the poorest land in what was once their own country.

The Descendants sent a message to Scott that in an effort to raise awareness about the broken treaties and the marginalization of Native Americans that began in the wake of Lewis and Clark, they intended to try to stop the expedition as it travels upstream toward Pierre, South Dakota. It was at Pierre that Lewis and Clark had their ugliest encounter with Native Americans, their closest call. When a Teton Sioux insulted Clark, he drew his sword, and immediately a party of warriors drew bows and arrows. It could have been utter disaster for Lewis and Clark, but the grand chief ordered his warriors to stand down, and the rest is history, good or bad depending upon perspective.

Scott, however, is also sanguine about the threats, and believes they fall within the framework of the objectives of the expedition. "Our goal is to educate, and bring heightened awareness about the cause and effects of Lewis and Clark. The First Nations want a voice, want their issues to be heard, and we might be a vehicle for such." And Bud Clark adds, "In regards the Native Americans, we want to help in the healing process."

William Least Heat-Moon has said that our nation "didn't learn what they taught themselves. Lewis and Clark went as students; they came back as teachers, and we failed to learn the lessons that they had learned."

Scott Mandrell and his scruffy band of rediscoverers have a

chance to help change that; to move consciousness and understanding in a better direction, and that, I believe, makes them
heroes of our time.

IN THE HEART OF THE HEART OF THE COUNTRY

Unwinding the Missouri, we whisk our hybrid into soybean and
corn country. We pass through Sioux City, Iowa, where the Corps
of Discovery, just three months into the journey, faced its first
fatality, Sergeant Charles Floyd, who fell ill and died, probably
from a burst appendix. Out the window we overlook a straight-
ened and embanked Missouri River, quite unlike the broad, shallow, oxbowing stream pocked with islands observed by the Corps
of Discovery. They were 450 miles from St. Louis by river then.
A different corps, the Army Corps of Engineers, channelized this
stretch in the 1940s and 1950s, cutting the distance by a third,
making it safe and efficient for barge traffic.

We stop in this stretch at a Dairy Queen, owned by Berkshire
Hathaway, and Pasquale's favorite confectionery. "Warren Buffet
owns DQ; that's why the Blizzards are so rich," Pasquale cracks.

Next stop is Omaha, where the captains' historic first meeting
with Native American leaders took place on a bluff overlooking
the river. We meet Mayor Mike Fahey, proud of a billion-dollar
renovation along the river under his watch, one that has turned
the once-seedy area into a modern meeting place for a mix of
cultures. Then we steer over to Gorat's Steak House for dinner,
Warren Buffet's favorite brain-food eatery, celebrating 60 years
serving the "Finest Steaks in the World." The fertile floodplains
of the Missouri through Middle America have allowed the fruit-
ful cornfields, which in turn have fed the cattle that make the
famous Omaha Steaks, and sate the second-richest man in the
world. When in town, Warren comes in most every day for a hot
beef lunch, and every Wednesday night for his trademark rare
T-tone steak with a double order of hash browns and a Cherry
Coke. His friend Bill Gates has also pitched into a dry-aged slab
here, as has Tom Brokaw, who once worked in Omaha. The place

feels frozen in the 1950s, evoking not only the Frank Sinatra-in-Palm Springs chic (it was in fact the Gorats' home in the 1950s), but staff from another era as well. The chef, Bill Caveye, has been sizzling in the back for forty years; five of the waitresses have been serving for more than twenty years. And almost everyone else is family. We meet Steve Branecki, who owned a DQ for thirty-six years but married into the Italian Gorat family, with blessings, and now helps run the shop that, he says, proudly serves billionaires and average Joes. I set in to sample a couple of their signature pieces, the French-fried paisley (oxymoronic fatty health food) and the Blue Ribbon Strip Sirloin (excellent, though this journey down the Missouri has been passing prime beef country throughout, and there have been some choice contenders).

We then truck on over to Independence, Missouri, once called Queen City of the Trails, a booming crossroads in the early nineteenth century. The city is located where the Missouri River veers north, so travelers heading due west would not continue by boat, but load onto wagons and continue on the Santa Fe or Oregon Trail. Although steamboats did continue all the way to Montana, the great majority of the river traffic was between St. Louis and here. And it was in this stretch that most of the river disasters occurred. Of the seven hundred steamboats that paddled up and down the Missouri River between 1830 and 1902, nearly three hundred were destroyed by trees or other river debris. The *Great White Arabia* was one of these causalities, and we meet the Bob Ballard of steamboats, Dave Hawley, who with four partners raised the 171-foot-long side-wheeler from its muddy grave. On the afternoon of September 5, 1856, the *Arabia* was plying the river bound for the new town of Omaha with 130 passengers and 200 tons of freight. Folks were having dinner when a snag ripped a gaping hole in the oak hull. One survivor's account of the disaster: "We felt the shock, and at once the boat started sinking. There was a wild scene on board. Chairs and stools were tumbled about, and many of the children nearly fell into the water. Several of the men seized the lifeboat and started for shore, but they came back and the women and children were put in the boat."

In the summer of 1987, Dave Hawley and his partners found the long-lost wreck buried in a bean field, using a proton magnetometer, a fancy metal detector, and started the protracted and expensive exhumation. "We borrowed $50,000, and it ending up costing over $1 million," Dave tells us. The treasure from the muck was worth it in a time-capsule sense, but not monetary: coffee beans from South America, guns from Belgium, and trade beads from Bohemia. There were crystal glasses, almond-scented hand cream, and bottles of French perfume, cognac, and champagne. They found butter, cheese, and spiced pigs' feet. There were a million nails and thirty-five thousand buttons on board. But no gold or payroll. As for cash, they found twenty-six cents. To pay off the debts for raising the *Arabia,* Dave and company decided to open a private museum along the Missouri, charging admission. In 1991, the Arabia Steamboat Museum opened its doors, showcasing more than 100,000 pieces of antebellum Americana, about half what the boat was carrying. And now Dave and party are in the black and using proceeds to continue work on preserving the rest of the artifacts, which will take another decade or so, says Dave. And he wants to raise other boats. He has a long map on the wall identifying where boats went down, his wish list for his reach of the Missouri River.

To end the day, we make a quick stop at the humble, white, Victorian-style home of Harry S. Truman, and his Library not far away, where we bump into a dapper ghost of the thirty-third president. Dressed in brimmed hat and double-breasted suit, carrying the trademark cane, it is historian and former Truman Library archivist Niel Johnson, who now earns his living as the impersonator who takes one as close to the living Harry Truman as can be done. I shake hands across history with the president, and when I ask who'll win the close presidential race, he pulls from his inside suit pocket the famous "Dewey Defeats Truman" newspaper, holds it above his head, and launches into a monologue of Harry's folksy quips and blade-sharp commentary.

Harry was profoundly affected by the big brown river that ran two miles from his home. He was also passionate for music, and one of his favorite pieces was Strauss's "Blue Danube" waltz, another song written about a river. Rivers have always inspired music, and the Missouri is no exception. Tomorrow we'll find its soul. Kansas City, here we come. . . .

The Missouri, unruly, bending, swooping, pouring downstream with a strong rhythmic drive, was jazz before it had a name. It was manifest destiny that the river would spawn the modal, chromatic sound that is the quintessence of American music.

With slavery abated after the Emancipation Proclamation of 1863, blacks began to move up the Mississippi River, away from the plantations and toward a new world of freedom, economic and artistic. Many turned west at St. Louis, heading up the Missouri, and many landed at the crossroads town of Kansas City. A large, segregated black community developed, based around the intersection of Eighteenth and Vine, and there they played music that had its roots in Africa: blues, ragtime, and a new, emerging polyrhythmic improvisational form. But it didn't fully emerge until the 1920s, during Prohibition, when Tom Pendergast's political machine controlled the town and looked the other way as liquor, gambling, and every other vice got it on. Clubs stayed open twenty-four hours a day, seven days a week, and black musicians around the country came to ply their trade and trade their styles. At its peak, there were twp hundred clubs in the Eighteenth and Vine district. It was the musical mecca for African Americans, a conservatory of jam, and here, jazz grew up. The bands of Andy Kirk, Count Basie, and Jay McShann would riff and vamp alongside vocalists such as Jimmy Rushing, Joe Turner, and Pha Terrell. Bennie Moten codified the KC swing here; Count Basie fused his big band sound; Charlie "Bird" Parker, born in 1920 along the Missouri River here, honed in the after-hours bars here the skills that would flower into his pioneering work in bebop.

But today, as we swing our way down Vine Street, it is a different scene altogether. Buildings are boarded up, windows shattered; a once-vibrant mural of great black jazz artists sits across a weed-infested lot faded, stripped, and stained. The neon is gone, replaced by hand-painted scrawls. It's a ghost of what was once the center of the universe for jazz. What killed it? Count Basie said jazz is like murder: "You play it with intent to commit something." But the death of the jazz scene was third-degree. The Civil Rights Act of 1964 ended legal segregation, and African Americans, as they could afford it, moved out. The clubs closed. The music died.

As we park our hybrid, however, at the famous intersection, we discover a pulse of reemergence in the heart of the district. The American Jazz Museum stands at the corner of Eighteenth and Vine, and is one of the few museums in the world devoted to America's signature musical idiom. It is an amazing tribute to the art form and a potent past. We meet Juanita Moore, the executive director, who gives us a tour of the snazzy halls, rich in interactive displays, films, recordings, replicas of the flashing club signs, and priceless artifacts, such as Charlie Parker's plastic sax. It's the only museum I've stepped through where everyone sways and taps in time while soaking in the sights and sounds. Paul Allen, the billionaire builder of the Experience Music Project museum in Seattle, could learn a beat or two here. But the truly unique facet of the place is the Blue Room, its own attached nonprofit nightclub that features live acts four nights a week. And we've hit the jackpot: saxophonist Bobby Watson is scheduled to play tonight with his reassembled band, Horizon.

So after chowing down on barbecue ribs at the fabled Arthur Bryant's (Calvin Trillin rated it best barbecue joint in the world), just up the street, we slide into the Blue Room and listen to Watson's alto sax interplay with bass, piano, drum, and trumpet in virtuoso rapport. I can't quite believe I'm sipping a Bombay and tonic in a *museum* and listening to great jazz. They got some crazy little rhythms here, and we went and got us some.

Lewis and Clark often wrote in their journals: "We proceeded on." Time for us to do the same.

As we head out of town, we pass near where the vehicle we're driving, the Escape Hybrid, is assembled, in a modern Ford plant. Everything's up to date in Kansas City, but we don't stop as our onboard navigation system has us pointed down the final stretch of highway to St. Louis, where the Missouri River ends as it conflues with the Mississippi River, and their waters then run to the sea in the Gulf of Mexico. We do make our last gas stop for the trip. Our total for the 2,654 miles we travel in the Escape Hybrid from source to mouth will be $192.78, almost a third less than with an ordinary SUV.

It's a fast, two-hundred-mile dash along limestone bluffs and vast fields of dreams, but we make a few stops, including at the Katy Trail, an abandoned railroad bed, now a biking path, that hugs the Missouri for more than a hundred fifty miles west of St. Charles. And we weave through the Weinstrasse region, toasting our final fling. Before Prohibition, Missouri ranked second among wine-producing states, with a hundred wineries in the Weinstrasse region alone. As early as the 1880s, Missouri was producing two million gallons of wine annually (surpassed only by New York). The Missouri mud, left from floods and former channels, filled with rich soil and nutrients, is an ideal marl for certain grapes, and more than sixty wineries prosper today in the region.

At last we reach St. Louis, where the two great rivers convene, and we pull from a pack the Nalgene bottle filled with the crystal-clear Missouri source water we gathered high in the Montana Rockies two weeks ago. With all the dams and diversions, little original water reaches this point anymore, so we thought it fitting to give a few drops back in our celebration of the Missouri as it was when Lewis and Clark made their traverse. It would be our own meeting of the waters.

But there is a problem. The entire river junction area and most of the banks of the Mississippi and Missouri around St. Louis are privately owned, mostly by large companies with factories or loading/unloading facilities along the strand. Searching for access across the joined river in East St. Louis we notice railroad tracks atop a twenty-foot-high levee. A sign says, "Private Property, Keep Out. Area Strictly Off Limits. Violators Will be Prosecuted." Yet this seems the only point available to make our offering.

As Pasquale makes his way toward the concrete levee, bottle in hand, a state patrolman suddenly appears driving along a road adjacent to the tracks. "You're not supposed to be here," he yells.

"We just traveled down the entire Missouri, and we're here to pour some water from the source into the river," Pasquale hollers up to the patrol car.

The patrolman glowers, considering the concept. He glances up and down the river, then asks: "How long will it take?"

"Five minutes."

He pauses again, then says, "I didn't see a thing," and drives off.

After climbing over the levee and stepping across five sets of abandoned tracks and down an overgrown bank, we see the turgid goal. In the background, the Gateway Arch glistens. And Pasquale pours the bright liquid we've carried across a continent to meet and merge with the mighty, muddy river, a fate that we share.

In a time before the only glimpse most see of America is from jetliners cruising six miles above the ground, Lewis and Clark were first to appreciate the vastness of the continent and its challenging—yet exquisite—landscape. Our road trip alongside the Missouri was but a light pencil tracing on the deeply inked map of Lewis and Clark's epic adventure. But just like they, we learned the character of the country, from its wide-ranging and picturesque landscapes, its varied wildlife, it multicultural mixing pot. We met people of all stripes and colors, all beliefs and values, all sharing one powerful ribbon that ties together and wraps up much of America into the beautiful and productive gift that it is: the mighty Missouri River.

13

QUEST FOR THE SOURCE OF THE ZAMBEZI

Zambia

Under a spreading sausage tree, a stone's throw from a sunning ten-foot Nile croc on a sandbar, with a pair of bushbuck across the river, we're sipping Mosi beer, which tastes like Coors, only worse. We're tourists in a place you can't find on a map.

Zambia, in south central Africa, has never been widely known as a tourist destination. Zambia, in fact, is not widely known for much of anything. What little global recognition it enjoys comes more from the antique cuts of the colonial penknife, from its borders with more newsworthy neighbors, the Democratic Republic of the Congo (formerly Zaire) to the north, Angola and Mozambique to the west and east, and Zimbabwe to the south. In the mid-1960s, after independence, it was the world's third-largest producer of copper. For a time, Zambia's currency was among the most valuable in the world, and per-capita income equaled 800 U.S. dollars, second to South Africa in the sub-Saharan region.

But with the crash of copper prices, Zambia is now very small beer in the mining world, and it has yet to find a viable refill. Kenneth Kaunda, founding president and overseer as the country slid into economic ruin over a twenty-seven-year socialistic rule, tried all sorts of schemes to bring back its glory, including backing an American con artist, Farley Winston, who sold the head of state on a contraption that ostensibly converted grass to diesel. KK, as the president liked to be called, had visions of a new sort of African OPEC and banned the burning of grass, until the scam was exposed.

Now Zambia is cited as one of the word's poorest countries, with 50 percent unemployment and 75 percent of adults living below the World Bank's poverty threshold of $1 a day. The nation is also occasionally in the news for its epidemic of "slow-puncture disease": 20 percent of adults are HIV positive. In a nearby village today, among a gaggle of giggling kids, we met a grim-faced eight-year-old, John Zulu, doing his homework in the dirt, both parents dead from AIDS. He's in a big club: nearly half of Zambia's children have lost one or both parents to the disease. Lately Zambia has also seen some ink for its southern drought and its politically charged rejection of Frankenfood, the genetically modified corn sent by the United States to feed a region where some have been reduced to eating dirt.

Perhaps tourism is the redeemer. Last month, Zambia's recently elected president, Levy Mwanawasa, announced that his government has placed tourism and agriculture at the center of the country's economic revival. Yet, even though Zambia has nineteen national parks and thirty-five game-management areas (30 percent of the country), and some of the greatest concentrations of wildlife in the world, the game has always far exceeded the gawkers.

Tourism has not had an easy way here, especially of late. Zambia Airways, the national carrier, is bankrupt, its planes repossessed. The perfect storm of global recession, the post-9/11 fear of flying, and the "Zim Effect" (the apprehension of being fair-skinned and being anywhere near Zimbabwe President Robert Mugabe) have conspired to bring holidaying visitation down as much as 85 percent from its already paltry levels.

Amid all this, though, is our host, forty-nine-year-old white Zambian Chriss Wienand, and his ratty optimism for a scheme to create an adventure farm in Zambia that is as exhilarating as

it is ecologically sound and maintainable. Chriss and his partner have negotiated a ninety-nine-year lease of fifty thousand
acres along the lower Luangwa River, a tributary of the Zambezi.
They have dubbed the property Mandevu ("man with beard" in
the local Cinyanja language). Their operating company, Mbizi
(zebra) Safaris Ltd., is looking to turn the land, upon which roam
elephants, leopards, lions, zebras, and a carnivore's dream sal-
ver of antelopes, into a private park that will serve overlanders
(the Bedford-vans set), photographers, birders, rafters, and some
hunters. Just five hours' drive from the capital, Lusaka, it will be
among the easiest big game parks to access, and it has ambitions
to be sustainable, which in this part of the world means keeping
out the poachers. Until the 1960s, more than one hundred thousand elephants roamed the Luangwa Valley, the largest focus of
the beasts in the world. Today, due to poaching, just 15 percent
of those herds remain. In the 1970s there were some twelve thousand black rhinos in Zambia. Today there are none.

So how do Chriss and company hope to achieve this balance between wildlife and the economic needs of ultrapoor
human neighbors? By supplying the villagers with income and
the necessities of life through tourist fees collected and private
donations. This has been tried many times before, as with the
Campfire program in Zimbabwe, and the Zambian government-
sponsored ADMADE (acronym for the wonderfully bureaucratic
name "Administrative Management Design"), but hulking corruption in the distribution chain has always contaminated these
efforts. The difference here is that the enterprise is thoroughly
private, and Chriss is overseeing all payments for goods and
services personally. Already, Mbizi Safaris has built a clinic and
a school for the locals adjacent to the property, and Chriss has
employed up to a hundred people at a time. And the project has
barely begun, its required circumference fence just posted this
year, and its entrance road improved so that it now takes ninety
minutes from the nearest town, Nyimba, rather than four to five
butt-banging hours.

In fact, we are among the first visitors to Mandevu and plan to spend the next few days hiking the grounds and witnessing the wildlife, which includes the panoply of African predators and a dozen varieties of highly poisonous snakes. In our group we have two software engineers, three PhDs in math, a pathologist, and a pediatrician, so I figure we're covered for all emergencies. Then we'll head upriver, to a couple of national parks, and finally across the watershed divide to the Bangweulu Swamps, the source of the Congo, the river that has become the overwrought symbol for the white man's descent into madness while on an extreme quest in Africa.

GAME THEORY

Several hours into the hike I hear him struggling, panting behind me with every footfall. Dov Harel, who in repose looks like a twinkling Talmudic scholar, now has a swollen red face so sopped in sweat it looks coated in Mylar. His heart rate is up to 150 beats a minute. I offer to take his pack, but between rasps he declines. He refuses the help of two other offers as well, so we do the right thing and stop for a swim . . . in the cool, crocodiled waters of the Luangwa River.

More people are killed in Zambia by crocodiles each year than by all other animals combined. Any meat that floats their way triggers their killing instinct, be it fish, hippo, antelope, or human. And just upstream we had seen a twelve-footer slip into the currents.

Crocs like to sneak up on their prey in water deep enough to hide, so we find a spot in a rapid, shallow enough to see approaching jaws or claws. Even then, Justin Seymour-Smith, who runs a private game park in Zimbabwe, and with recent events has time on his hands and has joined our holiday, stands ready on shore with a Rigby .416, a rifle big enough to drop an elephant at three hundred yards.

The dip cools and cleanses—a few of us even swim the rapids in the nude, our usually protected skin pale as crocodile bellies—and Dov is back to normal as we continue our trek, passing bushbuck, baboons, impalas, and bloats of hippos. About five feet tall, weighing in at about five tons, about the same as two of our four-wheel-drive vehicles, hippos are proportionally the fattest animals on earth, but for short sprints can run as fast as a horse. Although vegetarians, they too are quite dangerous and will attack if they feel threatened, easily snapping a human body in two with their carrot-sized molars and steam-shovel jaws. And with an average of about sixty hippos per mile, the Luangwa is the most heavily hippo-inhabited river in the world.

As we approach our goal, a twisting hot springs spills into the river, and another type of predator makes its appearance—the blood-hungry tsetse fly. It looks like a horsefly, but stings like a bee—its rapierlike proboscis can penetrate khakis, jeans, even tennis shoes. And, like Michael Myers in a John Carpenter film, you think you've killed one of these buggers, and it just keeps coming back. Chriss likes to tear off the wings and tell them to walk home. These tsetses, harmless to humans, carry nagana—bovine trypanosomiasis, a parasite that kills three million cattle, goats, and pigs a year in sub-Saharan Africa. For us they are merely a nuisance, and one to be tolerated knowing they serve a larger purpose. The wildlife we see wouldn't exist without them. Without such an effective guardian, wilderness areas such as Mandevu would long ago have been tamed, the wild animals cleared for domesticated ones. When Norman Carr, Zambia's conservation pioneer, was appointed a member of the Order of the British Empire for his life's work, he suggested the conservation award should really have gone to the tsetse fly. Where the tsetse flourishes, so does the great wildlife of body Africana.

Nicolas Kalembelembe, thirty-two, a former waiter at a game lodge, is our local guide, who interprets the bush through which we pass. We learn that trees communicate here. When a beast is gnawing at the bark of the mopane tree, it emits a pheromone that telegraphs to surrounding trees to stimulate an increased level of tannin, which makes the bark unappetizing. We learn that virtually every abandoned termite mound hosts a tamarind tree, as baboons like to sit atop the mud castles and chew on the pods of the tree, dropping the seeds, which take and sprout the tropical evergreen. The forest is a pharmacy here, and it seems half the plants are used for either back pain or erectile dysfunction, including the bark of the balanite bush, a local Viagra. But the sausage tree, Nicolas informs, is for the women. They like to mix the seeds from the sausage into a lusty porridge and eat it just before a tryst, as it makes them "warm."

We walk down the canyon single file, African style, and every now and then the front man, usually Justin, cries fowl, and the bush telephone sends word back one by one. But it never works right, and once when I was in the rear a sighting up front of a white-crowned plover ended up a leopard sighting by the time it reached me.

At the end of our six-mile hike, we're picked up by Chriss, who has been literally fighting fires on the property all day. We climb into the Toyota Land Cruiser and head back to camp, Chriss roughhousing the wheel. Along the way a sinister bouquet of tsetses finds its way into the cab, and we all start swatting. Chriss winces as he plucks one off his cheek. Robert Bismuth picks up a roll of toilet paper and slams it mightily at one on the window, but all he does is effect some tissue damage, and the little buzzer flies away.

THE HOT ZONE

There is a haunting backstory to a little-known film produced a few years ago, *In the Blood*. George Butler, director behind *Pumping Iron* and a pair of Shackleton films, decided to film a tribute to African hunting. But midshoot, while using a brushfire to flush out wildlife, a not-uncommon practice, the fire went beyond control, surrounded a game scout, and burned him to death.

I kept thinking of this scene as the wind kicked and the flames encircled us for a few hot and potentially deadly seconds as we swatted away at them.

Burning is a way of life in Africa. For much of the continent, there are two seasons, the wet and the dry. Since time immemorial, Africans have burned in the dry for many reasons—to refortify thin or spent soil for another round of planting, to create charcoal for cooking, to light the way for a night crossing, to drive out animals to poach, to keep predators at bay while walking or camping, or to exact retribution against property owners who fence in a place where land has traditionally been tribal, communal, and freely passable.

This is the end of the dry season in a drought year, and the tall *Hyperrenial* grass used for thatching is tawny, brittle, and tinder dry. We begin the day with an early call from Chriss announcing no breakfast. Put on high boots and socks (no sandals) and get into the trucks—there is a wildfire to fight.

Fire is huge concern for Chriss, not only because it could spread and wipe out the camp, but also because it can raze the natural habitat, chasing the wildlife off the protected property and into the arms of poachers. We trundle east down the Dam One Road for about four miles in pursuit of the burning bush. We park at the bottom of a parchment-colored hill, then thrash to the top. Off in the distance, along the next ridge, we see a whorl of smoke. We make our way toward it. Chriss figures a fisherman started the burn while taking a shortcut back to his village but admits there are half a dozen possible causes, including a disgruntled employee or a jealous neighbor. About halfway up, we see Nicolas Kalembelembe, our nature guide, and a team of nine other Mandevu employees whacking away at ragged lines of fire with the leafed branches of the *Combretum* frangrance tree. With a crude ax, Nicolas cuts off a series of four-foot branches for us, and it's clear what we're supposed to do.

We fan out and start beating at the fire, which seems to cover a couple of acres of lion-colored grasslands. We learn quickly the two most effective strokes: a strong, top-down spank, which momentarily snuffs out the oxygen, or a power golf swing that drives the flames back into the seared area. Both work on flames

less than a foot high, but when a gust sends a flame higher, we step
back and wait for the wind to take a breath, then begin bashing
again. Together we work our way around the furious periphery.
At some hot spots, clusters of square-tailed drongos and lilac-
breasted rollers hover above the flames, catching fleeing insects
in the thermals.

After an hour we snuff the last flame, take a few triumphant
pictures of faces streaked with soot, and head down the hill for a
well-deserved breakfast. There is something primally satisfying
about fighting a fire and winning before breakfast. I can taste the
coffee and bacon.

But three miles from camp, Chriss jolts to a stop and points
up a ridge. Another dark cloud of smoke is spiraling skyward,
and Chriss commands we get out. We arm ourselves with a new
set of tree branches and trudge up the rise to a necklace of low
flames.

It's just after 9:00 a.m., and the first heat of the day stirs the
wind. In short order we snuff out the lower reaches of this second fire, but as we work our way to the top, the wind nudges
the flames higher. Several times we almost contain the burn, but
whenever we've just about got it collared, it leaps around, crackles, snickers at us, then blasts on. We fight for another hour, hot,
thirsty, exhausted, but the fire is speeding ahead of us, devouring
the wheatlike grass like a herd of hungry horses. The flames continue to grow, some fifty feet high as they catch the trees. Finally,
Chriss calls us down for a regroup. "This is an exercise in futility.
We need a different tactic. We'll go to the Dam One Road and
back-burn."

Just after the rains, in June, with some moisture still in the
grass, Chriss had made controlled burns across the farm just to
avoid this type of conflagration. But now this blaze was leaping
over the fire lines with impunity. The road could be the last stand
to keep this fire from running west, to our camp on the Luangwa
River.

Down at the road, Chriss and Justin take clumps of grass,

light them, and spread them along the dry sward at the edge of road. The hope is that the back-burn (or side-burn, in this case, as we're on the long frame of the fire) will move toward the fire and stop it in its tracks with nothing to consume. But with a burst of wind the plan backfires, and the back-burn flies across the road. Fanned by an increasing wind, it becomes a towering inferno. We all jump back, then attack the edges, smoke tearing our eyes. We're coughing and clubbing the flames, making little progress. Chriss, a bush-version Red Adair, takes a team to the fire front, where another road transects, and begins another back-burn. For three hours we battle the fire on different fronts, retreating for slugs of water and brief rests under winterthorns, then heading back into the fray. The landscape, which yesterday was filled with thick, elephant-eye-high grass and woodlands, now looks napalmed, charred and barren, with blue smoke drifting like a deadly gas along the ground.

By midafternoon, everyone is fatigued and starved, throats burning from the smoke. But it seems we have stomped out the last flames on both ends. Once again we pile into the Toyotas, lusting for breakfast, but Chriss wants one last look at the perimeter before declaring victory. We drive back to where we started and see more smoke—the fire we thought we had snuffed is back, so we drag ourselves through the sharp grass up the knoll for another go. Everyone is spent, utterly bushed, but this looks as if it could be the closing round. So we swat some more, coughing in air thick with motes of ash, struggling with each swing. Then Chriss yells, "Man down . . . We've got a man down," and I imagine one of our group engulfed and burned. Halfway down the hill where the final flames had been licking, someone is lying on the ground.

It's Desmond Rabinowitz, the trip pediatrician, probably the fittest man among us, looking twenty years younger than his fifty-three years. He had stomped out the last of the embers and was heading up the valley when a sudden dizziness hit. Des has type 1 diabetes, insulin-dependent diabetes mellitus, and had been figuring throughout the day, like the rest of us, that we would be back for breakfast soon, where he would refuel on natural sugar. He was carrying a Luna Bar, as he does whenever exercising, and had pulled it from his pocket, peeled back the wrapper, and taken a bite, but it was too late. Down he went. Chriss heads back to fetch the Land Cruiser, while Justin and others administer to Des, hydrating him, covering him in shade. For a few chilling minutes, Des doesn't speak, won't respond to questions or comments, just licks his dry lips. Justin finds the Luna Bar on the ground, cleans it, and feeds it to Des, who begins to recover. By the time the Land Cruiser rumbles over the scorched earth toward us, Des is back on his feet.

An hour later, 4:00 p.m., we're at camp, ready for a shower and breakfast. The fire, which Chriss estimates burned five thousand acres, or 10 percent of the farm, is dead. For now.

THE VALLEY OF DEATH

High and beautified by the grace of their flight, the white-backed vultures signal the carcass, circling like, well, vultures. We steer off the road into the bush, where a dozen of the birds hang like dirty rags on branches. Steering closer, we see perhaps a score of the bald, hook-billed birds, wings clacking, beaks pecking at the animal, tearing out its insides in sharp bites. It is, or was, a warthog, noosed in a poacher's wire snare, and now, as we step around to get a view of the beast, its carcass reveals one-third skeleton, looking like the frame of a small boat hull, and the rest gray skin and coarse hair. It looks like the work of movie special-effects wizard gone for coffee in the midst of some sort of digital morphing effect.

The Kunda people here poach in the game management area primarily for food for their families (large ones; the average Zambian mother has seven children). There just is not enough *nyama* (meat) or arable ground to go around. Even though Zambia is one of the more underpopulated countries in the world (just 11 million people in an area the size of France, Belgium,

Austria, Denmark, and Switzerland combined), there is a disproportionate number of people here alongside the South Luangwa
National Park, more than the hardscrabble land can support. The
current theory has to do with the backfiring of a U.S. Agency
for International Development–backed program to share income
from commercial hunting with the locals who live in the game
management areas. As originally conceived, licenses for hunting
would be granted through the local chiefdom (a two-week classic safari runs as much as $25,000 per person), with a percentage
left behind to distribute among the villagers, imputing a sense
of worth to live animals. But with the launch of the program,
word spread quickly throughout the country: "Hey, they give you
money if you live in Luangwa Valley," and where once ten thousand villagers lived, now there are a hundred thousand. To top
off the problem, eighteen months ago, then-president Frederick
Chiluba banned all commercial hunting throughout the country, believing that hunting permits were being counterfeited, that
ministers were being bribed, and that licensing fees were going to
support the opposition. Even though there is a new administration, the hunting ban has yet to be lifted, and for almost two years
there has been no money from hunts for the now-overcrowded
villages. Poaching is on the rise.

Less than a mile down the road from the dead warthog, we
pass another aid project, this a village in a red moon of cleared
forest surrounded by an electric fence to keep elephants from the
gardens and crops. The fence is lifeless as clay, and the wire used
is the same we saw in the warthog snare. Atop the hill, a couple of
old female lions, scarred and scruffled, eyes streaked dark from
age, look down disapprovingly.

Along the river, in the game management area, we have lunch
with Craig Madden, thirty-nine, for the past five years a walk-
ing-safari guide in the South Luangwa Park. He doesn't hunt, has
never hunted, except for rabbits when he was a child in Australia. But like virtually everyone here, he is a strong advocate of
hunting as the best way to fund the needs of local peoples and to

keep the wildlife in an ecologically sound check. "Animal-rights advocates don't understand that commercial hunts come for the big animals, which are almost always the oldest and the ones that should be culled anyway, as they compete for food against the young. And the monies from these hunts not only go to help the local peoples, they also go to pay the salaries of the antipoaching rangers, and there are far fewer rangers today than two years ago. I can't think of a better way, unless Bill Gates contributes 1 percent of his wealth to wildlife preservation here." Craig, like most in this eastern piece of the country, is frustrated by the corruption and unfulfilled promises of the government in Lusaka and is especially critical of the recent cutback of game rangers. So he has made his own contribution. He has just released a CD of *African Bush Sounds* he recorded while walking the area. A percentage of the proceeds goes to RAT (Rapid Action Teams), a private army of antipoachers funded by the lodges in the valley.

When at last we roll into the bestiary of South Luangwa Park (where there is no hunting, but poaching persists), we see the show of life that is wild: Thornicroft giraffe, a subspecies unique to Luangwa, browsing on the leaves of a winterthorn tree while another struts by with the slow gait of a runway model; chorus lines of "pajama donkeys," Burchell's zebra, looking natty in pinstripes; impalas pelting around neurotically, vast almond eyes on slim necks; fluffy pukus, the colors of sunrise on their backs; waterbuck, kudu, bushbuck and baboons; and at one turn we see an old cow elephant, lying down under the searing sun on the cracked ground of a waterless oxbow, her genital area bleeding. She's dying, alone in the dust, her herd up the dry river bed a few hundred yards away. We watch her struggle to get up, but she is too exhausted. Her eyes, looking like the cracked glaze of village pottery, telegraph sadness. Death is probably just a few hours away, and then the vultures, lions, and hyenas will come for their gorge. The flies and beetles will quickly finish the transformation. Then, if they beat the poachers, the game guards will collect the tusks, to be stashed for the next time CITES (the UN Convention on International Trade in Endangered Species) opens for stock-piled ivory trading, as it did for some southern African countries last year.

We next stop at a bend in the river, where a hundred hippos are blowing their tubas and the turreted eyes of crocodiles patrol for prey. Downstream we see a collection of crocs snapping at the tail end of a hippo in the middle of the river. The hippo, half-sunken in the copper water, is dead, and the crocs are enjoying a beggar's banquet. Craig, the Aussie guide, told us he had come across nine dead hippos in the last day and suspected perhaps another outbreak of anthrax, the deadly spore-forming bacterium found in the soil here. In 1987, two thousand hippos died in a two-week period from anthrax. But, he says, they may have been victims of poachers. "With the downturn in tourism, there are more poachers here than tourists."

When Dr. David Livingstone crossed the Luangwa River near here in December 1866, in an uncharacteristic moment of inspiration he wrote, "I will make this beautiful land better known to men that it may become one of their haunts. It is impossible to describe its luxuriance." The way it has turned out is not what he imagined.

RED MEN WALKING

Two years ago July, a twenty-three-year-old, British-born safari guide was trampled and gored to death by an enraged female elephant while leading an American tourist on a walking safari along the Luangwa River. In a last act of valor, the guide distracted the charging animal from his client, an American engineer, who had tripped and fallen into the bush.

Now we are on a similar walking safari, stepping quietly into our own Discovery Channel special, tramping single file down the Luangwa to the confluence with the Mukamadzi River draining the Northern Province, the setting sun burnishing our already red faces. A herd of elephants parades across the water; in the river there are so many hippos it looks as though you could step along their backs to the other side. Last year, 754 hippos were counted in a quarter-mile section in front of the Wilderness Lodge, a project supported in part by the Cologne Zoo, and the only camp in this neglected park. We are the sole visitors in Luambe Park, a small piece of protection between the much larger South and North Luangwa parks. The last group here was a week ago, and the next scheduled party of two is a couple of weeks away. No traffic jams of tourist-stuffed safari vehicles here. We have two local game scouts hired to protect us, Peter Pastor, walking behind with a rusted machete, and, twenty yards ahead, Jason Nkhoma, an AK-47 slung across his shoulder, with ten rounds. Because of the small caliber, the Russian-made automatic will have a hard time dropping a charging elephant or hippo, though it is ideal to nab a band of poachers or take over the Comoros.

Then there are the solar-powered vehicles in the river, the crocodiles, fully charged at the end of the day, ready to go into high hunting gear. The dried mud bench we are traversing ten feet over the river has a hair crack above us, so it looks as if the path could snap off and pitch us into the currents any second. So the primary feeling when traveling on foot here is of some sort of exhilaration, a perverse frisson that comes with walking by the edge. In the Toyota, we are gods; walking, we are part of the food chain. This is exercise, but it is also an exercise in humility.

There are few places in Africa where one can walk on safari. It's considered too dangerous for the great national parks of East Africa and elsewhere. Animals attack, and the more touristed parks want the protection of a layer of motorized metal. But one of Zambia's distinctions is not only allowing this type of travel, but also making it signature.

The late Norman Carr is credited with commercializing the walking safari. Norman first came to the Luangwa Valley as an elephant-control officer in 1939, killing more jumbos than he could count. He ended up Zambia's Grand Old Man of conservation—eight thousand people, including former president Kaunda, attended his funeral in April 1997, and his tomb in an ebony grove is now something of a place of pilgrimage for his many disciples, including most of the safari guides we've bumped into, even Chriss Wienand, our host.

After serving as an officer with the King's African Rifles in North Africa during the Second World War, Norman returned to Northern Rhodesia (now Zambia) with a new idea—perhaps it would be possible for villagers to make money out of protecting, rather than killing, elephants and other animals. He realized that to make such a scheme work, the people on the land would have to benefit directly. He spoke to Paramount Chief Nsefu, who was mystified as to why people would pay to watch animals but was willing to try the experiment. In 1950, having built six simple rondevaals (round, thatched chalets), Norman brought the first visitors from Chipeta, a town one hundred miles away. They shot with cameras instead of rifles and during the first year paid the chief and his council about two hundred dollars for the privilege. Ecotourism in Africa was born.

Although politics, weather, economics, greed, and corruption have made Norman's dream less than realized, it did launch an industry of outback walkers, and it inspired Chriss with his Mandevu private farm project to try to learn from mistakes past and make the dream finally real. And one purpose of this trip is for Chriss to survey how other parks and projects are doing throughout the country.

Continuing our walking safari, we pass what looks like some sort of village shrine, but in fact it is a jungle gym—barbells and weights carved out of the heavy mopane, used by Jason and other guides to pump wood and keep in shape, not just for the day job, but also for catching poachers. Jason says he has caught ten to fifteen poachers in his ten years as a scout and guide in the area, and is paid twenty kwacha (four dollars) for bringing each back alive. Jason also invites us to listen to his village sing for us in the evening, an invitation born of the shared experience of self-propelled movement, not likely had our guide been segregated in the front of a vehicle, while we gawked in clouds of dust from the back.

A bit down the road, Justin Seymour-Smith, our very own David Attenborough, only more knowledgeable, picks up a clod of dirt and scratches it for us to reveal an ant lion, one of the Little Big Five, others being the rhino beetle, buffalo weaver, elephant shrew, and leopard tortoise. The ant lion waves its mandibles like a miniature Edward Scissorhands, and Jason informs us that it can walk only backward, a shame in these parts. But the detail, the slice of nature's exquisiteness, reminds that these are nuances of Africa we would have never seen riding in the back of a well-logoed safari vehicle. A minute later, a strange sound detaches itself from our footfalls. The leaves begin to rustle like wind before a storm. Walking fine-tunes our senses. And Jason crouches, readies his rifle. He waves for us to stop. Then a baby elephant crosses the path not a hundred feet in front of us. This is not good news, as a mother elephant protecting her young is among the most likely to charge. Glasser Conradie, the thirty-four-year-old manager of Luangwa Wilderness Lodge, tells us the best thing to do if the cow charges is run, though "elephants can outrun people." Suddenly this walking safari is in danger of becoming a running safari. Among the group we exchange glances, each recognizing that it is not so important that we outrun the elephant, but that we outrun one another. And I regret not having the green mangoes for breakfast, which we were promised would keep us running all day.

Bellies of the Beasts

There is a pattern to the passionately cobbled tales of journeys into Africa, be they biography, journal, or fiction. From *The Devil Drives* (the story of Richard Burton) to *The Strong Brown God* (the story of Mungo Park's explorations of the Niger) to *Through the Dark Continent* (Henry Morton Stanley's account of crossing the breadth of Africa) to *The Sheltering Sky* (Paul Bowles's saga of American couple Kit and Port heading south), the stories start with romance and hope and several characters, and along the way something of each is lost.

In Mandevu, the private game ranch on the lower Luangwa where we began nine days ago, we were ten travelers, not including Chriss, our host. Now, after trundling north, deeper into Africa, in a series of long drives totaling some twenty-five hours, we are down to seven (the missing three left legitimately, though one departure was unplanned). Along the way, as on any journey, things have gone missing, we've broken gear, we've been covered with cuts, blisters, and rashes. But worst of all, we're down to one mathematician, which has me concerned.

During the expedition along the MMBA (miles and miles of bloody Africa), we stopped and played football with the salami-shaped fruit of the sausage tree; we inspected a local hospital that thrives without electricity or refrigeration; we noshed on cream of tartar from the fruit of the baobob tree purchased on the side of the road; we passed a hundred men and boys on bicycles with no gears (but thumb bells, which keep the wildlife away); we signed a dozen "mabooks," logs of entries, an imperialistic leftover; we consumed gallons of gin and tonic and shandys (so much for nonconsumptive tourism); we slept under the Southern Cross, serenaded by hippos, hyenas, lions, and mosquitoes; and we have yet to meet an American, make that North American, anywhere on this tour.

So I thought I would share a bit of the conditions under which I've worked throughout this journey, turning out the words for this report.

First, electricity and light have been the greatest challenges. When not on the road, we have used folding portable solar panels to charge a twelve-volt, dry-cell battery, but it hasn't been enough to power my modified laptop for any reasonable duration. So as backup I've tapped into one of the Toyota vehicle batteries, awkward when someone needs the car for some chore. Night falls like a guillotine at six here, just twelve degrees south of the equator, and so I often work after dark, which is a mixed blessing as it is often hotter than 100°F during the day. After dark, I've used flashlights, which attract clouds of bugs, and kerosene lanterns, which emit enough toxins to keep the insects at bay, but also induce headaches and nausea after continued use. Pasquale Scaturro, Everest expedition veteran and field producer, spends about four hours each night downloading digital images taken throughout the day, and reformatting, enhancing, and captioning the pictures. I write the dispatch and record a digital diary. Then we zip the files and hook up the Telenor ISDN satellite system, which connects us to a geostationary Imarsat satellite over the Indian Ocean, which beams our signal to the Telenor offices in Bethesda, Maryland, which then connects us to the Internet, through which we can transfer the files to home, where the data is stored for later editing.

But we've really roughed it when it comes to where and what we've eaten. For instance, we stopped for lunch a couple of days ago at Tafika ("we have arrived!") Camp in South Luangwa Park, run by Remote Africa Safaris, owned and operated by John and Carol Coppinger, bush hospitality legends. The Rabelaisian repast included sliced papaya with lemon, salmon cakes, tuna rolls, deviled eggs, corkscrew macaroni, bacon quiche, freshly baked bread, and chocolate mousse. We pushed back chairs feeling as heavy as the leadwood trees under which we sat. Then we moved to dinner at the "fly" camp (torn down at the start of the rainy season, it's rebuilt from all-natural materials at the start of the dry) in Luambe National Park, The Luangwa Wilderness Lodge, where we snacked on samosas, fish cakes, and nachos before sitting down to a *grande bouffe* of T-bones, French fries, fresh salad, and a selection of South African wines. And the five-dollar hamburger at The Wildlife Camp was to die for. So even though we've done some serious walking and fought fires for hours at a stretch, the greatest workout on this trip has been exercising our palates, and we've become champions, competing with the hippos for bloat.

Today, about twenty miles from the entrance to the remote North Luangwa Park, after knocking through hours of pocked and cracked black-cotton soil road, we stop because our Toyota is leaking. And Chriss notices the front leaf spring bracket is broken on one of the vehicles. So we've lost another of our party, our trusty Toyota Land Cruiser 1HZ pickup, specially modified in Australia for outback conditions. In the 105°F heat, amid blizzards of nasty mopane flies (they seem to come here for vacation; their only delight in life is to bug us), we jury-rig a replacement out of a slab of mopane wood, strapped on with baling wire and "Zambian welding" (strips of inner tube). Chriss doesn't think the vehicle can make it to camp, as we have to cross the sand-bottomed Luangwa River, a punishing proposition that could bugger the steering arm. So he calls Dorian Tilbury, manager of Mwaleshi Camp, on the VHF, and asks him to meet us at the entrance to North Luangwa Park. ("Rats, I was hoping to do some ballroom dancing" is his response.) An hour later, we transfer gear and kits to Dorian's safari vehicle and grind through the desolate park, across the river, and to the bush camp on the Mwaleshi River, where we sit down to a simple bush meal of filet steak with sautéed potatoes, fresh salad, peas, carrots, and ratatouille with a chilled Nederburg sauvignon blanc and fruit pavlova for dessert. Pity us our privations here in the back bush of Zambia.

CHASING WATERFALLS

We hear a rumor there is another couple in the park, up from South Africa, staying at one of the other two camps in this 2,400-square-mile track of raw wilderness, and mild discontent seeps in with the concept. Because this land appears so empty, it is easy to imagine that whatever we see belongs to us. And simply because we have traveled so far, it seems natural to believe we have some special claim to this wilderness. So we head upriver, to a place little known, to escape the crowds.

Along the way we are reminded how arrogant a concept seclusion is. We pass a herd of some four hundred buffalo, trailed by a pride of lions. We skirt by yellow baboons, impalas, greater kudu, banded mongoose, Moloney's monkeys, puku, warthogs, Cookson's wildebeests, zebras, bushbuck, waterbuck, spotted hyenas,

and two rarely seen antelopes, Sharpe's grysbok and Lichten-
stein's hartebeest, which bounces along the savanna as though
on a trampoline. Sometimes a bit too close for comfort, we pass
elephants, several score in all, and it seems incredible that during
the late 1970s and 1980s, gangs of commercial poachers, using
high-powered rifles and automatic and semiautomatic weapons,
killed an estimated one thousand elephants a year for ivory in
this park alone. The park warden dealt in ivory, skins, and meat.
Foreign diplomats smuggled out contraband. North Luangwa
Park became known as "the second Ivory Coast."

A major turnaround began in 1986 with the establishment
of the Convention on Trade in Endangered Species, which dialed
down the international demand spigot. It was also around this
time that wildlife conservationists Mark and Delia Owens, best
known for their book *Cry of the Kalahari,* arrived in North
Luangwa to continue research on carnivores, having been
booted from Botswana in a dispute over fencing polices (they
were against the wire barriers they saw blocking antelope migrations). Appalled to find the North Luangwa landscape bloodied
and littered with elephant skulls, they set up the North Luangwa
Conservation Project (NLCP) and with funds raised from abroad
(they were gifted on the lecture circuit) began equipping local
game scouts. NLCP also targeted villages around the park where
poachers, like bush Robin Hoods, shared booty with the locals.
NLCP, like many of these schemes, gave economic and technical
assistance to the surrounding villages that in theory would give
an alternative to the poachers' largesse. To a degree it worked,
and within seven years poaching in North Luangwa had been
appreciably reduced, and elephant and other populations began
to rise.

Despite some good work, the Owenses didn't last here either.
After a time they were accused of running North Luangwa as
their own private kingdom, and they pissed off a lot of people,
including our host, Chriss, who once needed to use their air-
strip but was denied access. The manager of our camp, Dorian

Tilbury, says a television documentary crew caught a poacher being executed on camera, and fingers pointed at the Owenses, so in 1997 they retreated to the United States. Then management of the NLCP was taken over by the Frankfurt Zoological Society, which oversees the project today.

After stepping past this pageant of game, Dorian leads us up into the Chichenda Hills, to the upper waters of the clear-flowing Mwaleshi River. We stop in the shade of a sausage tree hanging with a hundred strips of faded fabric from knurled branches. Dorian gathers us around like a priest assembling his flock. This is, he intones with the ersatz reverence guides around the world have mastered, the burial place of Chief Mukungule, legendary head of the Bisa tribe, a tribe romanticized by some as having coexisted in idyllic balance with the wildlife for millennia before colonial days. The chief died a century ago, and each year in the fall the village elders come and pay homage by hanging a new piece of cloth. The nearby falls we hope to reach were once a favorite sanctuary for the chief, and now for us to pass we need to make an offering. At fifty-seven, Michael Kallay is the oldest in our group, and as such is appointed the profferer. A mixture of ground maize and tobacco is poured into his palm, and we are led to the back of the thick tree, where a yard-long, fist-wide vertical slit darkens the trunk, inside of which, we are told, is the wrapped skeleton of the chief. "Now, follow the ritual exactly, or the spirit of Chief Mukungule will ensure that something terrible happens. First, take off your hats. Now, kneel down and clap three times as Michael pours the offering into the crypt." We all do as we're told, but after the clap I put my hat on so I can take some notes. "Now clap three times more," Dorian instructs, and I follow suit, but forget to take my hat back off, an egregious violation of the ritual.

"Now you've done it," Sel Leyser, our chief nature photographer, notices. "We may have angered the chief."

Minutes later, we are lolling in a secluded riverine paradise, a section of the Mwaleshi that squabbles over a series of small, sparkling waterfalls. As we compare notes of secret paradises of our youths now overrun with resorts and touro-dollars, there is a keen appreciation that we are part of a rare trice in an over-charted world.

Below the falls is green pool, filled by a bloat of forty hippos and several large crocodiles. Dorian tosses several stout croc rocks into the upper swimming holes to check for errant reptiles, then we all shed and plunge. A couple hours into our bath, I decide to slide over a small waterfall that spills into a deep pool. It's a fun little slide, and I tell the others, who follow suitless. Sel has a sweet glide through and is laughing in the wake until he realizes he has let himself drift too close to the next waterfall and is now caught in the current. "Grab the rock," those of us watching Sel yell, but it's too late, and I see a look of pure horror in his eyes as the water breaks around his head like glass and he is swept over the falls and out of sight.

For a second the world seems to weigh on a dot of quiet, broken by the stridulations of insects. Fearing the worst—if the falls don't get him, the hippos and crocs below will—a couple of us scramble to the foot of the falls and there find Sel with a grin that looks dipped in a bowl of crystal. He's dog-paddling in a quiet pool still one pitch above the hippos and crocodiles, unscathed, exhilarated from the run. "I told you to keep your hat off," Sel scolds me. "You upset Chief Mukungule." On the way back, as a freak storm pelts us with cold rain and high winds, my hat is torn from my head and dispatched into the night, a final offering to the spirits of this place numinous and in many ways beyond belief.

THE MISSION

Larium dreams and buggered schemes have made men mad in Africa. But madness here is not all breakdown; sometimes, at the confluence of obsession and irrationality, it is breakthrough.

During an eleven-mile walk in the 100°F-plus heat, we are all in a poignant state of decay, but we still manage to get up close and personal with the area's headliners: lion, elephant, and buffalo. Although not twitchers, we see perhaps a quarter of the valley's four hundred bird species, and while we're focusing binoculars at a regal African fish eagle there is on the ground a blur and a bound: a leopard darts from a nearby tree into the reeds just a few yards away. It's a fantastic sight. Now we've seen the Big Five minus one (the rhino), the best Zambia can offer.

Not long ago, perhaps thirty years, there were as many as twelve thousand black rhinos in the Luangwa Valley, an ideal habitat. By 1986, all black rhinos here were gone, slaughtered by poachers, horns crushed to powder and brokered as a powerful aphrodisiac in the Far East or sold in solid state to wealthy Yemenis for decorative dagger handles.

Tourists come to Africa to see the wildlife, and the most popular draw is the Big Five, which can be ticked off in Botswana, Kenya, Namibia, South Africa, Tanzania, Zimbabwe, and others, but not Zambia, and Zambia suffers for it.

Enter Hugo van der Westhuizen and the Frankfurt Zoological Society, who are undertaking an ambitious plan to reintroduce black rhinos to North Luangwa National Park beginning next year. Hugo hails from South Africa, where he worked for several years in Marakele National Park and on the South African Game Capture Team. His experience with rhino, and his zeal for the cause, have made this effort possible, along with the $300,000 a year the Frankfurt Zoological Society has committed. Already an electrified fence is being constructed in the center of the park, where the first five rhinos, two breeding females and three males translocated from South Africa, will find their new sanctuary. Over the course of three years, fifteen more will be introduced. And if the official scouts and village patrols are successful in keeping poachers at bay, and disease and other disasters don't strike, the fences might someday come down, and rhinos will roam free again, for tourists and others to enjoy.

Hugo flies the Cessna 180, donated by the Frankfurt Zoo, down from Central Rhino Operations Control over to Mwaleshi

Camp to join us for a lunch of pork rolls and deep-fried veggies and describes the challenges he faces. There has been an increase in general poaching of late, he says, as the continuing ban on hunting licenses has robbed locals of expected income. The 140 scouts hired by the Zambian Wildlife Authority (ZAWA) almost went on strike last month because they hadn't been paid. Several of his best scouts have been lost to AIDS or have left to pursue more economically rewarding careers. The money he receives from Germany is only about 60 percent of what he estimates he needs to make the project and the park sustainable. "We'll never get this park to pay for itself," he says with a sigh. "We're just buying time, waiting for a solution to present itself." Perhaps a large endowment or a set of wealthy concerned donors could be the answer, he muses. I ask if Viagra may have reduced the demand for rhino horns in the Far East, and he says no, that there is still a robust market for other medicinal applications, and the demand from Yemen always far exceeded Asia's anyway.

But in the face of this, Hugo is improbably optimistic, almost obsessive in the rightness of his mission. Zambians can't believe he is working year-round in such a remote patch on a nonprofit project and keep wondering as to his real agenda. Some think he is mining gemstones; others believe he is in cahoots with poachers. Still others believe him mad. But Hugo envisions a day when local schoolchildren make field trips to see the rhinos and are awed in their breathing presences; he imagines volunteers patrolling the fences and reporting poaching attempts. He foresees an Africa here as it was a thousand years ago. "I don't know how, but I think we will succeed," he concludes, and heads back to his tiny plane with its doors stripped off, the better to sight poachers and downed wildlife.

Tomorrow we are off to visit the efforts of another man on a utopian quest in Africa: Shiwa Ngandu, The Africa House. One of our party, Paul Maritz, born in Africa but now living in America, has visited this house on the escarpment above us, and he writes this to describe the barmy endeavor:

Shiwa Ngandu sits above the Lake of the Royal Crocodiles, burial place of the Bemba Kings, in remote Northern Zambia. It is still over one hour's drive from the nearest telephone. It is a stately manor house, built in the style of an Italian villa. It looks down on a complete, feudal village, complete with workers' housing and workshops, all now decaying back into the African bush. Only the majestic gum trees that mark the formal steps up to the villa retain their glory. It was all the product of the dreams of one of the last of the Victorians, a testament to all that was good and bad about colonialism.

Sir Stewart Gore-Browne was a complete product of his nation and age. Emotionally deprived and sent to boarding schools as a child, from age ten he would weekly write to his favorite aunt for over fifty years. He kept a daily diary, documenting his war service during the Boer War in South Africa, and in Europe during the First World War. He would be refused in love early in life, but would wait until his forties, to marry the eighteen-year-old daughter of that first love (who would not surprisingly later walk out on him).

Trained in no profession save that of an army officer, he had the active mind and curiosity typical of late Victorians. His sketches and watercolors of the great buildings of Europe fill two volumes. He volunteered in 1910 to serve on the Anglo-Belgian Boundary Commission, which was chartered with tracing the watershed between the two great rivers of southern Africa, the Zambezi and the Congo, and in so doing setting the boundary between British and Belgian influence, and the two postcolonial nations of the Zambia and the Democratic Republic of the Congo.

Whilst on a side hunting trip, Gore-Browne discovered natural hot springs in an idyllic spot on a stream in the highlands of northern Zambia. He resolved to return to the spot. After WWI, using his aunt's money, he returned to commence building his vision of an ideal community: that of an English Lord, resplendent in his manor house, benevolently ruling over peasants engaged in useful work. Overcoming almost insuperable logistical difficulties, he gradually realized his dream. The huge brick Villa has a chapel with memorials to his ancestors, a large library filled with English and French volumes, a bedroom with a huge bathroom and small cubicle for his "batman" [servant]. Having seen the treatment of blacks in South Africa during the Boer War, he was determined to show what an enlightened but traditional English sense of fairness could do. So below are rows of neat brick houses for his subjects.

As his estate slowly took root, Gore-Browne became increasingly involved in the politics of the British colony of Northern Rhodesia. He favored consultation with, and inclusion of, native blacks in politics. This set him at odds with his fellow white settlers. It was typical of his aristocratic charm however, that he became lifelong friends not only with Roy Welensky, the rough-and-ready steam engine stoker who became leader of the white settlers, but also with the emerging black leaders, especially Zambia's first President Kenneth Kaunda. When Gore-Browne died in 1968, it was Kaunda who eulogized him at his funeral.

But it is to the enigma of this hulking mansion in the bush that one returns today. Only the mad confidence of a class of people convinced of the righteousness of their position could lead to its preposterous construction: the Italian dreams of an English mind in the middle of the African bush.

Then to the final leg of our journey, to the Bengwelu Swamps, the source of the second-largest watercourse in Africa, the scrimshaw beginnings of the River Congo, whose vital currents have carried for centuries stores of folly, and on occasion breakthrough, which is then known for that instant as apotheosis now.

THE SOURCE

> *It's not all pleasure, this exploration.*
> —David Livingstone, 1873

Herodotus in the fifth century BC and Ptolemy seven centuries later wrote about the "fountains of the Nile," the waters from which issued the greatest river in the world. To locate its source—*quaerere caput Nili*—was the hope of great captains and geographers from the classical age to the Victorian: Cyrus and Cambyses of Persia, Alexander the Great, Julius Caesar, Nero, and the mid-nineteenth-century rivals, Richard Burton and John Hanning Speke. After dismissing the geographical claims of Speke and Burton (both of whom he disliked, especially Burton, translator of the *Kama Sutra,* a man he considered morally bankrupt), Dr. David Livingstone set out in 1866 on his final expedition to Africa to claim the prize as the discoverer of the source of the Nile. He was convinced the "four fountains" sprang from swamplands in what is today northern Zambia.

Livingstone got it wrong and instead discovered the source of the Congo, second-longest river in Africa, and there he left his heart.

The Scottish missionary-explorer, who spent shy of thirty years seeking "God's Highway" (a water passage into the African interior that would allow colonization, the end of Arab slave trading, and Christian conversion of heathens), died of malaria, dysentery, and melancholia at the age of fifty-nine in the Bangweulu Swamps, desperately clinging to the delusion he was tracking the course of the Nile. His heart was cut from his body, placed in a box, and buried under an mpundu tree, while his body was carried to the coast and shipped to England. One of his last journal entries reads: "Dear God, I am oppressed that this may, after all, be the Congo. Who would risk their life for that dreadful river?"

We would.

First, some background. I have spent much of my career chasing great rivers and managed to organize first descents of sections of the Nile and the Zambezi (the latter picking up where David Livingstone left off in 1855, negotiating the quite wild course through the gorges below Victoria Falls in 1981). But I had never let my hand swirl the waters of the Congo. So quite keen I have been to see this source. Others in the group are enthused to see *Balaeniceps rex,* a rare, dodolike stork with a wedge-shaped bill, known as the shoebill, that hides in the swamps.

So we decamp and begin the two-day drive from one of the most remote parks in Africa to a place beyond remoteness, the trackless swamps of Bangweulu ("where the water meets the sky"). We wend our way for the final time across the Luangwa Valley, toward the Muchinga Escarpment, passing last herds of buffalo and several hyenas, including a couple courting under a wild gardenia tree (when they loped away, I plucked a bouquet as freshener for the Land Cruiser).

Up a rough track we wind out of this southern branch of the Great Rift Valley to the rim, then across the plateau, flat as a griddle. No more drama; no mopane (apologies to Mary J. Blige). With little notice, the watershed is crossed between the Zambezi and the Congo, and we bask in the hot breeze of a plateau nearly four thousand feet high (by average elevation, Zambia is among the highest countries in Africa). We camp at Kapishya Hot Springs, soak under arching raffia palms, swim in another crocodiled river, and listen to the eerie whoops of hyenas as we zip up our sleeping bags for the night. Lions and other cats have been known to attack campers at night, but hyenas are the only animals that assail fairly regularly. One of our party has a friend who lost an ear to a hyena while camping in Mozambique; many years ago I was camping in Awash National Park in Ethiopia, and a French tourist had her face bitten off. So we build a witch burner nearby and hug the bags together, and I take a spot in the middle.

In the sharp morning air we begin the long final stretch to Bangweulu. Outside the town of Mpika, which specializes in brokering salt, bananas, and cassavas, we pass The Clinton Night Club ("Your Pleasure Resort") but manage to resist. The Möbius strip of wildlife protection is presented in all its emptiness as we steer west through the miombo woodlands of Lavushi Manda National Park, a barren passage that reveals only a ragged troop of baboons. There are no game scouts here, no camps, as there are no tourists. Tourists don't come here—not enough wild animals, most poached. The circle of nonlife.

As we knock down the last few miles, we enter a corridor of villages and pass hundreds of children but few adults. The kids wave and yell and run to us, hoping we will stop and change their lives. Many are orphans, parents lost to AIDS. Even though this is not a trucking route or crossroads, where most AIDS is spread in Africa, the women here, we are told, perform dry sex, a practice in which the vagina is dried of its natural secretions, supposedly to give more pleasure to lovers. The extreme friction causes lacerations, which in turn make infection to both sides more likely. Add to this the refusal by many to use free condoms dispensed by health organizations and nongovernmental organizations, believing there is a white man's conspiracy to reduce black African population with dirty tricks, and you get a region where more than 50 percent of the population is younger than fifteen years old.

Late in the day we traverse a single-lane causeway above the floodplain, the dry-season entrance to the game management area that covers the Bangweulu Swamps, and head for a silver water tower, the only relief under the open sky. As with other places on this trip, we are the only visitors, and Gary Williams is pleasantly shocked when his old friend Chriss Wienand walks through the door. For ten years, Gary owned and operated Shoebill Island Camp, four canvas tents and a thatched dinning room catering primarily to trophy hunters. But he sold it last year to the Kasanka Trust, a nonprofit that manages an eponymous nearby park and attempts, with mixed results, to distribute proceeds directly into conservation and development in the park and nearby communities. Gary gave up after the Lusaka government stopped issuing hunting licenses, squashing his main clientele, and because of his frustration with the increase in poachers, who are destroying the main attraction, shoebills, not for meat or resale, but to keep tourists at bay so the poachers can hunt mammals without witnesses or interference. Now the camp receives birders in the prime season, November to March, and the odd ecotourist the rest of the year, not enough to make a business.

In the sweet liquid light of the African morning, we head out on our quest to see a shoebill, a wild stork chase. We drive for half an hour and pass two jackals and a thousand black lechwe, the ergonomically designed, swamp-loving antelope found only here. We slalom through crowded cemeteries of gray termite mounds, park at a temporary fishing village, then begin to walk. "Sludge" is a better word. Quickly we are knee-deep in gloppy mud, and the going is agonizingly slow, the temperature hovering around 100°F. This is not the magnificent source-spotting I had envisioned, and there is no transcendence in touching these waters. As for finding the bird, Chriss had mentioned earlier he had once spent sixteen days in the Bangweulu trying to fetch a shoebill for the San Diego Zoo, but all he got was a feather.

Three hours into the trudge we've seen saddle-billed storks, rufous-bellied herons, various egrets, marabou storks, black-breasted snake eagles, and African marsh harriers, and picked up a few leeches, but no shoebill. Two of our local guides tell us to stay put on what might be called a reverse oasis, a spot of dry land in a sea of cloacal mud and water. The guides will go ahead for fifteen minutes and check out the front lines. But forty minutes later, with no sign of the guides, we decide to turn back. We're low on potable water, and the haze of midday heat is kicking us down. The lamination on my hiking boots has gone, and the bill of my shoe is separating. Slowly we slog back, thirsty, overheated, and tired; the ingredients of a potential epic stew stirring. At one point Sel folds into a pile on the ground, exhausted with the swamp high-stepping under a sun that seems like thunder made visible. He hydrates, rests, recovers, and we continue through the muck. It feels as though we're walking wrapped in hot towels. Paul practically steps on a hyena, which scuttles away with angry eyes. Seven hours after starting, we arrive back at the Land Cruiser, shoebill-less. An hour later, our guides arrive back, saying they saw four.

As with good ecotourists, it is the experience of effort, not the goal, which counts, and we retire to the bar.

A few days ago, the Zambian minister of tourism, the Honorable Marina M. Nsingo, made a speech to her constituency: "Countrymen and -women: I am reliably informed that ecotourism is able to raise revenues far in excess of that obtainable from wildlife revenue generation [read: hunting]. If fully utilized, therefore, it may help us make our rural areas more prosperous and help us eliminate poverty by creating wealth."

That's the not the story we heard on the ground throughout this journey from outfitters, camp operators, and guides. "It would take two hundred ecotourists here to generate as much as one hunting safari," a staff member at the Wildlife Camp in the Lupande Game Management Area told us. The last year data was published, 1999, communities in Lupande received $220,000 from hunting fees, used then to build schools, wells, and clinics, and that's after the various parties in the string, including the central government, took their skim. Ecotourism makes a contribution, to be sure, but very little by comparison, at least now.

I have never hunted; never will. I'm not sure I understand the psychology of trophy hunters, but I know the market exists, and it remains significant. Accepting that, it's hard not to see the short-term benefits of managed, sustainable hunting in a country whose main asset is its considerable wildlife. Ultimately, education and population control will lift the boat, but tourism, of all stripes, may keep it from sinking.

Should you visit Zambia? If you want to see Africa the way Livingstone did, without herds of safari vehicles and bloats of khaki, then Zambia is the place. The variety and numbers of animals are among the greatest on the continent, and the land is as raw, wild, and beautiful as when the first Portuguese traders stepped over the horizon. And what about being so close to Zimbabwe? The biggest fallout from the country across the Zambezi is the cost of goods and services here. Zambian camps and lodges are offering discounts of 70 percent or more to entice visitors, and it is a better bargain now than perhaps ever. And it seems extremely unlikely that the politics of race overwhelming

Zimbabwe could happen here. The countries have about the same population, but while there are twenty thousand to thirty thousand whites in Zimbabwe, not long ago owning a disproportionate amount of land, there are just two thousand to six thousand whites in Zambia, and all land is state-owned.

The leap forward for Zambia, the reach to sustainability, may be with seemingly mad schemes such as Chriss's Mandevu Game and Adventure Ranch. Because it is entirely private, there are no subornations in the chain. Money in doesn't line pockets but instead pays salaries and goes directly to community works, which Chriss supervises personally. Yes, this can work only on a small scale, but it may prove a model, and if so, it may spread. Zambia proudly promotes its national parks, but more than half are derelict, with no management, no wildlife, and no tourists. Mandevu may be an alternative, a pioneer of some sorts.

We wind up our two-week expedition through Zambia at Shoebill Camp with a dinner of *nsima,* the gritslike mash made from maize flour, the national meal. On top is poured a tasty sauce of tomatoes, okra, peppers, and onions . . . at last we've reached the sauce of the Congo. And I sit back and sip a warm Mosi beer, which tastes a lot like the best Guinness, only better.

14

THE MOST POWERFUL PLACE ON EARTH

Macedonia

There was a time when this question begged no debate. For a dozen years in the fourth century BC, Alexander of Macedon set about on a shock-and-awe campaign to conquer and unite the known world, and with a core of some forty thousand men from his highland kingdom he did just about that, becoming the first and arguably the only world leader history has known. Virtually all the lands from Egypt to India fell to the sword of Alexander the Great, and no place was more feared or revered than the place from which he hailed, Macedonia.

Even before Alexander, the place called Macedonia evoked power of which to steer clear. When the ancient Greeks held the Olympics, they forbade participation from their mountainous neighbor to the north because the hunter-warriors there were too strong, too good—the geographic equivalent of steroids. It was believed the Macedonians were descendents of Zeus, after all. When Alexander decided to enter the Olympics, he proved the dread justifiable: he won.

After Alexander died, at the seasoned age of thirty-two, Macedonia became the *Catena Mundi,* the link between worlds, the mystic cultural crossroads, the nexus of epochs, the power junction coveted by all. And most everyone had a turn: the

Romans, the Huns, the Goths, the Normans, the Byzantines, the Bulgarians, the Ottomans, the Serbs, even the Germans during World War II. After the war, it became the southernmost province of Yugoslavia, from which it bloodlessly reimagined itself as a nation-state in 1991. Through it all a certain character persevered, a stolid grit, a rocklike steadfastness and resolve that transcends time and empires while at the same time assimilating the more sapid traits of conquerors and passers-through, creating a sort of *Makedoniki salata* of temperament and spirit.

Today, Macedonia is a place few Americans can find on a map. Students of the Bible know it as the place where the Apostle Paul introduced Christianity to Europe. Some think it a prehistoric address in North America where woolly elephant types, mastodons, roamed a million years ago. Many understandably confuse the landlocked nation with the northernmost region of Greece, also called Macedonia, and in fact the name share is a constant sore between the common borders, a fear fever for territorial irredentism.

There are no direct flights to Skopje, the capital of Macedonia, from the Americas. I fly via Moscow, and while in transit meet an Afghani who lives in Los Angles but is returning to Kandahar with his wife and daughter for holiday. When I tell him my destination he shoots a stare of shock. "You're going to Macedonia? Isn't that dangerous?"

The Balkans as a whole are still perceived by much of the world as mired in melee, powder-kegged and unsafe, when in fact the wars ended a decade ago, and Macedonia was sidelined for most of the action anyway. There was a brief flare in 2001, when ethnic Albanians, who make up a quarter of the population, made a bid for independence, but a resolution of greater autonomy and representation soothed the tensions, and now there seems a unified desire for peace and better business. There are determined efforts to turn the agrestic country into a high-tech center or a hub for ethanol and other alternative-fuel sources, and with its extravagant mountains, healing hot springs, and rich archaeological and religious history, a major tourist draw. We've come to explore Macedonia, to unturn its stones of adventure, to unlock a few of its treasures, and perhaps unmask some of its many, many mysteries.

Macedonia is fecund with archaeology. You can send a spade into the earth practically anywhere and turn up an antique coin, a shard, a helmet, even a golden glove, thousands of years old. There's a shadow industry of "diggers" who skulk about with scoops and shovels and trade their finds on the black market, sometimes for millions of denars. In the southwestern quadrant, on the dusty shores of the deepest lake in Europe, we meet the foremost over-ground archaeologist, Dr. Pasko Kuzman, who has been excavating three-thousand-year-old submerged cities and the first fortress of King Philip II, Alexander's father. He is a carbon-dated copy of Anthony Hopkins as the lost anthropologist in the film *Instinct,* a permanent, supernal glow to his face like a religious icon, long white hair airborne, chest hairs popping around his Neolithic cutting-stone pendant, and stray-dog restless, like his hero, Alexander, whom he admires as a "philosopher in action."

Pasko's signature tools include three weighty watches he wears on his left wrist, which he calls his time machines. With one he says he travels to the Bronze and Neolithic ages. With another, to the future. And with the third, his "archaeological watch," which has special sensors, he makes his finds. "If it beeps twice, it is silver; three times, and I've struck gold."

To prove his prowess, Pasko offers to take us to "Cabinet Troja," his attic lab up several flights of narrow stairs in a museum that looks designed by Frank Gehry without the curves. He flips on the fluorescent lights, and there along long tables and shelves are the fruits of his plow: rows of spears, shields, arrowheads, swords, necklaces, wine goblets, and rusted bronze battle helmets, including one with a wreath and curving ram's horns, similar to how Alexander is depicted on coins and plates. It amazes me that all these treasures are spilled about this loft like a boy's rock collection, ignorant of order, protection, and neatness, and we're allowed to fondle these artifacts, reaching back and touching the works of hands from more than two millennia ago.

Then, after we try to squeeze into the narrow helmets and imagine marching thousands of miles in such, not to mention doing battle, with a twinkly beam Pasko reaches into a pencil cup on his desk and pulls out a silver key. He opens a file cabinet and sets down a container that looks like the humidor for some sort of theatrical MacGuffin. We all lean over, and he snaps back the lip to reveal his greatest unearthing, the golden mask of Trebenista, along with a golden glove wearing a gold ring, all of which he discovered in 2002 in a tomb here beneath Ohrid, the oldest continually inhabited city in Europe, dating back some seven thousand years.

This is perhaps the most significant modern-day find in Macedonia, and it has made Pasko a bit of a celebrity, and we all know who will play him in the movie. Four other similar masks were spirited across borders, sold in black markets, and are now showcased in museums in Sofia and Belgrade. Pasko keeps this one in a cigar box in his musty loft. He insists I hold the delicate, fifth-century-BC visor, which I almost drop when he remarks it could fetch $18 million on the open market. But he seems none the worried, as though there are troves more where this came from. Two years before he uncovered this mask, his watch beeped three times, so he knew it was coming.

Pasko explains the mask was funereal, intended to help the dead communicate with the living. To further clarify, he waxes as precise and elusive as a Bashō haiku: "Through the archives of the earth, and the archives of consciousness, Macedonia threads both as legend and reality."

Pasko himself seems threaded in legend and reality, a man who uses the power of the past to understand the future.

"What do you see?" I ask.

"Macedonia will never disappear. It is a legendary place that will exist through time. Only when the basic elements of the universe cease to exist so then will Macedonia."

"What have you learned?"

"Alexander fused the world. He used his power greatly. He enabled the people of Iraq and Iran, Palestine and Egypt, India and Pakistan to live together, to live in abundance. We try to reach this ideal, but we cannot. We can only aspire to understand the world as Alexander. If we have one hundred years of peaceful development we will still be far back. But someday, if we use the lights of history to look into the future, we will be forward to the past."

And with that Pasko puts the mask back in the box, ushers us through the door, and with a swipe of his thumb turns off the lights and the power of this improbable place at the radius of the world.

Where Did Science and Religion Begin?

Two men in blue standing on a mountain in northeast Macedonia claim it began here, at an ancient sacred temple called Kokino. Just five years ago, archaeologist Jovica Stankovski and astrophysicist Gjore Cenev were poking about the Bronze Age ruins near the top of this three-thousand-foot-high neovolcanic shock when they noticed certain notches were aligned with positions of the sun and moon. A year later, their discovery was validated by NASA. Just beneath the summit of Taticev Kamen, the cut andesite rocks and hand-hewn thrones make up what is being marketed as the Macedonian Stonehenge, as one of the greatest megalithic observatories in the world, the only one so far discovered in Eastern Europe, ranking up there with Angkor Wat in Cambodia and Abul Simbel in Egypt.

Like boys on a treasure hunt, Gjore and Jovica scramble about this site, excitingly pointing to each marker and cut, oblivious to the 110°F heat, espousing their theories. It was, they believe, crafted by a pagan cult in one of the first known efforts to create a calendar. As in the illustrious scene in *Raiders of the Lost Ark,* the sun here would climb at the solstice and pour a ray through a slit in the rock. The rising beam would then illume the face of the high priest, who sat on a stone throne. The meeting of the sun and the mountain represented a marriage of two gods, and at that moment a series of sacrifices would begin—horses, bulls, rams, goats, perhaps humans, but certainly virgin wool. The blood spilled would fertilize the soil, promising abundance in the season ahead, and the union between sky and earth, between gods and people, would be manifest.

These rituals, set to celestial movements, allowed the first measurements of time and made possible an organized society that knew when to plant seed, when to harvest, when to move the goats and sheep to pasture. Before such, people lived in roaming tribes, living off what they could hunt and gather, with no discernible science or religion. But if this is where it all began, the archaeo-astronomical duo also proffer that this is where religion and science divided, as these ancient practitioners discovered that each had merits that evolved civilization separately from the other, and that split continues, ever widening, today.

Macedonia, as a vortex of deep history, boils with mysteries. While I am on this expedition a team announces that it has redeciphered the middle text of the Rosetta stone, and that it is written in ancient Macedonian, confirming the western reach of the empire, and that the Macedonians were the "masters of that time." It seems to make sense since the Rosetta stone was issued by priests to glorify Ptolemy V's coronation at the mouth of Nile, and the Ptolemaic dynasty had descended from Ptolemy Soter, one of Alexander the Great's generals, a Macedonian. But heretofore scholars had presented the Rosetta stone as written in just two languages, Egyptian hieroglyphic script and ancient Greek. And if there is one certainty with mysteries it is that such revisionist interpretations only make the mysteries murkier, and more debatable.

Then there are the wholly unsolved runes. Alexander the Great's golden sarcophagus, a treasure that would fetch untold millions today, has never been found, and there are theories it lies in a crypt yet uncovered. Along the Markova River just outside Skopje, where yellow flecks stipple the beaches, some archaeologists conjecture the Golden Fleece was cached in a cave. The Knights Templars marched down the Via Egnatia, the great Roman road that runs across Macedonia, on their way back from Jerusalem, where some believe they stole the Ark of the Covenant, which may be buried somewhere around here. A Macedonian village is named after the Bogomils, suggesting to some the heretical sect started here. Just above Lake Ohrid, which has risen hundreds of feet over the centuries, concealing lost cities, even perhaps Atlantis, archaeologist Pasko Kuzman leads us down an alley into a junkyard of rusted tools and auto parts. Here, Pasko worms down a dark warren and motions us to stoop and follow. Suddenly we are in a musty ancient tomb, and by its size, about the dimensions of a hotel suite, it was a sepulchre for royalty. Could it have been Alexander's?, I ask Pasko. In the darkness I can still see his impish eyes dart as he replies, "It is not for me to say." Regardless, the burial chamber is empty, perhaps the victim of one of the many tomb raiders who steal about this country smuggling antediluvian treasures to overseas buyers.

WHERE DID ART BEGIN?

Just outside the municipality of Kratovo, we meet Dr. Dusko Aleksovski, who holds advanced degrees in philology, archaeology, and paleolinguistics. He is renowned as the man who discovered rock art in Macedonia in 1991 and went on to locate more than a million prehistoric wall engravings and etchings. And he has the medals to prove it: one for practically every find hangs from his chest in the official portrait at the World Academy of Rock Art, based in Kumanovo, Macedonia, of which he is founder and president. He leads us to his most recent find, Tsotsev Kamen, a hellishly hot and hard-to-climb basaltic mesa fashioned for Neolithic fertility and wine ceremonies, where the mystery seems to be why anyone would build a temple here. On the back, we crawl up past a dead snake that once guarded the cave to a mural of petroglyphs some twenty thousand years old. Dusko raises his wrist, wreathed in a bead bracelet of rock art symbols, and points out a stick figure in a yahoo stance, then what he calls "the tree of fertility," and finally a man traveling with a chariot. Afterward, at his Rock Art Museum, crammed with as many testimonies to his finds as actual finds, he turns on his favorite rock star, Bob Marley, and raises a glass of *rakija*: "I believe rock art is the heart and soul of Macedonia. It is the beginning of all art."

WHERE DID WE TRANSITION FROM ANIMAL BEINGS TO BEINGS ABOVE THE ANIMALS?

Near the mountains called Jakob and David, in a golden wheat field, by a spreading walnut tree, there is an inauspicious ditch about ten feet deep and perhaps thirty foot square. It was here in the autumn of 2000 that Milos Bilbija, an archaeologist at the Museum of the City of Skopje, unearthed a clay figurine of a contemplative man, a statue that dates to seven thousand five hundred years ago, an effigy he calls Adam of Macedonia. The little sculpture is quite realistic, with human skin color, defined muscles, a visible spine, even a penis, with a flared disc representing the sun in his solar plexus, the great chakra portal. I am told this is the oldest carved figure of a man ever found. It is significant, says Milos, because it solves a great mystery: it tells us when people changed their consciousness about who they are. Prior to this, all figurines found around the world were of goddesses—some fifty were discovered deeper down in this trench. And in the layer above this ceramic man, metal jewelry and buttons were exhumed, marking the beginnings of the Bronze Age. Milos posits that Adam has his ass in the Neolithic and is facing the Megalithic, the tipping point where there is recognition that the difference between humans and animals is spirituality, the knowledge that we have a soul. And it happened here, in what Milos calls "the navel of the world."

"How did we make this leap?" I ask Milos as we kneel in this vital ditch sifting the sands of history.

"We have a thousand musicians but only one Mozart—then there were many priests but only one genius. It takes only one man to change the world."

"How do you know this is the truth?"

"You find the truth by digging. To me, the mystery of Macedonia is not a mystery . . . It is reality."

WHERE IS JESUS CHRIST'S CROSS?

For a place with such profligate history, it keeps itself quite masked. I could find mention in no guidebook, and there are no signposts as we wind up the leafy mountain pass in southwestern Macedonia and park outside a disconsolate-looking gate that states the house rules with a simple line illustration, slashed with a red X, of a man in shorts and muscle shirt, both of which cameraman Didrik Johnck is wearing. Nonetheless, the keeper of this monastery allows us a clothing exception, and we file into a nondescript block of a building to be dazzled within by the Church of Immaculate Mother of God, Sveta Bogorodica Precista. Like most Orthodox churches, its core is the bottom to a cupola with extravagant frescoes and a visual feast of Christian iconography wherever the eye falls. A parade of history has marched here. I'm told by Agnia, the diminutive custodian, that the Knights Templars trekked the Via Egnatia to this hill in the ninth century carrying Moses's sarcophagus. Richard the Lion Hearted wintered here in the late twelfth century on his way to Jerusalem. Even some of the relatives of the last Russian czar, Nicholas Romanov, found refuge here during the Russian Revolution, and the last one died, still cloistered, just ten years back.

But the piece that catches my eye, or rather not, as I am not qualified to open the lid, is a cloaked stone box in the back of the church that supposedly holds a splinter from the true cross of Jesus Christ. Just a couple of months back, I met an eminent biblical archaeologist along the Jordan River who said there simply was no physical evidence that Jesus actually existed, and if what lies within this box is what they say, then here lies proof. Nobody I can find in the monastery has actually seen the artifact, and there seems no photographic substantiation, but the faithful of this monastery have absolute conviction it lies in state in the small chamber in the recesses of this little-known Macedonian Orthodox Church.

Few countries have such an abundance of hidden apologues, spiritual relics of dynasties and conquests, furtive monuments filled with seals, codes, parchments, icons and frescoes, arabesques and crescents. Ever since humans began to wander across these fertile hills some twenty thousand years ago, it has been a labyrinthine crossroads of cultures and religions, and there are testaments almost everywhere in Macedonia.

CAN THE DEAD CURSE THE LIVING?

Spirituality before Muhammad, before Christ, came in all stripes, as it does today.

As we slash our way through stinging nettles, fire plants, and wild strawberries up the unreasonably steep Tajmiska River Valley, I'm told I am about to witness something few outsiders have ever seen, the unmapped Spirit Cave of Macedonia. After two hours of bushwhacking in brutal heat, we clamber up a craggy wall and peer into a coolly enticing cave entrance the size of a refrigerator. Enticing for the fact that just within its mouth are strewn several human bones, including a tibia and fibula that seem to point outward like a warning. Our guide is Koyo Koyocku, secretary of the local speleological club and one of the discoverers of this cave. "Discover" is a relative term, as it is clear it has been used for centuries, mostly, Koyo says, by nearby villagers who come here to pray to spirits not described in any book. When conventional religion, medicine, or science fails, they scale to this fissure to beseech the supernatural for health, for fertility, and for peace in the afterlife, as quite a few, it seems, drop in here and never come out. Not fifteen yards into the cave, we pass a bleached human skull, its black sockets seemingly staring at us from the floor; then we pass another, and three more, then piles of human bones and scatterings of skulls. Never have I passed through such a creepy place, or one so fairylike. As we screw our bodies deeper into the twisting ossuary, I sweep my flashlight by flowstones that look like melting cake icing, helicites like soda straws, crystals like frostwork, and skulls like nightmares. There may be as many as a thousand skulls here, so supposes Koyo, dating back two thousand years, many deposited during battles with the Romans. But one spiritual aspect transcends the ages and cosmologies: superstition. As Didrik asks to move a skull for a better shot, Koyo says we mustn't disturb the dead: "Bad things happen." Then he tells the story of four folks from a Skopje television station who recently came to record the contents of the cave. Against the advice of the villagers they took four skulls back to town to film under studio conditions. Three months later, two of the crew died under mysterious circumstances. The other two found themselves quite ill, yet even in a weakened condition they hiked back up to the cave and returned the skulls, whereupon they returned to health.

There is power in these hidden places. The power of belief, the power of myth, the power of symbols. One such place is invisible: Mother Teresa's birthplace at the edge of a city mall in Skopje. Nothing remains of the hallowed address but a plaque, the home having been leveled in the 1963 earthquake, yet the power of the imagined imagery of the "Saint of the Gutter" is such that this nothingness is a tourist attraction.

Religions have competed for supremacy here for centuries. For five hundred years the Ottoman Turks ruled, and that legacy punctures the sky with the white needles of minarets throughout cities and countryside. During the Ottoman era, churches were not allowed to reach higher than a mosque. Now Macedonia is primarily a Christian enclave, and the Macedonian Orthodox Church erected a giant electric cross in 2002 on Mount Vodno, looming over the capital of Skopje and the neighborhoods of the minority Muslim Albanians, a sign of the times. One resident of the capital told me the only time she feels comfortable is when the crescent moon rises next to the Millennium Cross and hangs for a moment in harmony.

It is said there are 365 holy sites around Lake Ohrid. During the Ottoman rule there were efforts to loot and burn many of the Christian churches, and when that happened, relics and records were spirited away to hide in the thirteenth-century St. Clement's Church of the Holy Mother of God Most Glorious. The curator, Jana Popovska, has been showing off the medieval paintings and artifacts for twenty years, yet her enthusiasm for these treasures bubbles as though this is the first day on the job. When I ask her about the power of this hidden spiritual vault, one that escaped the tyranny of rivals for centuries, she, instead of invoking divinity, pounds her chest three times with her fist, and through a beatific tear proclaims, "The real power is here . . . in your heart."

IS THERE A FOUNTAIN OF YOUTH?

The residual mayhem of one of geology's greatest crashes, the point where the African, Asian, and European tectonic plates collide, is the gift of a lavishly fertile land of volcanoes and mineral hot springs, a land perhaps more gracious to health and healing than any other, and yet it is so little known as to be almost abstract.

Almost 80 percent of Macedonia is mountainous, and herein gurgle and effervesce some sixty-five identified thermo-mineral healing springs. Just twenty-three kilometers southeast of Skopje, where the river Pchinja passes through the Katlanovo Hills, is the Katlanovska Banja, a "center for prolonged healing and rehabilitation." It seems the antispa, no sandalwood incense, kukui-nut massage oil, lavender-scented candles, or Enya here. Its outside is distinguished by the number of broken windows and cracks running down the crumbly walls. The delicate perfume of rotten eggs wafts. Inside is equally appetizing.

But people don't come here for the ambience; they come for the waters.

In her starched white uniform and sensible shoes, Dr. Stefonkos Mateuska, the chief rehabilitation specialist at Katlanovska, tells me the water is hypermineralized, with a unique cocktail of sulfur, chlorides, carbonates, calcium, iron, magnesium, and more. Since the second century BC, the Romans and subsequent cognoscenti have used these baths to cure rheumatism, arthritis, and a host of chronic, neurological, and orthopedic diseases. It's also considered a fountain of youth, and villagers come from all over with plastic bottles to fill for timely consumption. In the main bathhouse, which is gender segregated, I strip and ease into the hot water, which is indeed blissfully soothing. In the pool I meet two enthusiasts, Koce Sokolov, who was in an awful car crash that broke his back and has found near total healing here, and Dusan Antovski, who shows a six-inch scar on his knee from a basketball accident. He says he hobbled here on crutches, and after twenty days of treatments he threw his crutches away, and now he runs.

Later, Dr. Mateuska tells me she has never seen an American at this spa; it is just not known beyond these borders. But she compares its waters with the spas of Vichy, with one noteworthy difference: whereas treatments in France often go for two hundred dollars, or even two thousand dollars, here the soak I just enjoyed was two dollars.

CAN PLANTS REALLY CURE?

Wherever one sets a foot in Macedonia, there are brilliant plants and flowers with naturopathic powers. One of the secrets of Alexander the Great's success was that he and his soldiers knew these properties. There are endemics, such as *zolta koskoina*, which went into a poultice for battle bruises; *Stellaria media*, a decoction of which could heal a sword cut; *Arnica montana*, which helped with swelling from a javelin wound. *Narthecium ossifragum* was particularly effective in healing fractures from bludgeon blows, and when battles went bad, a tonic from saffron was used to alleviate post-traumatic stress syndrome. Then there was the lobe-leafed *cemerika*, a toxin used by witches, and conspirators. It may be that one of the world's first ethnobotanists was done in by a plant, as some theorize that cemerika poisoned Alexander the Great.

We have occasion to test at least one of the special elixirs here. After we thrash through the forest on the way to the Spirit Cave, Didrik's leg is on fire from brushing against stinging nettles. He's screaming in pain when I hand him a bottle of locally brewed kantarion oil, from the yellow perennial of the same name. It doesn't immediately ease the pain, he says, but I can vouch for the fact that he is almost instantly less irritable and anxious, and that pesky jaundice is just gone.

CAN WATER MAKE MIRACLES?

High in the blue mountains above the village of Drugovo, inside the walls of the Monastery of Sveta Bogorodica Precista, there is a cool mountain spring that serves all denominations with its healing powers. The nun who is caretaking when we arrive tells us the water here regularly performs miracles. I ask if she has witnessed any, and she nods vigorously and cites a seventeen-year-old girl who suddenly went mute. She came here and drank the water, washed some over her face, then spent the night in the adjacent church with her mother next to her. In the morning, she opened the door, and her voice rang over the hills. The nun herself is living testament. In 1999, she and six others, including a three-month-old baby, all three of whom had partaken in the holy water, left the monastery for a road trip. On the second curve going down the steep mountain the car veered off a cliff. It crashed into a tree and was totaled. Yet miraculously all seven, including the baby, were thrown safely from the car before impact. The police later puzzled over the impossibility as they found all the doors locked and the windows rolled up in the smashed vehicle.

The nun says also that many have journeyed here for fertility, and after imbibing these sacred waters, which she says are blessed by Jesus Christ, then crawling three times through a low stone arch and worming thrice through a rosary rope the size of a hula hoop, they almost always create the miracle of new life.

After bouncing about this wild and determinedly declivitous country for a week, my bones are feeling a bit jarred, and

I decide I need to go see the doctor. I need some Macedonian healing. So up a stony hill outside of Ohrid I go, and in front of a little clapboard house with a grand view of the scintillant lake, I meet Dr. Nikola "Feelgood" Julovski. From a crude, steaming still that dominates his driveway, a copper tube crosses several feet to a cooling container with a spigot. The good doctor puts a tulip glass beneath the spout, and out decants the most widely used home-brewed therapy in Macedonia: the Slavic Tonic, double-distilled rakija. He tells me the secret to a long life is a glass of rakija in the morning, a glass of Macedonian red wine at lunch, and glasses of both in the evening, sharing that his ninety-five-year-old mother, who has religiously followed this protocol since becoming an adult, is planning on "catching a hundred."

I can almost see the vapors as he hands me the glass and pre-scribes I must swallow the clearly potent remedy in a single shot. He offers to demonstrate with his own glass, and I follow. The dosage is apparently not sufficient for what ails, and he prescribes several more, each time leading the way. Soon I'm stuck between rakija and a hard place, about to become part of the cultural sedi-ment, looking for ways to retreat before the cure becomes the complaint, but not wanting to offend the hospitality of the doc-tor. Each time I stand up to depart he grabs my sleeve and pulls me back to the chair for another, doctor's orders.

If there are miracles in Macedonia, one is certainly that I woke up in my own hotel bed the next morning, before noon, phenomenally unlooped, with bones not broken, and actually feeling a bit better for the treatment. In this sanitorium coun-try that is a whirlpool of high tectonics, rakija, I believe now, is indeed the low-tech tonic that heals.

WHERE PASSIONS RULE
With a population of just two million people in a country the size of Taiwan (which has twenty-three million), a culture of biking and walking, and no real heavy industry, Macedonia has the cleanest air and water in Eastern Europe. Combined with its

voluptuous mountains and urgent canyons, that means the country is designed for adventure. In our brief stay, we set out on a too-ambitious schedule to scuba dive in Lake Ohrid (among its underwater ruins), rappel the ninety-foot-high Smolare waterfall on Belasica Mountain, spelunk the galaxy of caves, paraglide over wineries, jeep-safari the Sara Mountains, and hike the blossoming highlands, and more, but we can't squeeze them all in.

My cohorts John Canning and Jon Brick get up one morning at two to head out with Boris the Balloonist and ride the dawn over the Towers of Marko, a medieval fortress, and the elegiac landscapes featured in the Milcho Manchevski's films *Before the Rain* and *Dust*. When they start to descend into a graveyard, a set of toothy dogs yip at the approaching basket, so Boris fires the burner and lifts the balloon, only to have it plop into a farmer's backyard, where the alien gondoliers are treated to the hospitality that infuses a place that has accommodated more landlords than Manhattan. At 8:00 a.m., they are implored by strangers to sit down and share Turkish coffee, breakfast sweets, and rakija.

Didrik and I sleep in and at a reasonable hour make a four-wheel-drive trundle through the Mavrovo National Park, up Mount Bistra to the Mavrovo Ski Resort, where we hook up with superfit and Lycra-decked Zlatko Sapundzija, at fifty-six the top mountain biking guide in Macedonia. We take a ski lift to a denuded summit that sprawls in the shadow of the country's highest peak, Kobilino Pole, on the Albanian border, 9,068 feet above the Aegean. From here we start our whorling dervishlike descent, unwinding the Alpine mount, passing long streams of sheep and into herds of galloping wild horses. These hills breed tough people, and animals, and some say it was here that Alexander the Great gathered his battle-worthy horses, including his legendary steed, Bucephalus.

We continue riding down, down, down, until we glide into the abandoned Vlach village of Galicnik, literally hanging over the Radika gorge. Our guide, Nora Buklevska, summers here at her mother's hundred-year-old house, and she tells us the hamlet once thrived as it produced a special sheep cheese that was exported to Egypt, even America. But, Nora says, the socialism of the former Yugoslavia took away the spirit, motivation, and incentive to live in this scenic fastness, and the residents, including her mother, moved away to more hospitable climes, and now it appears as a faded postcard of an aerie remembrance.

ARE WOMEN EQUAL TO MEN IN ADVENTURE SPORTS?

Up another river valley, the Treska, the water does a *danse de ventre* through a series of green-and-red-striped gates, one of the world's top wild-water slalom runs. It was built in 1975 by champion kayaker Mico Popovski, a competitor in the Munich Olympics, and has been used for training and international competitions since. Mico is now the coach for the Ilinden kayaking club, named for the rebel spirit of the Ilinden Uprising of 1903 when a little mountain village beat back the Ottomans and created the first nation state in the Balkans, the "Krushevo Republic," one that lasted all of ten days.

When I ask Mico who is the best boater on the course today, he doesn't hesitate a second to point out a hunched paddler who is playing a sharp wave like jazz: "Lazar. He came in seventh in the Athens Olympics."

"What's his last name?" I hang my pen over my notebook.

"Popovski"

"Same as yours?"

"He's my son."

Lazar, as it turns out, actually finished sixteenth in Athens. A proud father's memory may be exaggerating his son's accomplishments. Still, it seems this river has produced one of the few, if not the only, father and son Olympic kayaker duos, as both competed in the Barcelona Olympics. Lazar went on to vie for gold in Atlanta, Sydney, and Athens and is now training for Beijing. He has a brother who is also a keen boater, and when I scan the windmilling pageant of kayakers, I ask Mico why there are no women on this river.

"It's a problem for women to be in a kayak. They are very scared."

It's true that in all the adventures we've explored in Macedonia, we have yet to encounter a woman participant, which may be something prenatal, or just unfair sampling, or a vestigial artifact of the old ways as this young mountain country transitions from a peasant to a modern culture. You wouldn't know that visiting the cities, however.

After a week of exploring and adventuring, we take to Skopje for deserved pampering. We sample the rightly praised wine Alexander the Grape, the plumply applauded tomatoes, and other organic foods (most everything is naturally organic as the farmers can't afford pesticides) along the corridors of riverside cafes and in the alleys of the Turkish Old Bazaar. And we head to the freshly opened Vital Beauty Center, a space-age spa that uses high-tech French-manufactured machines that look like surface-to-air missiles to ease some of the aches and pains.

CAN LOVE KILL?

And we head to the Capri bar, for 22 years the watering hole for the fashionable and famous, and meet the proprietor, Dragan Muratovski, who with his bald pate, body shirt, and single earring is the simulacrum of Mr. Clean gone hedonistic. Dragan orders up some rakija, and after a shot I ask why he named his haunt "Capri."

He drops his head toward his glass and sighs: "It is because of the biggest regret of my life. The biggest mistake of my life." He then tells the story, one as florid, romantic, tragic, and optimistic as Macedonia itself.

When Dragan was a young man, he traveled to the island of Capri and met a beautiful Italian woman, Laura. They fell madly in love and spent the perfect summer together. They resolved to continue the relationship, to take it to a higher level. Dragan had to return home for a spell but was able to make his way back earlier than expected, and he set out to surprise his love. He called ahead and reserved a suite and had it filled with flowers and champagne. But when he walked into the hotel he heard Laura's laughter wafting from the pool. He rushed outside and saw her splashing about and playing with another man. He couldn't hold back his anger and pulled the man from the pool and beat him up. Dragan then hastened to the suite for his retreat, where he received a call from his lover's father, who informed him that he had just bloodied his daughter's visiting cousin. The father forbade Dragan to see his daughter again and disappeared with her.

Dragan returned to Macedonia and opened this bar in her tribute. He lost himself in collecting expeditions to Africa and Asia and brought back a capuchin monkey from Thailand as a companion. But he was depressed and anxious, still pining for his lost love. When after five years the monkey suddenly died, he went to a psychic to understand why. She said the monkey absorbed his stress and it was too much for his little heart, so he suffered a fatal stroke. Dragan had the monkey stuffed, and he hangs today in an apartment above the Capri with a little smile curled across his face.

After telling the tale and showing me the monkey, Dragan belts back another rakija, puts on some Caprian music, and sits down facing the door as he always does, hoping, he says, that someday his long-lost Laura will walk through it.

It might be said that Macedonians, like many from every state in the Balkans, are wistful for the time when their borders had the longest reach and their power was at its apogee, and each naturally claims that political lines should now resolve to this time. Like Dragan, they continue their lives, rich with adventure, ardent with passions and the never-ending quests for the good drink and brilliant memories. But they remain always watching, waiting, and hoping that the greatness of the past will once more walk through the door, and the world will be right again.

15

ED VIESTURS AND HIS IMPOSSIBLE DREAM

Annapurna, Nepal

The paramount moment in mountaineering history was when Edmund Hillary and Sherpa Tenzing Norgay stood atop the apex of the earth in 1953, the first to crown that glory after a half century of attempts.

The second-most-hailed event in such narrations was when an American team, led by Jim Whittaker, summited Everest in 1963. For America, Whittaker's achievement was treated like putting a man on the moon.

But these seminal achievements pale next to the objective I am accompanying: the attempt by Ed Viesturs to be the first American to summit all fourteen peaks in the world that are more than 8,000 meters (26,250 feet), above what climbers call the death zone, all without bottled oxygen, the ultimate in physical and mental challenges. The final summit in Ed's odyssey is the 26,545-foot (8,091-meter) Annapurna, perhaps the second-most-famous Himalayan mountain after Everest and notably more difficult and dangerous to climb. Statistically it is the world's most hazardous mountain. One climber dies for every two who reach the summit.

Only a handful of people have ever attained this utmost coronet (Italian Reinhold Messner blazed this conceit in 1986), and no other American has come close. Ed, who is known for his judicious approach to mountain safety, has twice turned around on the five-mile-high frozen monolith of ice and stone that is Annapurna, citing suboptimal conditions. But the stakes are higher now than ever before in this eighteen-year pursuit. Ed is on the far side of his middle forties and has a wife, Paula, and three young children: Gil, seven; Ella, four; and now Ana-bel, born just last October, awaiting his return. He now climbs to come home.

I first met Ed in 1996 when David Roberts, the renowned mountaineering author, brokered a get-together in Seattle. I was so impressed with Ed's soft-spoken demeanor, his sensible style— the antithesis of the swaggering, feverish, mountain-sized-ego, risk-it-all personality that infuses so many extreme adventurers (sometimes fatally)—that I decided to become involved in his quest. At the time I was a founding executive at Expedia, and so I arranged for the company to sponsor Ed on his attempt at Annapurna—twice. And I was mightily impressed that despite the sponsorship dollars and a watchful press, he turned around within tantalizing sight of the summit. If there is a man who knows and breathes the management of risk, it is Ed Viesturs. In 1988, on his first attempt on 29,035-foot Mount Everest, Ed turned around 300 feet from the crest. On 26,300-foot Shisha-pangma, he stopped 20 feet shy of the top.

"The mountain decides when you go up, not you," Ed likes to say.

Ed sometimes calls himself a "freak of nature." Although he hails from what he calls "the great mountaineering state of Illi-nois," Ed possesses a phenomenal physiognomy and a unique mental toughness. He was tested at a physiology lab at the University of Washington, with results showing his lungs much larger than normal, allowing an abnormally high intake of oxygen at altitude. Whereas climbing stairs at sea level takes the wind out of most of us, he doesn't find the wheeze until he's halfway up the Himalayas.

He's climbed Everest six times and has broached other

mountains more than 8,000 meters high twenty-one times to date, a world record. Some, in a green-eyed way, call it serial summit disorder.

In character, Ed has devised a plan to iron out as much risk as possible in the cloth of this next climb. Along with longtime partner Veikka Gustafsson, of Finland, he is doing a series of high-altitude practice runs on nearby Cho Oyu (which Ed topped in 1994 and 1996), a mount on the border of Tibet and Nepal that reaches even higher than Annapurna, but is considered a less-pernicious peak. Also with Ed is Wyoming-based photographer Jimmy Chin, who joined Ed last year on Everest as they were shooting scenes for an upcoming feature film based on *Into Thin Air,* the best-selling account of the 1996 Everest disaster that killed Ed's pals and climbing partners Rob Hall, of New Zealand, and Scott Fischer, of Seattle, along with seven others.

Ed was on the mountain on May 10, 1996, working on the IMAX film *Everest.* An unexpected storm blew in, lashing climbers near the summit with 100-mile-per-hour winds that obscured their route down the mountain. Ed and the rest of his crew had decided not to attempt the summit that day, so instead were reduced to communicating over the radio as Rob Hall slowly froze to death, trapped high on the mountain. Ed tried to cajole his friend to his feet, but it was too late.

"We knew he was going to go to sleep that night and that he wasn't going to wake up," Ed remembers. "We started crying. We felt so helpless."

In the days that followed, Ed and other members of the IMAX team became rescuers. Then Ed had to face the next question: Would he attempt to summit Everest in the aftermath of so many deaths or back out and in the process put the multimillion-dollar project in jeopardy? Ed decided to attempt the summit, which he achieved on May 23. He also found Hall's and Fischer's bodies in the snow.

"Coming down, all I could do was sit there and spend some time with them," Ed recalls. "Both their wives had asked me to retrieve some personal items—Scott's wedding ring and Rob's Rolex—but I just couldn't do it."

This time, Ed and his team plan to acclimatize on Cho Oyu for several weeks, and then on or about May 1, they hope to helicopter to the base camp on the north side of Annapurna, where Frenchman Maurice Herzog set his epic first ascent of an 8,000-meter peak in 1950. The now-classic story was chronicled in the all-time best-selling mountaineering tome, *Annapurna,* which inspired Ed to be a climber when he read the grisly account in high school, checked out from the public library. Shortly thereafter he started climbing at Devil's Lake, Wisconsin, a regular haunt for members of the Chicago Mountaineering Club. During college at Washington State University, Ed became a guide on 14,410-foot Mount Rainier and climbed it nearly two hundred times. Then in 1989, he reached the summit of 28,169-foot Kanchenjunga, the third-highest mountain in the world, his first 8,000-meter peak, and he was hooked. "I decided then to go for all of them," he recollects.

If all goes as planned, my support team will have trekked in from Pokhara, the hill town to the west of Kathmandu, and will rendezvous with Ed for his final push to the top of the world. Ed is hoping to make that last step in a little more than a week, after fixing ropes and studying the mountain from as many vantages as possible. When and if conditions are ideal and the mountain calls, the team will make the attempt alpine style, with no Sherpas or extra gear, light and fast, hoping to close at last the gap between human limits and the summit of the last 8,000-meter peak.

The last thing Ed said to me before departing to Nepal was his personal mantra that he recites at practically every public appearance, and in private conversations: "Getting to the top is optional, but getting back down is mandatory."

It all started with Annapurna. And one way or another, it will end with Annapurna.

ED'S QUEST
1. Kanchenjunga (28,169 feet), 1989
2. Everest (29,035 feet), 1990
3. K2 (28,250 feet), 1992
4. Lhotse (27,939 feet), 1994
5. Cho Oyu (26,750 feet), 1994
6. Makalu (27,765 feet), 1995
7. Gasherbrum II (26,360 feet), 1995
8. Gasherbrum I (26,470 feet), 1995
9. Broad Peak (26,400 feet), 1997
10. Manaslu (26,758 feet), 1999
11. Dhualagiri (26,794 feet), 1999
12. Shishapangma (26,300 feet), 2001
13. Nanga Parbat (26,658 feet), 2003
14. Annapurna (26,545 feet), May 2005?

* * *

When there is a split in the path ahead, always take the hardest route.

—Nepalese proverb

While Ed Viesturs is somewhere on the slopes of Cho Oyu, a nearby 8,000-meter peak, battling high winds and trying to adjust his body to altitude in preparation for the main event, his third try up Annapurna, I'm in the idyllic western hill town of Pokhara, on the old trans-Himalaya trade route, sprawled along the edge of Phewa Tal, Nepal's second-largest lake. With me is a group of associates and friends, all hoping to make the difficult trek to Annapurna North Base Camp, up a trail first blazed by Maurice Herzog and his team in 1950 when they achieved, at great cost to fingers and toes, the first ascent of an 8,000-meter peak. If weather, health, and other conditions permit, Ed plans to helicopter to base camp on May 1, ready for a fast and light shot at the summit of the mountain known for its deadly avalanches and horrible storms. And if we can make this trek, which spirals steeply up and down sheer gorges and over dizzying passes, then we hope to rendezvous with Ed and be there to celebrate his cardinal climb.

Pokhara is something of a phantom town these days. Despite this being the height of the trekking season, many of the lakeside lodges, guesthouses, gear shops, cafes, and restaurants are shuttered and the streets empty of backpacks and hiking boots. The Maoist insurgency has taken its toll. Last week, *Time* magazine declared Nepal's civil war "the deadliest conflict in Asia" and the nation at times "the single most dangerous place on earth."

The world's only Hindu kingdom opened its doors to tourism in 1950 and saw an exponential rise in visitation as climbers and trekkers came to be among eight of the world's highest peaks, including Everest and Annapurna. The Annapurna Conservation Area saw more than seventy-five thousand trekkers in the year 2000. But by the next year things began to turn. In 2001, just twenty-five thousand showed up. And in 2002, the number was a measly sixteen thousand. This year, predictions are for fewer than five thousand. "Our business is probably down 98 percent" from its peak, says Stan Armington, who has been running Nepal operations for Mountain Travel Sobek, our outfitter for the trek, since 1969. Where not long ago tourism was the country's top foreign-exchange earner, it now trails carpet and garment making. Even though we count several veteran adventurers in our little group, all are leery of not just the physical challenges, but also the political. Two days ago, a Maoist bomb blew up a private school here in Pokhara. Just as we departed from the United States, there were rumors that the Maoists had planted land mines along our route.

The war with Maoist rebels has claimed around eleven thousand lives over the past decade, and by some estimates the rebels control 80 percent of the countryside. In 2001, the entire royal family was massacred by the drunken Crown Prince Dipendra, who then put a bullet in his head. The Shakespearean orgy of regicide and suicide placed King Birendra's brother on the throne.

In February of 2005, King Gyanendra seized power, sacking the entire government and ending the frenzied fourteen-year experiment with democracy. He declared martial law and for a time cut off all communications with the outside world. Even longtime ally India suggested that Nepal might be declared a failed state. America, the United Kingdom, Japan, and Australia have all warned their nationals to stay away, and the U.S. State Department has labeled the insurgents "terrorists." The rebels, who draw inspiration from China's Mao Tse-tung and Cambodia's Khmer Rouge, want to end Nepal's constitutional monarchy and replace it with a communist republic. Rebel leader Baburam Bhattarai has vowed to "hoist the hammer-and-sickle red flag atop Mount Everest," but so far nothing said about Annapurna.

Ed is considered to be the most cautious of climbers, though these matters did not keep him away, and so we have followed. Once at a certain altitude the mountains know no politics, only the whims of the gods.

Irish adventurer and writer Dervla Murphy once called Nepal "The Waiting Land." It lived up to its name early this month in Pokhara, Nepal's second-largest city, when the Maoist rebels executed a *bandh* or strike that halted all bus and air traffic in and out of the city. Now it seems the land has inhaled and is waiting, waiting. Waiting for the next strike, the next avalanche, the next undoing. We wait to leave here tomorrow for Jomsom, 3,000 meters high, a way station on the centuries-old Tibetan trade route alongside the Kali Gandaki River and the beginning of our literally breathtakingly trek.

Looking north from Pokhara, beyond the tea plantations and tiered rice fields, we see little, as an unseasonable rain and attendant clouds have thwarted the views. But the posters in the empty hotel curio shops show a scene of dazzling clarity, the grand march of mountains that are the Annapurna Himal, just beyond our touch. It would be easy to drop into the romantic delusion that by stepping into these great massifs of rock and ice we achieve some form of empathy with them, as if something so brightly oversized must somehow be gracious. But they are anything but. Nothing can live above 8,000 meters; it is the death zone. Just standing still at this altitude you are dying—brain cells vanish, the mind mushes, the body deteriorates.

Annapurna is the consort of Shiva and a Hindu goddess of harvest and providing food, yet she seems to take away as much as she creates. There are more than fifty-five known climber deaths on Annapurna, a 50 percent ratio of deaths to summits. Anatoli Boukreev, the talented yet controversial Russian climber who was a key character in the Everest disaster of 1996, was killed by an avalanche on Annapurna the following year's Christmas Day. Alison Chadwick-Onyszkiewicz and Vera Watson disappeared on the mountain in 1978, during the first American women's expedition to an 8,000-meter peak. I was almost swept away by avalanches when I made a trek to the Annapurna Sanctuary ten years ago. Ed Viesturs, in his heroically judicious way, turned around twice on Annapurna because conditions were not optimal. This time the stakes are higher. In his midforties, he's touching the ceiling of extreme athleticism; his family has grown; his finances depend upon his mountaineering successes; and the world will be watching as he makes this perhaps final attempt. But Ed is nothing if not courageous, and sometimes the greatest courage is to turn around from a fight you may not win.

KNIGHTS OF THE SKY

> *In such country there is no monotony.*
> —H. W. Tilman

It seems we're interleaved between the events of fifty-five years ago, to the day, when Maurice Herzog and team wandered about these flanks desperately looking for a route up Annapurna, and the events before us as we try to find our way to Annapurna Base Camp and watch as Ed Viesturs makes his try. But already, as with many well-planned mountain expeditions, things have started to go to wrack. Ed called from his satellite phone to share the news that while his partner, Veikka, made the summit of Cho Oyu, photographer Jimmy Chin was stricken with cerebral edema, a sometimes-deadly altitude sickness, and so Ed sacrificed his summit bid and instead carried his friend down the mountain to save his life.

On the trail to base camp we've had our own confronts. John Rosinki, the technician from Cisco who hopes to operate some cutting-edge communications systems at base camp, has been feeling the effects of altitude (he's from Florida), while Dave Shore, the expedition logistic manager, seems to have picked up an amoeba. Jonathan Chester, a veteran Himalayas photographer, is having trouble with his knees, and I have the Khumbu cough. Russ Daggatt, our satellite authority, is trekking with two broken ribs, which can be immensely painful if he slides downhill, or if someone tells a bad joke, something not too uncommon. We're hiking up a trail rarely taken—it does not exist on any trekking plates—somewhere in the belly of the world's deepest gorge. Today, as the group spread out, Russ and I somehow took a wrong spur and found ourselves winding up a yak path into the snow, lost just as Herzog and his men were many times in the two months they spent seeking out a route to the top. We couldn't see human footprints anywhere (though perhaps a snow leopard or yeti print . . . hard to tell), so after this folly we unwound the mountain and implored a village *amala* (wise woman) for the true path. Eventually we caught up with the rest of the team and made our way to camp, a dung-infested patch above the Kali Gandaki River, between the two bright blades of Dhualagiri and Annapurna, just as a savage hailstorm hit (right around 2:00 pm, which Herzog wrote happened regularly at this hour).

But the weather is the more disturbing with the news from our sirdar, Kul Dhoj Magar, who informs that the col we are supposed to climb the day after tomorrow, named by Herzog the "Pass of April 27" may be unpassable. He's been told that an Annapurna expedition tried to cross the breach a week ago and was turned back. The hail and rain that has pummeled us since we began doesn't bode well for clearance at higher altitudes, and of course there is no other way to base camp. Well, perhaps. As I pore over the maps I see that a tributary called the Miristi Khola approaches base camp beyond the pass, and in fact Herzog and team crossed the upper reaches of the tight, tearing river on their approach after clearing the pass. Though there is no evidence that anyone has ever tried to work up the Miristi Khola from its confluence with the Kali Gandaki, in theory it seems possible. This is low-water season, and it looks to be about a nine-mile scramble up the steep river. But there are three hitches, at least. The first is that the map's contour lines show steep cliffs along the river, and it could quite easily become impenetrable. The second is that the daily afternoon deluges could cause inopportune flash flooding. Lastly, in order to reach the mouth of the Miristi Khola we would have to trek down the Kali Gandaki into the heart of Maoist-controlled country. It's here that Maoists have held up trekkers in recent months and exacted a "rebel toll" for passage. But things have gotten worse of late. Just earlier this month two foreign trekkers were victims of a land mine. Maoists have threatened tourist facilities throughout Nepal, and rebel leader Baburam Bhattarai has warned travelers they could be "caught in the crossfire of the contending armies." So, if we turn back at the pass, our only other choice to meet Ed at base camp is to run the rebel gauntlet and make a pioneering ascent up an unknown river, much the way Herzog did his reconnaissances during the 1950 expedition.

To put pepper in the mill, we are in a communications stand-off. I'm hoping to report Ed's climb in as close to real time as possible, but the three bags containing the three satellite systems needed to uplink the dispatches and photos and videos never arrived in Kathmandu. I have an Iridum phone with me, but it is voice only, and our plan is uplink rich data. Didrik Johnck, an Everest veteran and a field producer for this project, has stayed behind in the capital working the phones and streets to track down the missing gear, or find replacements. But for days he has come up naught. The current crackdown by the king has shut down all cell phone service and embargoed satellite phones without a lengthy and expensive permit process. So, we have implemented a "sneaker net," wherein we burned media onto a CD and gave it to a runner, who sprinted to Jomsom and gave it to a pilot with instructions to arrange shipment back to the United States, somewhat similar to the method James Morris used when he sent his dispatch to the *Times* of London with the report that Ed Hillary and Tenzing Norgay had summited Everest, though his was entirely analog.

But I have just gotten news via my Iridium that just as Didrik had given up all hope, he got the call that the satellite gear had been located, and so he grabbed the kits and the first flight to Pokhara, then a flight to Jomsom, and then he rented a tractor to head down the first part of the trail, and now he is somewhere trekking madly through the thunder and hailstorm trying to catch up.

We're hovering in tents at the start of a near-vertical trail that rises four thousand feet to the next encampment. We're beyond the last village, on the edge of Annapurna's wilderness fortress. Nepal is very poor country, among the fifty poorest countries in the world, yet it thrives on an overabundance of beauty, wonder, and adventure. And we're in the middle kingdom of it all.

MOUNTAIN MADNESS

> *Thou hast a voice, great Mountain, to repeal*
> *Large codes of fraud and woe; not understood.*
>   —Percy Bysshe Shelley, "Mont Blanc"

North Annapurna Base Camp

"It's a very, very hard trek; maybe the toughest in the Himalaya," Ed Viesturs warned a few weeks ago when I proposed taking a team to North Annapurna Base Camp to cover his climb. Ed is not one to overstate.

This is all too evident when we find ourselves breaking trail by postholing in waist-deep snow just shy of fifteen thousand feet, inching along icy ledges barely boot-wide with sheer, half-mile drops, getting lost in a whiteout with fifty-mile-per-hour winds on a plateau that offers vertical and absolute relief on three sides, and hacking steps with an ice ax on slippery slopes throughout. If we could pull ourselves out of our bodies and view our little expedition from a distance, it would seem much like the terrifying scenes from *Lost Horizon,* the film based on James Hilton's book about a trek to a legendary Himalayan valley called Shangri-la. Only here there is no portal to paradise, just a terminus at a rocky, adiathermanous outcropping in the long shadow of Annapurna, a raw and seldom-seen camp Maurice Herzog and his team first established fifty-five years ago.

On Herzog's expedition, a porter fell to his death along these trails. We have our share of near misses. Several of our forty porters skid about in precarious exposed sections but always make recovery. Kristy Severance, a seasoned Himalayas digital photographer, toddles along a slight and tapered ledge high above a thousand-foot-deep canyon. Ball-bearing-sized hailstones pelt the tracks of those in front. Kristy steps on an icy patch, falls, and starts the steep slide to oblivion. But just behind her, Alex Welles, a longtime member of the Seattle-based Mountaineers and a veteran of expeditions to Sikkim and Kashmir, drops to the trail, scoops his hand downward, and snags a loop on Kristy's pack as she is spilling into the void. Kristy is pulled back to the thin ledge, her legs "like spaghetti," but she gradually straightens to her feet and cautiously steps forward. There is no alternative. We are yet a day away from base camp, and to turn back here would be even more taxing and treacherous.

It all gives greater appreciation for what Ed does, which is almost unfathomable to those who have not experienced the Himalaya. As we stumble along in strobelike winds and swirling snow, we look down to the deepest gorges in the world and up to the highest mountains. Ed kicks about another two and a half vertical miles higher than our highest pass, in conditions far more severe, and manages to make it look easy. It is not.

When we reach one pass, atop a snow-slicked wedge shiny as fresh paint and sharp as a luge run, there is a Buddhist chorten marking the crown, well-coated in offerings of prayer flags, rice, and stones. I place a flat rock on a shelf, a common offering in such high sanctums, and pray for safe passage, for us and for Ed and his team.

Finally, we clamber up a giant moraine slope, past the skull of a Himalayan thar whose bleached horns point the way, and at the crest we look down to a high valley that seems made more of the maria on the moon than anything on earth. At the far end, on a plateau spotted with edelweiss, a string of prayer flags flaps above a scattering of tents . . . It's the Italian expedition that was turned back a week ago on the pass we just negotiated. Even with fixed ropes and seventy porters, the pass was too dangerous, so they returned to Pokhara and hired a helicopter to lift them into this grand fastness at the foot of the chilling, two-thousand-foot moving spill of Annapurna North Glacier, alongside of which is the route to Camp I, where the serious climbing begins.

We stumble down the last slopes of gray scree and gather to high-five and hug: we made base camp, with close calls but ultimately without serious accidents or injuries. Tents are pitched, *tatopani* (hot water) with lemon served, and our own version of prayer flags, Brunton solar panels, rolled out. But even here, about as close to the sun as one can get on earth, we can suck down little power, as the day is smitten with heavy snow and thick cloud. So we fester and shiver in our tents, waiting for a spot of sunshine, waiting for Ed.

That night it is so cold, my water bottle freezes in my tent. Sometime before dawn there is an eerie howl outside, perhaps the wind, perhaps a glacier crying, perhaps a Yeti. But at breakfast, Lhakpa Nurbu Sherpa, our chief guide, claims the peculiar sound was that of a snow leopard lurking past, the rare cat that

Zen author Peter Matthiesson stalked unsuccessfully in his eponymous epic tale, as elusive as the apex of Annapurna.

About 9:30 a.m., the distinctive *whop-whop-whop* funnels up the mist-enshrouded Miristi Khola canyon, and minutes later a rusty Russian Mi-17 breaks into view. It circles over our camp, over to the North Annapurna Glacier, then settles in a gravel basin a hundred yards away, the downwash spitting particulates into our tents.

As the giant rotors turn, out leaps Ed Viesturs, looking very much the rock star he is. Several others follow in his wake: photographer Jimmy Chin, still not wholly recouped from his bout of edema on Cho Oyu; Veikka "the Flying Finn" Gustafsson, so famous in his own country he has his own action figure in stores; and David Breashears, the director of the IMAX box-office record breaker *Everest,* which happened to star Ed. A mountain of gear is tossed out the chopper doors, and, whoosh, the clunky contraption is off down valley, leaving behind a booming silence.

Unlike most high-altitude climbers, who tend to weathered hatchet faces, hollowed cheeks, and wolflike eyes, Ed looks cherubic , his face more oblate than chiseled, and his five-foot-ten-and-a-half-inch frame more boxcar than streamliner. He looks so ordinary, he seems out of place in this zone of fragile existence. But he telegraphs confidence and competence, and after a quick hug and an expression of awe that we actually made the trek, he immediately sets about pitching his camp.

Ed tells me he hopes for a quick ascent this round, though his permit lasts until June 1 and he'll stay that long if he has to. It turns out there are two Italian teams on the mountain this season, sharing the wide swath of base camp with us. One of the Italian teams has been waiting a week for the weather to break; the other has been waiting forty-one days. Both have members who have been turned back from summiting Annapurna before. The mountain is like a narcotic that irresistibly draws back, no matter the menace, no matter the cognitive rebuff. "Many of them do it again and again, in spite of danger, fatigue, hunger, or thirst. It is a passion similar to gambling," wrote Viollet-le-Duc in 1870 about those addicted to dangerous places. In 1997, David Breashears and Ed cofounded "Everest Anonymous," a kind of twelve-step program for those who had spent too much time on the world's highest peak. The penalty for returning was $1,000 to each member remaining on the wagon, and when last spring Ed and David returned, they ponied up.

Inside Ed's dining tent, he goes over his plans. Unlike the old-style siege assaults on big mountains, in which a pyramid of gear is established at high camps and the hopeful summiteers come down to sleep low each night in an attempt to acclimatize, Ed climbs simply and economically. His is a light, alpine-style, linear ascent. He and his teammates are fully acclimatized from their time on Cho Oyu, and once they begin going up they want to keep going up, until there is nothing but sky.

So we head to our respective tents and hope for good weather on the morrow, good fortune in the days ahead, and blessings from the mountain gods.

INTO THE THRONE ROOM OF THE CLOUDS

For three days, Ed and Veikka share a tiny tent at 22,500 feet as a high blizzard rages. They are running low on food, and their bodies are slowly breaking down.

Although Ed Viesturs has been waiting most of his adult life for this moment, he will wait still until conditions are just right, or turn around one more time, likely the last time. As he waits in the tent, sharing a sleeping bag with his comrade, munching on banana chips and cashews, there is a steady stress between the fire of courage and the contract to kin; between the searing danger and the cold comfort of caution. He is caught in the waiting room to greatness.

Then the weather finally breaks, and on May 12 at 3:00 in the morning, the team sets out, including several from the Italian expeditions. After two hours, one Italian turns back, citing the extreme cold and exhaustion. Then another Italian turns around. The rest climb for eleven hours nonstop, up the last four thousand feet of the mountain, gasping for breath in the thin air. Then, at 2:00 p.m., Ed Viesturs finally steps atop the blazing white coronet of Annapurna, and becomes part of the heavens. There are no more steps to climb. He is on cloud fourteen. Now he gazes upon the same breathtaking panorama that Maurice Herzog had beheld fifty-five years before. "It is like Christmas. It is a moment I'd dreamt about and thought about for so long."

When Ed makes it back to base camp, he collapses in his tent, but before the salve of sleep he counsels to all who can hear: "If you can dream it, you can do it."

16

SLEEPING WITH THE ELEPHANTS
THE *State* OF *Dreams*

If there is a common element to the blue riband of adventure in Africa, it is the frisson that comes from facing the maw. At the moment of capsize on the Zambezi, or the dodge of a rock fall on Kilimanjaro, or the facing of the feral eyes of a large beast, we are febrile but also unlocked in a way that never happens in the comfort zone, so that the slightest tap makes us shiver to the bottom of our beings.

It is the last night of our exploration of remote Zambia, the little-visited heart of Africa. We had supped on a meal Mexican, probably the only tacos and hot sauce in a five-hundred-mile radius, and were sipping gin and tonics around a mopane-wood fire (the hot-blazing hardwood "burns as long as your passion") as the gibbous moon began its bright sweep across the southern sky. Much of the conversation is about how to deal with African wildlife encountered unexpectedly. Earlier in the day, we had taken a hike, probably the first westerners to do so, up to the top of Mount Shongon, which means "the place no one goes" in Nyanja, the local language. Along the way we stepped along the footpaths of an array of herbivores and predators. So the fireside talk concerned what to do when surprising a beast while wading through high grass or the tangle of thorn trees. Professor Justin

Seymour-Smith, lifetime owner of a private game reserve in Zimbabwe, is our guide and authority on wildlife behavior, and he counsels across the flames: "You never know what a wild animal will do. Meeting you without warning on its turf, it might turn and go away, or it might charge. There are no shortages of tales in Africa of folks who have been on the wrong side of animal whim. But there are some general rules. If you encounter a big cat, never run. Stare it down and slowly back up; otherwise it will chase you like a house cat to a mouse. If you chance upon a gorilla, crouch down and bow your head as though praying. If you bump into a hippo or croc or poisonous snake, run like a rat. However, if you happen to face down a rhino or an elephant . . ."

Exhausted from our aggressive wanderings that had taken us from the secluded Busanga Plains in the west to this hidden preserve on the Mozambique border, I announce an early retirement, before the professor has finished his dissertation, and toddle to my little North Face Lunarship tent pitched on the high mud banks of the Luangwa River. The others are staying in "chalets," grass huts with beds, showers, and flush toilets, but because I am a world-class snorer, I courteously offered to pitch a tent a hundred yards from the rest. Besides, I like looking up through the mosquito netting to the Southern Cross.

For some reason, sleep is not forthcoming, and I roll about in my bag for some time. I feel the cold air from the canyon downstream creep in. I hear the sighing of the river, the whir and chirp of crickets, and later, the voice of an owl, like a dark brushstroke on the night.

Then about 10:00 p.m., I hear some rustlings upriver. I sit up. The moon showers the desolate glow of a dream onto the scene; the light on the winding river is shimmering as a shield, and the upstream trees seem to be swaying. Hippos, I think. The night previous I had been awakened when a couple of river horses were snorting in the shallows not far from the tent. Hippos graze at night, eating as much as two hundred pounds of grass a setting, but they enter and leave the river at well-trampled paths, and my little tent is pitched a prudent distance from any such corridor. So I roll over and again attempt to force sleep. But the crackling continues, and is getting closer, or so I imagine. But after a time, the sound abates. Something, though, seems not right. I sit up again and peer through the mosquito netting. The ridges of the hills are crowned with a moonstone radiance, melting into a profound blue in the shadowy ravines. Everything—hills, woods, ancient rocks—hangs in chasms of blue air; the whole valley is floating veiled in quivering fluid light. Cloud shadows drift imperceptibly across the sea of trees, deepening the blue to indigo. It seems I am looking at the ghost of a world, a lost world.

I squint and scan the horizon. At first I detect just a gray blur against the dark foliage upstream. It might be a tree. Or a cluster of bushes. But it moves. It disappears and reappears again farther down the bank. At last it lumbers out of the surrounding tangle of shrub and creeper and emerges at the edge of the riverbank. It is no longer just a blur but has shape and form . . . an elephant form. *Loxodonta africana,* a thunderhead of flesh and huge, rolling bones with long white tusks flashing in the moonlight. Slowly, almost imperceptibly, it crosses the bank toward my outpost, with pauses now and then to fan out its ears, and perhaps meditate, or dream.

The jumbo treads closer and closer; my heart begins to pound. Never have I seen a beast so big so close. If life is measured not by the number of breaths taken, but by the moments that take breath away, I am extending my life by a load. About five feet from the entrance to my tent, he halts and stares inside with a look of wildness no civilization could endure. I remain as motionless as I can, and look back into eyes like clear brown water. Then a cramp in my leg develops, so I try to reposition it without making a sound, but I rub against the sleeping pad, which makes a squeak. The elephant stretches his trunk toward me, and I can see the symmetric ridges decanting, like poured geometry. He sniffs, then steps back a foot and flaps his ears, they way elephants do when angry or about to charge, or so I think I recall from documentaries and picture books. Is he about to charge? I wish I had stayed to hear more of Justin's animal-escape advice. Should I try to unzip the tent and run? Should I clap my hands like a rifle shot and see if he will run? Should I shine my flashlight in his eyes? Should I lie down and play dead? I have my Iridium satellite phone in my fanny pack. I wish I could call David Attenborough. Or Justin. Or Simon, a professional hunter sleeping on the other side of camp. But I have no numbers to call and am certain the elephant would hear my voice if I did. So I just freeze in a sitting position and watch as the elephant circles my blue cocoon to the other side and begins to make long siphonings on the sausage tree that spreads above me. Whew. I relax a bit. He is ignoring me. But then I hear what sounds like sawing upstream. I look and see a huge acacia swaying in the moonlight, like the treetops in *Jurassic Park* before a sauropod appears. Another elephant is rubbing his back against the tree on the camp perimeter. Then he steps from a palisade of thorns onto the campgrounds following the footsteps of his predecessor, along the rim of the river toward my tent. He is bigger than the last, an animal magnitude from another time, and the glint of his tusks brighter. With smooth, rhythmic strides he moves to the very edge of my tent, and he too stops and glares inside. His great fanned ears move slowly to and fro. His breath pours through the netting and presses down on my shoulders. As he alters his position in the moonlight, the shadows show the structure of his great body, immensely heavy, slung from mighty backbones, supported by columnar legs. I can't help but think he looks like a baobab come to life.

Now there is one bull chomping on the tree next to me and another on the other side staring me down, two oversized, rolling bags of horror. And my stomach starts to growl. The Mexican meal is starting to process, and I can't hold back a sound. It pipes from my tent, and both elephants turn to glower and flap their giant ears. My God, I think, I am about to be stomped to death by elephants. Genuinely frightened, I feel my heart fly around my insides, my mouth go dry as a winterthorn, and my limbs shudder. I think about rolling the tent down the bank into the river, but then remember I had tethered it to the sausage tree so as not to blow away. And besides, the river is filled with crocs and hippos. The tether rope then makes me quiver. The first elephant is a yard away; if he moves forward and trips on the tether, he will fall on my tent, crushing the ingredients. I consider again making a run for it, but then remember how much noise the zipper makes, and know it will cause the elephants even more alarm. Then I hear a sound like Niagara by the tree. My bladder is full as well and is beginning to howl. Too many gin and tonics. I am terribly tired. But I dare not close my eyes. The thought of being trampled with eyes open wide is bad enough. But I know if I fall asleep I will snore, and I can think of nothing worse than a squashing while snoozing. So there I sit, stiff as a log, as the elephants scoff and sniff and chivvy about me. Elephants can eat for twenty hours a day, then rest the rest. A long night this might be. But then after a couple of hours of munching, the two leviathans lie down in a sandy spot below my tent and go quiet. I take advantage of the respite and also lie down, but command myself to not fall asleep. But my eyelids are heavy, and my mind wanders about in a haze of unbeing. I hear some crunching, sit up, and look through the mesh. Did I nod off? The moon has crossed the sky and sunk behind the trees. In the now quite dark landscape I can barely make out a silhouette shambling back upstream. With an unhurried pace it moves back into the shelter of the trees, entwines itself within branches and leaves, and then it is gone.

There is no other sound, save the litany bird, whose call seems to cry, "Good Lord, deliver us." There are no more hulking specters. So I presume both are gone, at last. But a silent presence still hangs in the air. I am about to burst, so I unzip the tent and leap outside to relieve myself. Just as I finish, there is a basso profundo bellow that rips open the night just a few yards from me. I had stirred the other beast. I dive back into the tent, rezip it, and hurtle into my bag. There is a subtle spark to his tardigrade pace as the elephant clambers up the bank, to the frame of my tent, and fixes a walleyed stare. Our eyes lock, and for a second I think I see a hint of empathy for a small, vulnerable creature wrapped in nylon.

Then the elephant turns and plods back into the bush. And into a deep and anodyne sleep I fall, returning with the dawn to a more managed, if less noble, wild place.

Index

A

Abboud, Solieman, 84, 85, 87, 100
Aborigines, 185–186
Abulkharim, Hapip Khlil, 97
Akakus Mountains, 88, 91
Alas Basin, Sumatra, xi
Aleksovski, Dr. Dusko, 301
Alexander the Great, 295, 299, 300, 307
Ali-Alzalet, Al-Mabrouk, 88
American Jazz Museum, 259
Ancon Expeditions, 126
Andaman Islands, and Thailand, 61–79
Angape, Joloma, 209–210
Angerer, Willy, 107
Annapurna (Herzog), 318
Annapurna, Nepal, 315–336
Antovski, Dusan, 307
Arabia Steamboat Museum, 257
Armington, Stan, 320
Arnst, Mike, 239
Aswan Dam, 10, 18–19
Atchan, Phra, 70–71
Attenborough, David, 205
Australian outback, 163–182
Aviam, Dr. Mordechai ("Motti"), 152

B

Bacon, Francis, 1
Balboa, Vasco Núñez, 124, 130, 132
Baro River, Ethiopia, 3–4
Barrera, Betto, 141
Barrie, J.M., 140
Barth, Heinrich, 93
Basie, Count, 259
Bastidas, Rodrigo de, 130
Bates, Bob, 188–189
Beard, Peter, 3
Beatrice River, Australia, 170
Becirovic, Enver, 50
Beringe, Robert von, 23
Bhattarai, Baburam, 321, 324
Biblioteca Alexandrina, 6–7
Bigirimana, François, 27–28, 29
Bilbija, Milos, 302
Bill and Melinda Gates Foundation, 29
Bismuth, Robert, 268
Blachford, John, 214, 216–220, 223
black rhinos, xv, 285
Blough, Lahav, 151
Blue Nile, 1–2, 6, 230
Blyth, Chuck, 215
Bond, Edward, 223
Bonington, Chris, 104

DEAR CUSTOMERS AND FRIENDS,

SUPPORTING YOUR INTEREST IN OUTDOOR ADVENTURE, travel, and an active lifestyle is central to our operations, from the authors we choose to the locations we detail to the way we design our books. Menasha Ridge Press was incorporated in 1982 by a group of veteran outdoorsmen and professional outfitters. For 25 years now, we've specialized in creating books that benefit the outdoors enthusiast.

Almost immediately, Menasha Ridge Press earned a reputation for revolutionizing outdoors- and travel-guidebook publishing. For such activities as canoeing, kayaking, hiking, backpacking, and mountain biking, we established new standards of quality that transformed the whole genre, resulting in outdoor-recreation guides of great sophistication and solid content. Menasha Ridge continues to be outdoor publishing's greatest innovator.

The folks at Menasha Ridge Press are as at home on a white-water river or mountain trail as they are editing a manuscript. The books we build for you are the best they can be, because we're responding to your needs. Plus, we use and depend on them ourselves.

We look forward to seeing you on the river or the trail. If you'd like to contact us directly, join in at www.trekalong.com or visit us at www.menasharidge.com. We thank you for your interest in our books and the natural world around us all.

SAFE TRAVELS,

Bob Sehlinger

BOB SEHLINGER
PUBLISHER

Richard Bangs' Adventures With Purpose

American Public Television is the distributor of RICHARD BANGS' ADVENTURES WITH PURPOSE —"Egypt: Quest for the Lord of the Nile." In this special, explorer and adventure travel writer Richard Bangs sets off for an incredible adventure on the great Nile River to uncover the history, myths and culture of the lost crocodiles of ancient Egypt. Known as "Lords of the Nile," these crocodiles shaped Egyptian tradition and influenced religion, daily life and even the pharaoh.

Bangs' voyage up the Nile tells the tale of a civilization inextricably bound to the waters of the river and its creatures. From Alexandria to Cairo, from the pyramids at Giza to the Valley of the Kings, Bangs explores the way the river and its fearsome "Lord" molded a society. Further upstream, he visits a temple dedicated to Sobek, the crocodile god, and looks for the beast in the waters of Lake Nasser.

Richard Bangs often has been called the father of modern adventure travel and a pioneer in travel that positively impacts the world. He has spent 30 years as an explorer and communicator and, along the way, led first descents — from source to sea — of 35 rivers around the globe, including the Yangtze in China and the Zambezi in Southern Africa.

RICHARD BANGS' ADVENTURES WITH PURPOSE television special is expertly crafted, with creative and effective shooting, editing and an outstanding script. Bangs is highly informative and engaging, revealing the culture and history of this area of the world with intellectual and cultural substance far beyond the typical television travelogue. The television special is planned for September 2007 release on public television stations across the United States. Check local listings for the special's airdate.

For 46 years, American Public Television (APT) has been a prime source of programming for U.S. public television stations. APT distributes more than 300 new programs per year in a variety of genres including history, biography, science, nature, performance, cooking, travel, gardening, arts & crafts, drama, comedy and classic movies. It is responsible for many public television milestones including the first high definition series and the 2006 national launch of Create™ — the 24/7 digital television channel featuring the best of public television's how-to, travel and lifestyle programs. APT is known for its leadership in identifying innovative, worthwhile and viewer-friendly programming. It serves as an essential distribution option for talented producers. APT Worldwide, its international sales division, has become a leading source for U.S. public television programming in countries around the world. For more information, visit www.APTonline.org.

EX⊕FFICIO®

Since 1987, Seattle-based ExOfficio has been the category leader in the travel clothing market, offering performance apparel combining technical features, fit, functionality, and style. To the untrained eye, most will see ExOfficio clothing and not be aware of all the innovative features and performance technologies. Which is the point. ExOfficio prefers subtle features, the ones you almost forget are there until you realize how comfortable you are because of them. Smart travelers pack ExOfficio to lighten their load, yet they wear it for everyday to simplify their life. For more information visit **www.exofficio.com/purpose.**

ABOUT THE AUTHOR

Richard Bangs is a world adventurer, international river explorer, Web pioneer, and award-winning author of over a dozen books and hundreds of magazine articles. He is also founding partner of Mountain Travel Sobek, America's oldest and largest adventure travel firm. He has a number of first descents to his credit, including the Yangtze, Euphrates, and Blue Nile. In the mid-1990s, Bangs launched Microsoft's Mungo Park, a pioneering Web site that featured live dispatches from expeditions around the world and that later evolved into the travel site Expedia. His book, *Riding the Dragon's Back,* won the Lowell Thomas Award, Best Travel Book of 1989. Other books include *Mystery of the Nile* and *The Lost River.*